# Painful Forms

# Painful Forms

## *Aesthetic Violence in American Literature and Art, 1945–2001*

Anna Ioanes

The University of North Carolina Press  CHAPEL HILL

Set in Merope Basic by Westchester Publishing Services
Manufactured in the United States of America

Library of Congress Cataloging-in-Publication Data
Names: Ioanes, Anna, author
Title: Painful forms : aesthetic violence in American literature and art,
    1945–2001 / Anna Ioanes.
Description: Chapel Hill : The University of North Carolina Press, 2025. |
    Includes bibliographical references and index.
Identifiers: LCCN 2025015221 | ISBN 9781469688930 cloth |
    ISBN 9781469688947 paperback | ISBN 9781469688954 epub |
    ISBN 9781469688961 pdf
Subjects: LCSH: Violence in literature | Violence in art | American literature—
    20th century—History and criticism | Violence—United States—History |
    BISAC: SOCIAL SCIENCE / Violence in Society | ART / Criticism & Theory |
    LCGFT: Literary criticism | Art criticism
Classification: LCC PS169.V56 I58 2025 | DDC 700/.4552—dc23/eng/20250528
LC record available at https://lccn.loc.gov/2025015221

Cover art: Kara Walker, *Cut*, 1998. Cut paper and adhesive on wall, 88 × 54 inches
(223.5 × 137.2 cm). Artwork © Kara Walker, courtesy of Sikkema Malloy Jenkins
and Sprüth Magers.

A previous version of Chapter 4 appeared as "Disgust in Silhouette: Toni Morrison, Kara
Walker, and the Aesthetics of Violence," in *Journal of Modern Literature* 42, no. 3 (2019):
110–28. https://doi.org/10.2979/jmodelite.42.3.07. © The Trustees of Indiana University.

A previous version of Chapter 5 appeared as "Shock and Consent in a Feminist Avant-Garde:
Kathleen Hanna Reads Kathy Acker," in *Signs: Journal of Women in Culture and Society* 42,
no. 1 (2016): 175–97. https://doi.org/10.1086/686757. © 2016 by The University of Chicago.
All rights reserved.

For product safety concerns under the European Union's General Product Safety Regulation
(EU GPSR), please contact gpsr@mare-nostrum.co.uk or write to the University of North
Carolina Press and Mare Nostrum Group B.V., Mauritskade 21D, 1091 GC Amsterdam,
The Netherlands.

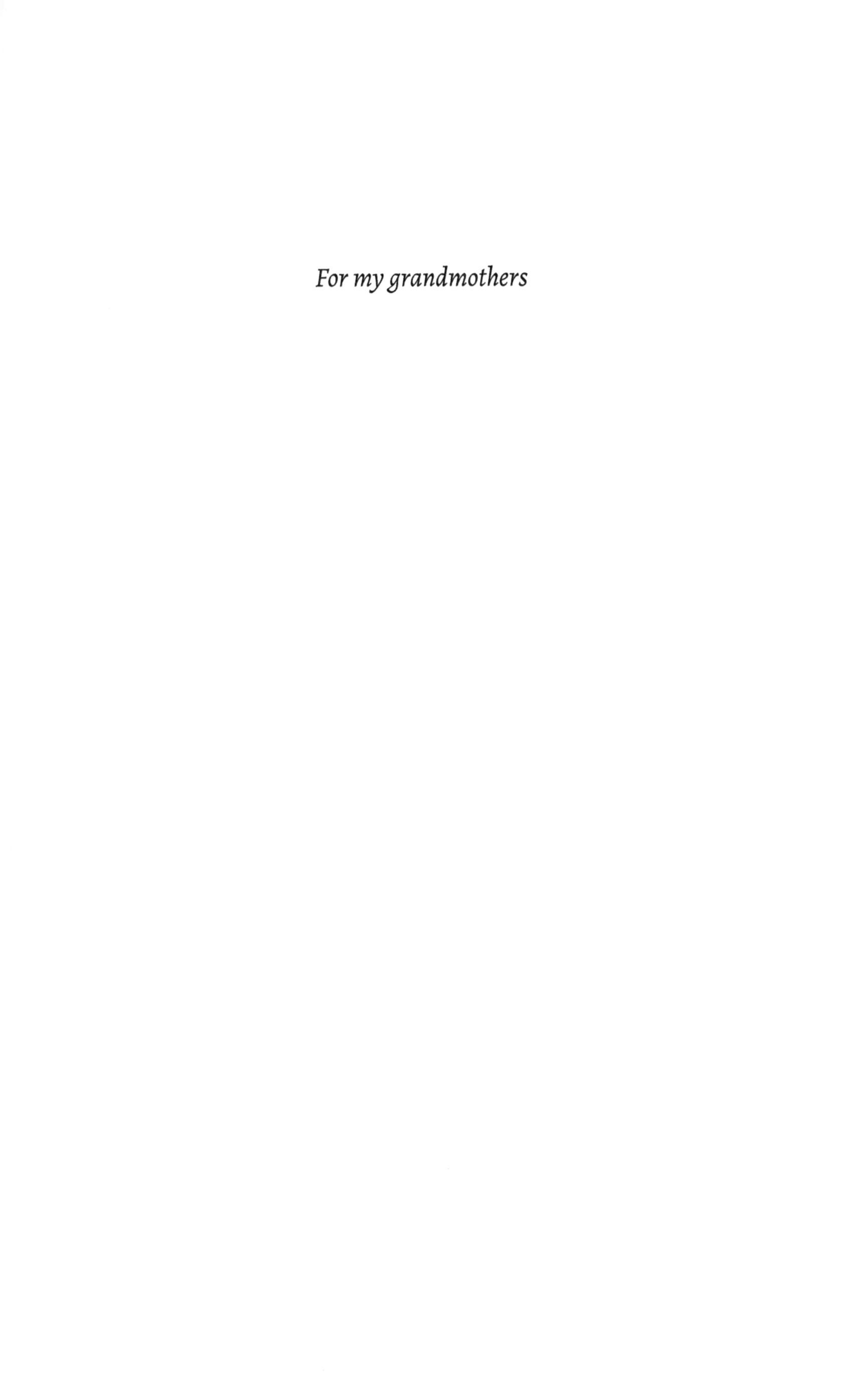

*For my grandmothers*

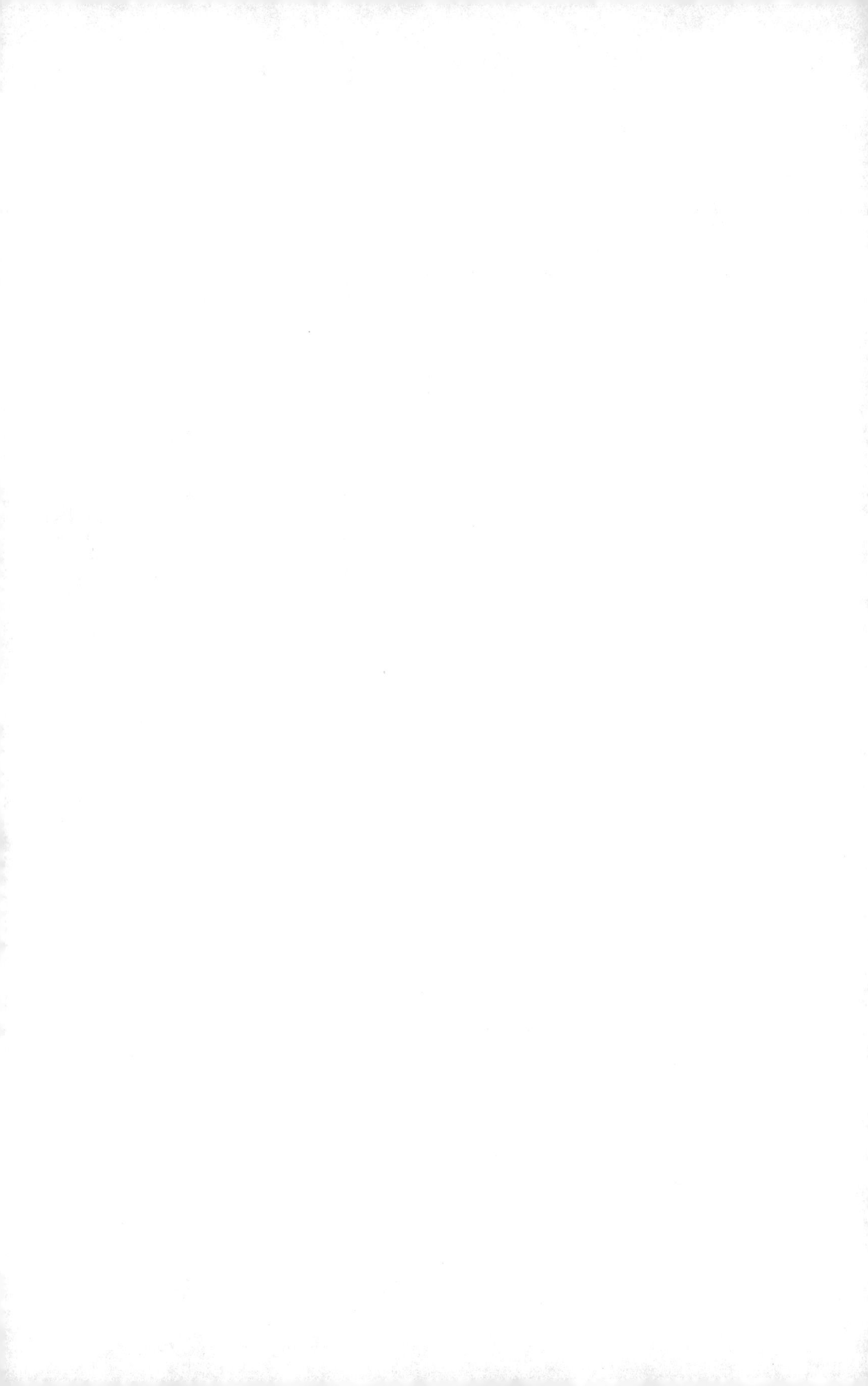

# Contents

# Illustrations

## *Acknowledgments*

This book bears the trace of many interlocutors, beginning with my undergraduate professors at Duke University. Janice Radway sparked my initial interest in riot grrrl zines and has been an inspiration ever since. Antonio Viego introduced me to theory, to scholarly monographs, and to the idea that I might write one someday. At the University of Virginia, I was incredibly fortunate to work with Rita Felski. I could not have asked for a more generous, incisive reader of my work, and I'm eternally grateful for her mentorship and the example of academic professionalism she set for me. Thanks to Marlon Ross for his brilliance, encouragement, and patience. My thinking about James Baldwin, in particular, has been shaped by his insight. I am grateful to Sandhya Shukla for her guidance and encouragement and to John Lyons, who offered generous feedback on my writing and enthusiastic support of my work. I owe a debt of gratitude, as well, to Eric Lott, Christopher Krentz, Jennifer Greeson, Hanadi Al-Samman, Victoria Olwell, Cynthia Wall, Clare Kinney, John O'Brien, and Mollie Washburne. For their friendship over the years and impact on this work, I thank Jean Franzino, Laura Goldblatt, Lindsay O'Connor, Jenny Braun, Dorothy Couchman, Tim Duffy, Jason Eversman, Kristin Gilger, Audrey Golden, Nick Rego, Will Rhodes, Drew Scheler, and Melissa White.

Early thinking about this project was shaped by my time as a postdoctoral fellow at Georgia Tech, and I thank Rebecca Burnett and Andy Frazee for their support. I was especially lucky to meet Nihad Farooq during my time in Atlanta; her brilliance, compassion, and generosity are unmatched. My community in Atlanta shaped this project as well. Thanks to Amy K. King, Andrew Marzoni, Adriane Quinlan, Ruthie Yow, Ben Shirley, Jennifer Forsthoefel Mollberg, Lauren Neefe, Kristin Allukian, Matt Dischinger, Hyeryung Hwang, Monica Carol Miller, Sarah O'Brien, Ellen Stockstill, and Tobias Wilson-Bates. Thanks to Owen Cantrell, Tina Colvin, Rachel Dean-Ruzicka, Rebekah Fitzsimmons, and Sarah Whitcomb Lozier-Laiola, who read the first version of the proposal for this book.

In its early stages, this project was supported by a Mary Lily Research Grant at the David M. Rubenstein Library at Duke University and a Short-Term Research Fellowship at the Stuart A. Rose Manuscript, Archives, and

Rare Book Library at Emory University. I owe a debt of gratitude to Kelly Wooten and to Courtney Chartier for their expertise and assistance. I am also grateful to Lisa Darms for her knowledge and assistance with the Kathleen Hanna papers at the Fales Library at New York University. Attending the Making Modernism summer institute at the Newberry Library, funded by the National Endowment for the Humanities, shaped the project indirectly, deepening my knowledge and providing brilliant interlocutors to think alongside. Thanks to Liesl Olson for convening such a dynamic program and to Keelin Burke for her assistance. Rachel Kyne's brilliance sharpened my thinking about the relationship between textual and visual arts, and I'm grateful to all the seminar participants for their collegiality and perspicacity. Early work on the project benefitted from feedback at the Futures of American Studies Institute, and I am grateful to Soyica Diggs Colbert for leading our seminar. Thanks to Sandy Alexandre and the seminar participants for their generous engagement with my work. I am also grateful to Sophia Bamert, Steph Brown, Aaron Colton, Douglas Dowland, Amy E. Elkins, Shannon Finck, Margaret Konkol, Heather Love, Melanie Micir, Lauren O'Connor, and Keja Valens.

I could not have completed this book without financial support from the Teaching and Professional Growth Committee at the University of St. Francis. I'm grateful for the funding and the work of the committee members who steward these resources. Thank you to Beth Roth for ongoing support and encouragement. Beth McDermott has been an unflagging supporter of my work and an unflappable model of a writer, teacher, and scholar; I am grateful for the example she sets and the wisdom she offers. Kevin Spicer has supported this project in innumerable ways, and I'm forever grateful. Thanks, too, to Karen Duys, Veronica Popp, David Veenstra, Kristi Macek, Trina Zeitz, and the librarians and staff at the LaVerne and Dorothy Brown Library at the University of St. Francis.

I would like to thank the editorial team at the University of North Carolina Press for the enthusiasm and care they have given to this book. In particular, I am grateful to Andreína Fernández, whose insights not only strengthened this project but also helped me see it through. Thanks to Lucas Church for supporting the project and walking me through the publication process with such transparency. I would also like to thank the editorial, production, and marketing teams at the press. Thanks to Amron Lehte for preparing the index. I am especially grateful to the anonymous reviewers, whose feedback has formed and re-formed this project, strengthening and clarifying my argument. Jean Franzino offered astute editorial guidance and her characteristic wisdom throughout the life of this project, and especially when I was preparing the manuscript for submission. I am grateful to Katherine Fusco and Laura Portwood-Stacer for their generosity and guidance.

An earlier version of chapter four originally appeared as "Disgust in Silhouette: Toni Morrison, Kara Walker, and the Aesthetics of Violence." *Journal of Modern Literature* 42, no. 3 (2019): 110–28. © The Trustees of Indiana University. An earlier version of chapter five originally appeared as "Shock and Consent in a Feminist Avant-Garde: Kathleen Hanna Reads Kathy Acker." *Signs: Journal of Women in Culture and Society* 42, no. 1 (2016): 175–197. © 2016 by The University of Chicago. Thanks to Indiana University Press and the University of Chicago Press for permission to include revised versions of the articles here. Excerpts from *Grapefruit: A Book of Instructions and Drawings by Yoko Ono* as well as the unpublished "Script for Striptease" are included with permission from Yoko Ono Lennon via Jonas E. Herbsman, Power of Attorney. Thanks to Connor Monahan for his assistance with these excerpts. Archival material from the Kathy Acker Papers is used with permission from Matias Viegener, literary executor for the Estate of Kathy Acker. Thanks to Siobhan Donnelly for her assistance with images from the Andy Warhol Foundation and to Monica Truong for assistance with images of Kara Walker's silhouettes.

Finally, I want to thank my family. I could not have written this book without their care and support. Thanks to my mom, Staley, for everything. Thanks to my da, Jim, for endless support and love. Thanks to my father, Tom, for his love and encouragement. I am grateful to the Rettberg and Clayworth families, and especially to Paul, Barb, and Deb. Thanks to my Nance, Jordan, and Ioanes family members. To my sister, Ellen: thank you for your friendship, brilliance, and bravery. Thanks to Wiley, who taught me so much about love. And for his love, I am always grateful to Eric Rettberg. Thank you, Eric; I love you.

# Painful Forms

# Introduction

In her zeitgeist-capturing essay "The White Album," composed over ten years from 1968 to 1978, Joan Didion weaves together observations on pop culture and politics, setting the Manson murders alongside the arrest of Huey P. Newton, her own injuries alongside the assassinations of 1968. Thus assembled, these experiences present this time and place—America, the 1960s—as one characterized by senseless violence, an increasingly rapid and decontextualized series of violent events that thwarts attempts to understand, to assimilate into a stable story about how the world works. The essay's iconic opening line, "We tell ourselves stories in order to live," is illustrated by a thought experiment that reflects a broader cultural grasp for meaning: imagine a "naked woman on the ledge outside the window on the sixteenth floor."[1] She is about to jump, and Didion claims that this image provokes a desire to impose meaning, to tell a story that would make sense of the violent act. Is this a personal experience of anguish, a political protest, or something else? Didion claims that "we look for the sermon in the suicide, for the social or moral lesson in the murder of five. We interpret what we see, select the most workable of the multiple choices."[2] She speaks of concerns that suffused the cultural moment of the 1960s, when it felt particularly urgent to determine explanatory mechanisms for what might end up, after all, being an "authentically senseless chain of correspondences."[3] The human desire to impose meaning by telling stories transcends the 1960s, but in a moment when violence was increasingly visible in mass media, the impulse to make sense of seemingly senseless acts of violence came to the fore of cultural consciousness and took on new meanings in relation to power and identity. In framing the American 1960s as a time and place in which it felt increasingly difficult, yet increasingly urgent, to make sense of senseless violence, Didion's essay indexes new ways of thinking and talking about violence that took shape after World War II and through the period of social change referred to as the long 1960s.

## Senseless Violence, Structural Violence, Aesthetic Violence

After 1945, American culture responded to changing scales and forms of violence: the world wars; genocide; the looming threat of nuclear annihilation.

Likewise, forms of political and social violence became newly legible and contested in the context of the liberation movements of the long 1960s, a period characterized by the increasing visibility of the civil rights movement, second-wave feminism, the antiwar movement, and gay liberation. This period saw new ways of thinking and talking about violence and ranges roughly from 1945, with the end of World War II, to the September 11 attacks in 2001, a period bracketed by wide-reaching media circulation of spectacular suffering in the form of the Holocaust and the 9/11 attacks. These two events, particularly as they were taken up through a mainstream US perspective, were frequently framed as an exceptional break from history in ways that could maintain a myth of US innocence in relation to geopolitical and ideological contexts.[4] The immediate postwar period was shaped by mass media imagery of spectacular and exceptionalized suffering that was highly visible while ongoing geopolitical violence of Pacific expansion took place. As distinct from the clear "imposition of a hurt" made legible by war, Cold War skirmishes and occupation in the Pacific were experienced, as Sunny Xiang has put it, as "hardly war," an ongoing experience of "war as hardly intelligible rather than spectacularly violent."[5] The postwar moment was shaped by geopolitical entanglements that were both overwhelming in scale and inscrutable or systemic. With spectacles of suffering increasingly available to audiences through mass media, the question of what registered as violence became culturally significant.

This book focuses on aesthetic responses to these changing conversations around violence in the long 1960s, characterized by concepts including senseless violence and structural violence. Tracing formalist renderings of suffering in literature, art, and performance through the 1990s, the coda turns to September 11, 2001, an event that shifted cultural concepts of suffering once again. The immediate aftermath of 9/11, which would eventually cohere into the war on terror,[6] marks a retrenchment of discourses of violence that sought to silence critiques of the United States as agent of suffering under a sentimental banner of exceptionalism around an attack imagined as singular. September 11 marks a shift in cultural understanding of suffering, an event that also coincided with the widespread adoption of the Internet and development of digital media, a moment that roughly coincided with the rise of mass shootings signaled by the Columbine massacre and attendant discourses of senseless violence.

This book explores how writers and artists took up the problem of representing suffering between these two important moments, in the context of emerging discourses of violence characterized by concepts of the senseless and the structural. One thread of this response, which I call aesthetic violence, built on modernist aesthetic strategies to restage and defamiliarize structures of violence, producing experiences of senselessness that gave audiences space to feel violent dynamics at a new and generative scale. The book traces a period heretofore undertheorized in the literary history of violence. The long 1960s in the United States forms an important chapter in this history. It continues the modernist tendency, theorized by Sarah Cole, to explore the intermingling of "private, subjective, and personal" experiences of suffering "rooted in the body" and "the representative, where larger political readings are invited."[7] In the subsequent historical moment, conceptions of violence as senseless speak to the experiential and personal, while notions of systemic violence point toward politics. Both of these frameworks, however, are insufficient for apprehending their intertwined nature. Both can occlude, as much as illuminate, ways of knowing about pain and the systems that cause it. Queering forms of state-sanctioned violence through aesthetic technique, works of the long 1960s remade pervasive forms of violence into sites for feeling differently about suffering. By committing to a primarily aesthetic project of exploring a feeling of senseless violence produced by systems of inequality, these works undo overdetermined approaches to violence and resist being instrumentalized for straightforwardly political projects.

Rhetorics of senselessness go hand in hand with new conceptions of violence as systemic or structural; *senseless* can name the experience of trying and failing to grasp the scope of systemic violence that exceeds human agency. The concept of senseless violence can be adopted to obscure or illuminate, to name the experiences of a victim or to hide the motivations of a perpetrator, to preserve a violent status quo or resist it. To claim that an act of violence is senseless is a rhetorical and political gesture, demarcating certain kinds of violence as preventable, beyond the pale, meaningless, or irredeemable. In turn, the notion of a "senseless" violence implies its inverse: some violent acts, according to this logic, are rational, necessary, or redemptive. As discussions of real-world violence increasingly drew on the framework of senselessness to make such rhetorical moves, writers and artists occupying minoritarian subject positions were developing a counteraesthetic of violence. These aesthetic techniques allowed for powerful affective responses in audiences while intervening in protocols of interpretation that see violence against marginalized people as all too familiar and legible, ultimately defamiliarizing forms of common sense that maintain a violent status quo.

As an alternative to questions of sense-making, artists and writers of the long 1960s employed what I call aesthetic violence. Aesthetic violence forecloses some avenues for interpretation or meaning-making in order to encourage alternate forms of sensory engagement. I borrow the term "aesthetic violence" from Leo Bersani and Ulysse Dutoit, who define it as a difficult perceptual encounter with art, in which the challenge of making sense of the work is experienced phenomenologically as a kind of pain.[8] Bersani and Dutoit defined this aesthetic violence in a 1979 *October* article, later expanded into a short book, which took a formalist approach to the violence depicted in ancient Assyrian palace reliefs. More recently, filmmaker and scholar Kamila Kuc has defined aesthetic violence as the destructive acts inherent in art-making (such as the filmmaker's cut or edit) that also generate new aesthetic and political insights.[9] As these theorists suggest, violence is inherent to the aesthetic experience: artists exercise force on their materials to create their works, and in turn, the emotional and cognitive demands artworks place on audiences can be a violating or painful experience. Perhaps it must be, if art is to move its audiences. I will say more about the concept of aesthetic violence below, delimiting its definition to focus on specific formal techniques that produce ambiguities about the suffering depicted, but here I want to linger in the conceptual murkiness of the term. Is all aesthetic experience a kind of violence? And does that claim overlook important distinctions between physical acts of violation and difficult emotional experiences? A novel cannot break my leg; a painting will not starve me. Yet theories of violence often treat the agential infliction of force by one body on another as the prototypical definition of violence, obscuring other ways to see how suffering is distributed in the world.[10] Complicating this definition, aesthetic violence inheres in the force of forms.

Aesthetic violence interrogates the concept of senselessness, and the arts are uniquely fertile ground for exploring the possibility that any experience can be "authentically senseless." The *Oxford English Dictionary* tells us that "senseless" can mean unfeeling or insensate, incapable of sensation or perception. In some usages, "senseless" means to be rendered unconscious or insensate through an act of violence. When not used to define a quality in a person or object, "senseless" describes events that are foolish, pointless, purposeless, or meaningless.[11] To be senseless can mean to be unfeeling, and while senseless aesthetics can prevent some kinds of feeling, like the release of catharsis, they also produce forms of feeling that are difficult to resolve or that sustain discomfort around a scene of violence, straining against commonsense understandings of the world that enable us to assimilate violence into a familiar, if still disturbing, mode of representation. Two notions of senselessness coincide in the aesthetics of postwar literature: senselessness can manifest as a kind of "unfeeling" as it has been defined by Xine Yao, which is to say, a feeling that is not recognized as feeling in a framework of dominant power structures.[12] Another notion, of senselessness as pointless, stupid, and meaningless, unintelligible or so extreme as to no longer be sensible,[13] points toward the rhetorical utility of calling violence senseless while also pointing us back to Didion's question about when and whether it is possible to make sense of violence. In contemporary colloquial usage, senseless violence is typically invoked around mass shootings and other forms of gun violence, though it is also invoked to describe terrorist attacks—violent acts that are clearly purposeful and politically motivated.[14]

Contemporary colloquial usage tends to invoke senselessness when describing spectacularly violent encounters. Tracking a prehistory of contemporary senseless violence through its aesthetic formation in the long 1960s, this book offers resources for bringing aesthetic awareness to bear on overdetermined discourses of violence that reaffirm a violent status quo through approaches that emphasize spectacle, sensationalism, and sentimentality. As Rob Nixon puts it, "our rhetorical conventions for bracketing violence routinely ignore ongoing, belated causalities."[15] As we will see, aesthetic queries into senselessness unearth the systemic or structural nature of violence disproportionately experienced by minoritized groups. Aesthetic violence heightens attention to the fuzzy boundaries between violence and nonviolence, the spectacular as well as the unrecognized elements of violence. Although senseless violence as a concept and turn of phrase dates back at least to the eighteenth century, its usage in American writing increased significantly after World War II and grew, across the second half of the twentieth century, alongside the concepts of structural violence and systemic violence.[16] The discourse of senseless violence developed alongside increasingly prevalent understandings of violence as enacted by a system or structure, suffering inflicted not by human actors but by systems operating according to their own logic. The sociologist Johan Galtung coined the term "structural violence" in his 1969 article "Violence, Peace, and Peace Research," defining structural violence as a kind of violence in which it is "no longer meaningful" to attempt to "trace[]" a violent effect to an originating actor; instead, "there may not be any person who directly harms another person in the structure. The violence is built into the structure and shows up as unequal power and consequently as unequal life chances."[17] With the rise of these conceptual frameworks around suffering, two seemingly contradictory concepts of violence were in fact intertwined. "Senseless" can be a rhetorical technique for ignoring structural causes; it can also be a description of the experience of suffering within violent systems. Rather than unearth a series of authentically senseless events depicted in literature and art, however, this book identifies formal strategies that structure violence and respond to discourses of senselessness, sometimes by making sense of seemingly arbitrary acts of violence, sometimes by heightening experiences of senselessness to focus attention on the feeling of encounter with violent systems.

As it developed in postwar mass media discourse, the concept of senseless violence was frequently used to suggest that new kinds of crime were proliferating uncontrollably. Stuart Hall's landmark study of the 1970s "mugging" phenomenon in Great Britain illustrates the broader ways that the concept of senselessness came to play a role in Western society's understanding of itself as threatened by violence. The mugging discourse, Hall claims, arose in the 1970s not because new forms of crime were actually developing, but as a new name given to a familiar criminal behavior. This phenomenon was better understood to reflect white British anxieties about changing economic conditions and the increasing visibility of Black and Brown people in their communities than a real change in how crime happened. Borrowing from American discourses of crime, sensationalized media reporting on mugging helped to create "a new construction of the social reality of crime" that also "provoked an organised response, in part because it was linked with a widespread *belief* about the alarming rate of crime in general, and with a common *perception* that this rising crime was also becoming more violent."[18] Not only reflecting these shifting beliefs about the violence of society, but shaping them as well, mass media reporting on "senseless" attacks also reflects an assumption that society is basically "consensual," with members generally sharing a belief system about how society functions.[19] This consensus renders some forms of violence (like mugging) senseless and other forms of violence (like increasingly punitive prison sentences for muggers) rational. Operating on this assumption, the broader cultural work of media discourses of mugging also helps to produce a hegemonic notion that society is increasingly violent and, moreover, that this violence must be contained through increased policing and other forms of "'soft' law-and-order."[20]

In the United States, a similar dynamic developed at this time concerning "riots," which Elizabeth Hinton has argued would be better thought of as rebellions.[21] After 1968, when Lyndon Johnson inaugurated the so-called war on crime, violence in Black communities came to be seen as anarchic, senseless outbursts, when in fact they were frequently organized or motivated responses to increasing police violence within Black communities. Noting that throughout American history, much more of our country's extralegal violence has been committed by white groups than Black, Hinton shows how "it was only when white people no longer appeared to be the driving force behind rioting in the nation's cities, and when Black collective violence against exploitative and repressive institutions surfaced, that 'riots' came to be seen as purely criminal, and completely senseless, acts. 'Law and order' became the main response from the white establishment."[22] Discourses about senseless violence in this period did little to reduce that violence; instead, increased cultural concern about senseless acts of violence frequently authorized new forms of state-sanctioned violence or surveillance to manage the crisis.

That said, while the cry of "senseless violence" was frequently voiced by an implicitly white mainstream who refused to see the social forces that might motivate (Black) people to steal, break a store window, fight back against police, or perform other acts of violence, the concept of senselessness was also invoked by those sympathetic to Black freedom movements. Editorials in progressive white newspapers in Mississippi, for example, decried the "senseless" violence committed by white supremacists who protested James Meredith's matriculation to the University of Mississippi.[23] Although this editorial invoked senselessness to advocate for integration, it also advocated for "law and order"—in this case, the ordering force of the National Guard troops brought in to protect Black citizens from white mob violence.[24] Harnessing the concept of senselessness to indict the violence of white supremacist protestors, this editorial still reflects the strange paradox of senselessness: its rhetorical force can serve a number of different political commitments, and it can be invoked to deflect or set aside clear motivations for violence, whether those motivations derive from a desire to maintain or to resist oppressive social systems. As Hall has put it in his discussion of mugging, media discourses of violence in the long 1960s often "rais[ed] the wrong things into sensational focus, hiding and mystifying the deeper causes."[25] These media discourses often obscured power relations that shaped violent phenomena, but a counter-aesthetic of formalized violence, developing in literature and visual art of this period, purposefully obscured some aspects of violence in ways that could ultimately illuminate the workings of power and affect in violent dynamics.

The converging discourses of structural and senseless violence set the stage for a specifically *aesthetic* phenomenon that complicates attempts to find "the sermon in the suicide," foregoing representational protocols that

explain violent phenomena in favor of producing an experience of senselessness in audiences. Inflicting forms of disorienting violence on audiences,
this aesthetic violence invites a mode of sustained feeling that unsettles commonsense notions underwriting violent social systems. Aesthetic violence
is a formal development, but it can also be defined as the experience produced by texts that do not just *represent* violence, but which *enact* it by producing experiences for readers that can be painful in their disorientation and
lack of resolution. Though they inflict a form of pain, these texts defamiliarize everyday acts of state-sanctioned violence, facilitating more capacious
feeling and thinking about the violences of everyday life. This aesthetic project disrupts *rhetorics* of senseless violence through formal innovation:
sometimes, these forms surface structures that explain seemingly senseless
suffering. Sometimes they offer a counter-discourse that emphasizes the
senseless experiences produced through legitimate, state-sanctioned violence. And sometimes these forms reproduce the senseless experience of
being subject to structural violence. The forms pain could take in this context also defamiliarized the commonsense notions of violence being invoked
in discourses of senselessness. In an era of sensationalized media reporting
on violence, aesthetic violence offered an alternative to sense-making in order to produce different types of knowledge routed through the body, ones
that ultimately provide new insight into various forms of power and readers' relationship to them.

Drawing on modernist strategies for producing aesthetic engagement,
aesthetic violence offered a strategy for addressing political questions but not
necessarily protesting political circumstances. James Baldwin limns the limitations of protest in his 1949 essay "Everybody's Protest Novel." Criticizing
*Uncle Tom's Cabin* and *Native Son* as two sides of the same sentimental coin—
one that maintains an illusion of white moral purity even in its condemna-
tion of white supremacy—the essay claims that "the 'protest' novel, so far
from being disturbing, is an accepted and comforting aspect of the American scene."[26] Its display of social injustice does not force an authentic confrontation with our material and emotional implication in that injustice, but
simply provides "a very definite thrill of virtue from the fact that we are reading such a book at all."[27] Just as the essay's title "implies that the actual function of protest novels was not to reform society but rather to produce
discourses of certainty,"[28] so does Baldwin's broader argument reflect the
dangers of certainty when confronted with representations of violence. Operating in line with a sociologically informed episteme of racial and gender
difference, the protest novel, as Jodi Melamed has demonstrated, reaffirms

those categories of difference as well as the hierarchies of oppressor and oppressed against which it protests, ultimately producing "a new form of normative and rationalizing violence."[29] It also extends demands on marginalized groups to make those appeals according to specific, limiting representational strategies of legibility. This "politics of explanation" places marginalized people "in the position of defending the[ir] humanity," a position that unavoidably affirms the very dehumanizing logic it seeks to contest.[30] The audience for the protest novel, in other words, only recognizes the suffering of marginalized people when it aligns with received narratives about society and produces the "thrilling" emotions that feel morally superior yet do little to confront violence in all its complexity. As an alternative to the legible language of protest, Baldwin would favor an emphasis on the "incoherence" of the United States' racist, sexist, and homophobic logics.[31] In addition to theorizing this incoherence in his nonfiction political critiques, Baldwin, like other midcentury writers aestheticizing violence, explored this incoherence in his fiction, inviting audiences to attend to, rather than disambiguate, such incoherence in order to help "germinat[e]" new ways of thinking and feeling about violence and power.[32] Sidestepping or torquing representational norms of the scopic regime of race and gender,[33] the aesthetic offers an alternative grounds for thinking through suffering.

This book traces a postwar literary formation that turns away from protest yet engages the "incoherence" of state violence that was being protested at the time. This literary formation unsettles readings of minoritarian creative works that tend to treat these works as *"all content and no form* — overdetermined by the artist's biography and isomorphic with the sociopolitical."[34] The works I bring together in this study take up "the structural conditions of social violences" as part of their violent imagery in order to draw attention to their aesthetic properties and to the sensory, sensuous engagement they demand of audiences. Although they might seem to abdicate political and ethical responsibilities to the groups that disproportionately experience structural violence, those writers and artists who commit to an aesthetic project above all else demonstrate a feminist, queer commitment to form that creates space for the wide-ranging affective responses those groups might feel in the face of violence. Deflecting the spectacle of suffering, a spectacle that frequently affirms social hierarchies of race, gender, ability, and sexuality, aesthetic violence often clashes with, rather than reflects, social organization. Formalist approaches to suffering thwart interpretations that violently and "prematurely fix the meaning of minority artistic production within prefabricated narratives."[35] Canonical yet marked in different ways by minoritarian gender, racial, dis/ability, and sexual identities, texts that aestheticize violence mobilize form to discourage interpretations that produce moral clarity, clear-cut social critique, or cathartic release. In so doing, artists and writers working with aesthetic violence produce aesthetic innovations, take a political stance against overdetermined representational protocols, and create a queer form of soliciting sensory engagement.

A formalist approach to the problem of pain, however, operates differently than sensationalism or sentimentality, two of the primary strategies writers and artists have historically deployed to protest injustice. The sensational heightens the brutality of suffering to whip up outrage, while the sentimental displays suffering to provoke pity or sadness.[36] Both modes represent violence in an effort to move audiences to a predictable form of feeling and, ultimately, to action. Aesthetic violence, by contrast, forecloses some emotional responses, especially sentimental responses that produce the satisfaction of "feeling right"[37] rather than fully reckoning with what is being represented. In protesting violence, a marginalized figure must all-too-frequently offer up a spectacle of suffering to make their rhetorical case, and this spectacle can become pleasurable for audiences, or can affirm the naturalness of the violence it seeks to undo.[38] Instead of instrumentalizing their violent scenes, these works sought to emphasize the often-illogical ways violence is experienced by victims, shifting the rhetorical work of the violent scenes from protest toward a kind of difficult and sustained aesthetic engagement.

What I am calling aesthetic violence overlaps with other modes of modulating or refusing feeling in the postwar era, signaling increasing interest in the limitations of appeals made through sentimental or sensational representations. This book shares with Deborah Nelson's account of "toughness" an interest in the unsentimental. A number of midcentury women writers and artists, including Didion, were committed to an aesthetic practice of toughness, an "outlook they shared on the questions of suffering and of emotional expressivity that preoccupied the late twentieth-century United States and, in many ways, continue to do so now. What makes them tough is their self-imposed task of looking at painful reality with directness and clarity and without consolation or compensation."[39] Though they share a skepticism toward the comparatively easy dynamic of sentimentality, toughness often appears in realist representations of suffering. Aesthetic violence, by contrast, draws on more stylized strategies coming from avant-garde and modernist traditions. Instead of eliciting emotional responses that would solidify group identity or cohere in a predictable way of feeling, formalized pain seeks to hold audiences in ambivalent or unclear modes of feeling, unsettling the notion that scenes of violence do predictable political work. Like Sianne Ngai's theory of ugly feelings that register ambivalent or blocked political agency,[40] aesthetic violence helps us theorize affective responses to historical conditions of structural violence. Similarly, recent scholarship in Asian American studies has detailed how the supposed inscrutability of Asian affect and identity not only reflects white mainstream crises of interpretation around racial identity but also might inform an identity politics that does not rely on essentialist categories of race.[41] Likewise, a politics of "unfeeling" that can be traced back to the nineteenth century offers a counterformation to the culture of sentiment,[42] informing aesthetic practices that hide characters' expressions of affect in order to refuse the command performances of feeling that mainstream audiences implicitly demand from representations of marginalized suffering.[43] Like modes of toughness and uncertainty that also developed in the postwar moment, an aesthetic approach to violence seeks to maintain, rather than resolve, interpretive problems that characterized the time period in order to surface aspects of suffering elided by commonsense notions about violence.

## American Cruelty

Scholars of post–1945 US literature and culture have analyzed the social functions of violent imagery, connecting cultural fascination with violent spectacles to innovations in media and technology.[44] In addition to the rise of abstract expressionism and the shift from Paris to New York as the epicenter of the visual arts,[45] changes in print journalism and the rise of television made the postwar period an image-saturated era. With the invention of photography, images of war could be brought close to a civilian, reprinted in newspapers, and later circulated as video footage on television.[46] The televisual relay of violence and catastrophe also reproduces images of suffering that are decontextualized from their origin point. They lack much of the necessary information that would help audiences make sense of them, yet television also purports to inform, to straightforwardly convey the news of suffering, and to unpack or explain the latest catastrophe.[47] Ostensibly stabilizing both the meanings of violence and the differences between victim, perpetrator, and witness, the photographed or filmed image of real-world suffering would also seem to build our consensus around how we understand violence. Yet as Susan Sontag cautions, "No 'we' should be taken for granted when the subject is looking at other people's pain."[48] Mass-mediated images of other people's pain purport to communicate clearly and directly, to produce predictable emotional responses and do clear-cut ideological work, but like sentimental appeals, these images can all too quickly slip into spectacle, eliciting forms of pleasure that do little to undo the violence they depict. This media landscape formed a backdrop against which literary culture reckoned with ways to ethically represent suffering, but one important facet of that culture drew on familiar forms shared by the visual arts in order to carve out space for thinking and feeling about violence in a different register. As television and mass media reshaped the scopic regime of violence, race, and gender, aesthetic violence emerged to counter the commonsense notions around suffering that were also being concretized at this time.

In response, aesthetic violence cultivated a particularly American form of avant-garde cruelty. In his theory of cruelty, French writer and artist Antonin Artaud insists that mimetic fidelity to real life limits artistic possibility and distracts from the embodied, subconscious, and sensory engagement audiences have with art.[49] In the wake of World War II, aesthetic violence could produce a form of Artaudian cruelty emerging in distinctly American portraits of violence directed at marginalized people. Postwar literary commitments to form—to privileging the aesthetic effect in a representation of violence—engendered a wide range of affective responses, rather than eliciting predictable responses that could be funneled into a coherent political project. Such an open-ended aesthetic project, however, could produce defamiliarizing effects that encourage audiences "to question the 'naturalness' not only of the aesthetic representation but also of the social facts to which it alludes, thereby opening them to active and potentially salutary revision."[50] When audiences are caught off guard by such "abstractionist" elements in a work, they attend to the strangeness of the effect and register the distinction between representation and reality.[51]

Opportunities for defamiliarization arise because language must follow certain rules in order to make sense.[52] Certainly, any art form may be more or less legible because of the ways it either adheres to or rejects formal and significatory conventions. From the cultural associations we make with different colors to the sense of closure provided by musical structure, elements such as patterns, recurrences, and structures—in short, *form*—enable audiences to derive meaning from artistic productions. Innovations in form might produce an audience experience of senselessness or nonsense, as when new listeners hear a minimalist composition by Arnold Schoenberg or uninitiated viewers see not a bird but a kitchen utensil in a Constantin Brâncuşi sculpture.[53] But the relation between formal familiarity and semantic legibility is particularly prominent in writing. Radically experimental writing can, of course, elicit novel kinds of engagement with text, even if signification is stripped away.[54] But narrative in particular relies on both relatively stable sign systems and a logic of continuity across the reading experience to produce meaning—indeed, to be *read* at all. Given the close relationship between language and sense-making, then, forms that trouble interpretive protocols are particularly poised to affect readers, both defamiliarizing the violence they represent and sparking a powerful phenomenological engagement with the text.

Mining the tension between visual spectacle and narrative coherence, this book tracks the mobilization of five forms shared by fiction and visual or performance artworks that aestheticize violence. These forms—the frame, the happening, the grotesque, the silhouette, and the collage—give shape to experiences of suffering in the long 1960s. Like other unsentimental or unfeeling aesthetic strategies, formalized violence intervenes in a cultural history that has frequently imagined both affect and identity to be legibly written on the body, visible to audiences who are receptive to sensational or sentimental displays of suffering.[55] To get at the affective work of formalized violence, I proceed from the notion that an inquiry into violent *imagery* in literature is enriched by comparison to violent *images* in the visual arts. Like the film theorist Eugenie Brinkema, I think that formalist approaches to violence might help resolve some of the challenges of an affective critique of violence.[56] Such an approach, though, need not sidestep affect or the phenomenological encounter with the image. Rather, analysis of form can work in concert with attention to audience experience. The abstracting possibilities of visual representation, as Leo Bersani and Ulysse Dutoit have explored, can produce a "kind of aesthetic violence" that demonstrates how violence is an aesthetic problem in general: this is a "'violence' of multiple contacts producing multiple forms," which effects a "perceptual wandering" in the viewer's eye that undoes attempts at interpretation, frustrating audiences.[57] More than frustrating, this perceptual wandering can become painful, an unresolvable phenomenological encounter with art that will not yield to the closure of interpretation.

Aesthetic violence is produced by formal arrangement of elements that set representations of violence within colliding or proliferating visual elements that keep a viewer's perceptual apparatus in motion, struggling to locate the narrative movement of the violent act. Bersani and Dutoit, noting that the perceptual disruption of abstraction is common in modernist art, also find it in the ancient Assyrian palace reliefs that depict war, lion hunting, and other violent scenes. Yet the violence depicted within the scenes is obscured or "contravened by visual abstractions which disrupt the spectator's reading of the subject."[58] The violence of an image is its displacement of violence: the difficulty of locating and reading the impact of force being represented produces a phenomenological struggle against the force of forms that obstruct one's view. Bersani and Dutoit's choice of the verb "reading" here is important, as it emphasizes the function of narrative in our sense-making protocols. When spectators cannot read the scene, they struggle to determine the narrative action being portrayed and settle on a fixed interpretation of what is happening. This aesthetic violence disrupts narrative approaches to violence, which imagine it to be contained to its emplotment, to be an act of force that is locatable, interpretable, and containable. The "narrative space" of an image uses foreground and background to direct audience attention to story elements and move them from beginning to middle to end. By contrast, an aesthetic violence offers a "continuous . . . space of related forms," demanding that viewers engage the interplay and collision of specifically formal elements.[59]

The tendency to see violence as story (or perhaps, *pace* Didion, to tell ourselves stories about violence) can naturalize violent dynamics and provoke fascination with violent spectacles that are erroneously imagined as a rupture of basically peaceful life.[60] Both violence and the image are fundamentally ambiguous and are primed to facilitate the experience of senselessness. In the formation of an image, a unity is created through a kind of force, and in creating unity from disparate elements, the creation of an image "tear[s] apart a closed intimacy or a non-disclosed immanence."[61] In this way, then, "not only violence but the extreme violence of *cruelty* hovers at the edge of the image, of all images."[62] Though representation seems to fall short in accounting for the senselessness of violence or the experience of pain, ample evidence contradicts the notion that violence is unrepresentable.[63] Western art is full of depictions of violence. Even more fundamentally, the manipulation of form and feeling that coalesces in any image per se might be understood as a kind of violence. Viewed through this lens, represented violence can be seen to do affective work that does not resolve itself in a purgation of violent feeling or the impulse to repeat violence.[64] Formalist approaches to violent imagery illuminate epistemic questions about violence and representation.


## Unsettling Common Sense

Since the advent of aesthetic discourse in the Enlightenment era, debates about beauty and form were also often debates about how society should be organized. For Russ Castronovo, the concept of aesthetic judgment involves impulses toward both democracy and fascism: can a multiplicity of competing judgments exist? Or does aesthetic judgment necessitate a hierarchical arrangement of power? As he puts it, "When aesthetic form shapes political possibility, violence appears at the edges of the discourse on beauty."[65] Aesthetic choices about how to depict violence could affirm or undermine violent social dynamics: as interrogations of modernism and fascism have shown, the risk of aestheticizing violence is that horrific acts become a kind of common sense, naturalized and celebrated when they are seen as questions of form, rather than human suffering.[66] At the same time, aesthetic discourse may be reworked to make violence ugly, and therefore to advocate for its prevention.[67] Aesthetic violence interrupts some of the common sense that crystallizes around suffering, such as the notion that the law has a natural monopoly on exercising violence.[68] By heightening and maintaining unresolved, often ambiguous feelings, aesthetic violence can also heighten attention to what Jacques Rancière calls "the distribution of the sensible," or the ways aesthetics shape the terrain of what individuals can apprehend via their sense perception.[69] Experimental or otherwise highly stylized aesthetic practices that announce their commitment to form open a view to what might be disallowed or illegible in the sensus communis. Scenes of aesthetic violence instantiate a moment of hermeneutic impasse by failing to follow legible scripts about violence, opening new perspectives that can undo the naturalized logics, or the common sense, of suffering.

My attention to the aesthetics of violence in the postwar era might raise alarm bells for modernists, who will recall Walter Benjamin's admonition at the end of "The Work of Art in the Age of Mechanical Reproduction." Benjamin writes that "All efforts to render politics aesthetic culminate in one thing: war."[70] In an essay celebrating the political possibilities of new artistic media, Benjamin situates an aesthetic of violence as a product of fascism, one in which, as Susan Buck-Morss glosses it, "sensory alienation lies at the source of the aestheticization of politics," and our disconnect from our own senses also allows us to take pleasure in "viewing our own destruction."[71] Rather than advocate for a propagandistic, "political" art, however, Benjamin seeks an art that can "undo the alienation of the corporeal sensorium [and] restore the instinctual power of the human bodily senses for the sake of humanity's self-preservation."[72] Reminding us of the roots of the "aesthetic"—which lie not in the bloodless forms of the artwork itself but in the sensory apperception of stimuli—Buck-Morss claims that Benjamin's theory of modernity might actually point toward ways aesthetics can ground anti-fascist responses to the world.[73] A formalist approach can make violence beautiful, or at least compelling, and in doing so, aesthetic violence can awaken sensory attention. Though representations of suffering that are indeterminate or noncathartic can produce painful feelings in audiences, these senseless experiences also help audiences to occupy the edge of knowing, a place before comprehension that can activate new attempts to understand. Distinct from a will to knowledge that would fix meaning and the social categories underwriting that meaning, this senseless experience of not quite or not yet knowing, mobilized through affect and sensation, is an experience of the "proto-political" work of the aesthetic.[74]

Without directly encouraging action as a response to the violence represented, aesthetic violence participates in new structures of feeling that might disrupt the naturalized logics of structural violence—violence that does not always appear as such. Here, I want to highlight the historical convergence of structural violence and Raymond Williams's theory of structures of feeling. Appearing in the interstices of social life, structures of feeling name places where ideology has not yet hardened and social relations might yet be reimagined.[75] Aesthetic debates have long been terrain for debates about how society should be organized and what democracy really looks like, yet the aesthetic is a volatile site, one that is generative for thinking through social arrangements precisely because it tends to produce unpredictable responses in audiences.[76] While resisting an instrumental approach to art that values it only for the direct impacts it might make on actors in the world (and particularly on the public arena of political life), aesthetic violence nevertheless intervenes in the social by disrupting interpretive tendencies that rely on familiar narratives about suffering. Aestheticizing violence became one way for these writers and artists to theorize and reflect on how language and image can produce commonsense understandings of suffering and, in turn, to elicit rich affective responses in audiences that might revise that common sense.[77] Reproducing a kind of avant-garde cruelty through a commitment to form, frames, happenings, grotesques, silhouettes, and collages could articulate nascent structures of feeling taking shape in response to discourses of senselessness and structural violence. When invoked by activists, politicians, or journalists, senseless violence is claimed as further evidence affirming an already settled worldview; it is a moral judgment or an abdication of the responsibility to judge. When explored via aesthetic technique, however, violence can upend the certainty of common sense aligned with state control of force, producing interpretive impasses that encourage more open-ended thinking and feeling.

## Painful Forms in the Long 1960s

The forms of aesthetic violence explored in the chapters to follow withhold, make ambiguous, or erase some strategies for knowing about violence in order to open up other forms of knowledge about suffering. Like other scholars associated with new formalism, I draw on the notion of affordances to name the ways formal strategies can elicit or encourage certain audience responses. Introduced by the psychologist James J. Gibson, an affordance of a given object names the ways it can be used—including uses not imagined by the creator of the object. Similarly, the affordances of literary form allow it to "do so many different, even contradictory things"[78]—and to produce a wide range of audience responses while affording some responses more readily than others. The concept of affordances clarifies how particular representational strategies produce uncertainty[79] and similar feelings of senselessness, demonstrating that limitations on interpretation can be built into a text designed to be interpreted. In this way, aesthetic violence disrupts the hermeneutic closure of the reading process and cultivates a difficult or painful phenomenological experience. For Namwali Serpell, an uncertain reading experience forces an ethical struggle with the questions raised by the text.[80] An uncertain reading experience where violence is the primary dynamic in question, I contend, also cultivates an aesthetic awareness of the forms of violence in our texts and our lives as well as the opportunity to build new structures of feeling around old forms of violation.

Moving promiscuously across image, text, and performance, each chapter of this book focuses on a form suffering has taken in the postwar era, tracking how literary and visual culture participated in emerging epistemic shifts around violence. *Frames* undo rhetorics of law and order that justify violent policing and capital punishment; *happenings* primarily give shape to the feeling of being subject to state violence as collateral damage; *grotesques* theorize the dynamic between knowledge and accident; *silhouettes* outline scenes of Jim Crow vigilante violence to resist spectacle; and *collages* formalize the fragmentation of sexual violence. While I occasionally track lines of influence between writers and artists, I am more interested in the ways text and image converge in their use of a formal structure for aestheticizing violence. Each of these forms deploys techniques of ambiguity, abstraction, inversion, or withholding as a way of rerouting the burden of feeling from marginalized victim to implicated audience member, in turn affording the experience of affective connection across reading audiences. If "affect [is] a relation unfurled by aesthetic objects,"[81] then hermeneutic impasses staged by form are not stultifying, but potentially generative. The works I analyze in this book are united by their relationship to modernist lineages and their commitment to an aesthetic project of representing violence, even those authors, like Baldwin and Toni Morrison, who have clear political commitments and records of activism.[82] Indeed, the first half of the book explores how writers and artists with radically distinct political commitments may nevertheless formalize violence in parallel ways to invite difficult affective experiences. When I compare Baldwin's use of framing to Andy Warhol's in chapter one, for example, I demonstrate a shared formal provocation that defamiliarizes state violence without necessarily making claims about how to respond to that violence. Indeed, a comparison between Baldwin and Warhol shows how these forms are ideologically portable. By emphasizing form in my approach to representations of violence, I show how aesthetic commitments can offer resources for thinking more deeply about violence, contesting notions that aesthetic criticism abdicates a responsibility to politics.[83] Indeed, I believe that in a moment characterized by debates about trigger warnings and the role of trauma in contemporary literature and the teaching of literature, careful attention to the aesthetic work of form must inform our understanding of these issues.

The first half of the book demonstrates how aesthetic violence metabolized new conceptions of structural and political violence, theorizing two forms that could contest rhetorics of senseless violence that affirmed state power. The first chapter shows how aesthetic violence can redirect attention from the spectacle of senseless violence and toward state structures that violently police social spaces and categories of race and gender. Frames highlight and upend rhetorics of senseless violence by shifting audience attention toward the boundary between random and state-sanctioned violence. Whether describing the physical structure holding a painting on the wall or a narrative feature in which a story is told from a vantage point of looking back on the past, the frame is a common form that has long been shared by visual art and fiction. Heightening attention to visual and narrative frames that are always at work in representation, the stylized frames of chapter one destabilize familiar assumptions about victims and perpetrators of violence, highlighting the violent effects of law-and-order rationality. Comparing visual techniques of framing in the work of Andy Warhol with James Baldwin's frame narrative in *Giovanni's Room*, this chapter argues that the frame is a form of attention that provides an alternate view of structural and senseless violence.

The book's second chapter argues that the form of the happening took shape as a way to articulate new epistemologies of suffering in a time of technological change that increased precarity. The name given to chance-based, unpredictable performance art events that began to develop in the 1950s, the happening also formalized the dynamic of waiting for violation that may or may not come, cultivating a feeling of suspension in audiences. The chapter takes up Yoko Ono's chance-based performance events as a lens through which to see how chance-based artistic processes responded to the wide-scale violence of potential nuclear attack and other forms of being collateral damage in a violent geopolitical system. I situate the happening in aesthetic innovations by John Cage and Allen Kaprow, then show how this form of violence appeared in literary technique, turning to Kurt Vonnegut's *Slaughterhouse-Five* as an example of literary deployment of the happening. A form that is rooted in both rule-bound procedure and anarchic chance, the happening not only names aesthetic innovations developed in the wake of abstract expressionism but also offers an aesthetic language to understand suffering that is experienced as random but produced by systems working as they are designed to. By inflicting aesthetic violence on audiences by suspending them in uncertainty, the happening invites deeper inquiry into the experience of embodiment in a precarious historical moment.

These two chapters form the first half of the book, which explores how the aesthetic defamiliarizes mainstream discourses of senseless violence and makes sense of structural violence. The third chapter, "Grotesque," functions as a hinge in my argument. The grotesque is often understood as a style of exaggeration, characterized by faces that appear frozen in intense pain. Yet as the cultural history of the grotesque indicates, this pain may in fact be a matter of perspective. Grotesque images may convey suffering, but they may also be misrecognized as images of pain. A term that clusters around mass media spectacles of suffering such as photographs of car accidents, the grotesque formalizes the epistemological challenge of making sense of accidents. Flannery O'Connor and her close friend, playwright Maryat Lee, used grotesque aesthetics to theorize the boundary between chance and design in experiences of suffering. The first half of the book offers some aesthetic techniques for making sense of senseless violence, and through the transition of the grotesque, the book shifts attention to ways form can thwart cathartic or hermeneutic responses in favor of exploring the uneasy affects of the senseless.

The second half of the book theorizes painful forms in order to show how aesthetic violence facilitates new responses to suffering by participating in structures of feeling. Aesthetic violence echoes and defamiliarizes forms of state violence, articulating structures of feeling that emerge in relation to those forms. Chapter four argues that the *silhouette* is an empty form that takes shape around lynching imagery. The silhouette outlines scenes of interpersonal violence to make them fundamentally ambiguous. Traditionally, silhouettes are a form of portraiture that renders a shadow or outline of the subject in black on a white background. A form that developed in the Enlightenment era and was closely connected to the assumption that physiognomy revealed character, the silhouette also carries with it the ideologies of race and gender that developed in that period and helped to rationalize the violences of transatlantic slavery. Mobilizing the silhouette to subvert dynamics of looking at Black suffering, the work of Toni Morrison and Kara Walker refuses to provide the spectacle of violence that can "immure" observers to suffering as easily as it can provoke outrage.[84]

The book's fifth chapter turns to collage works that blend text and image and explores the reception of these works to show how aesthetic violence can produce affective connections that not only unsettle the common sense of systemic violence but also underwrite new responses to that violence. The *collage*, a modernist form that developed in the visual arts and was adopted by writers, shocks audiences through radical, often mystifying juxtapositions. A practice of cutting and pasting found objects together on a canvas or, later, in a written work, the collage recontextualizes its materials through new arrangements. Producing a phenomenological experience of senseless shock, the collage was adopted as a feminist practice in radical literary movements unfolding as third-wave feminists debated the politics of both representing and responding to sexual violence. Comparing the collage work in Kathy Acker's fiction with the collage zines of riot grrrl artists, I show how the disjunctures of the collage become a formal container that could create space for taboo responses to sexual violence. In rendering sexual violence senseless, the collage affords emotional experiences of shock, recognition, and love that not only foster feminist community but also help to rewrite what Sharon Marcus has called the "grammar" of sexual violence.[85]

In charting the aesthetics of postwar violence across the forms of the frame, the happening, the grotesque, the silhouette, and the collage, I hope to show not only that a new way of navigating the aesthetics of violence emerged in the long 1960s, but also that attention to the aesthetics of violence can help us, ultimately, to make sense of violence and representation across a number of fields. In fields that study minoritarian literature and cultural production, such as queer studies, Black studies, critical race studies, and disability studies, a formalist approach to violence decouples the expected alignment between minoritarian art and protest, resisting attempts to interpret minoritarian art through a strictly sociopolitical lens in favor of more experimental modes of representation. In the field of post–1945 literary studies, aesthetic violence reveals an important way that some writers and artists responded to historical phenomena like the rise of the civil rights movement, second- and third-wave feminism, the Cold War, and the rise of mass visual culture. In tracking aesthetic violence across this period, I also trace the lineages of abstraction and post-abstraction through American literary culture, highlighting the persistence of modernist aesthetics in a postwar era typically characterized as a standoff between postmodernism and the return to realism. Broadly, a theory of aesthetic violence contributes to ongoing conversations about form and method by insisting that form does work in the world. This work is not, however, in a mode of straightforward critique but in the vein of affective, embodied engagement named by the aesthetic. Aesthetics are not merely on the page, but also in the body, and they do their work in subtle ways. Finally, scholars interested in affect studies can draw on the notion of aesthetic violence to see how affect can be a site of meaning-making, with the phenomenological experiences afforded by texts offering new insights on topics ranging from state execution to rape culture to the spectacle of Black suffering. By inviting audiences to encounter the limits of their own understanding, aesthetic violence also draws attention to the ways suffering is so often shaped by and bound up in sociopolitical dynamics of power and identity but is not reducible to stories we might tell about the social meaning of violence.

## CHAPTER ONE

# Frame

## *Rhetorics of Senseless Violence*

Think of a guillotine. Think of it empty, its slanted blade raised to form a kind of window; looking at the guillotine, viewers also look through this space to see a framed image of wherever they are. Below this, a circular frame; this is where the head goes. This is where death happens. Used for state executions in France until 1977,[1] the guillotine is a weapon, but it is also a form, a frame. Within the frame, death is imminent. When introduced in the 1790s, the guillotine "embodied revolutionary and Enlightenment ideals of humanism, science and efficiency" along with "a certain aesthetic appeal. The frame in which the blade runs is rectangular, the angled blade (*couperet*) appears triangular and the head collar (*la lunette républicaine*) makes a circle. This geometrical combination of rectangle, circle and triangle can be read as embodying an abstract, remote and mathematical beauty that is consistent with Enlightenment ideas of reason and universality."[2] The frame not only frames the victim, but is an aesthetic object by design. It is the guillotine that takes the life of Giovanni, a character in James Baldwin's 1956 novel *Giovanni's Room*. The form of the guillotine also informs the structure of the novel, for just as the guillotine's victim is only in frame up until the moment the blade falls, so is the novel framed through the moment of Giovanni's imminent execution. Frame narratives, nearly as old as storytelling itself, are temporal structures that contain an unfolding narrative within the context of one orienting moment: they shape perspective both spatially and temporally. The frame is a form of attention, and its aesthetic violence manipulates audience attention to challenge narrative certainty.

In this chapter, attention to the aesthetic work of framing will help us explore how competing perspectives on state-sanctioned violence played out in the long 1960s, when the rhetoric of senseless violence could be invoked to authorize or to contest the use of force by the state in an era of mass spectacle. With the rise of photojournalism in the postwar era, American audiences were experiencing the events of the long 1960s through mass-mediated images. By establishing a framework for viewing suffering, the photojournalistic image directs audience attention to a "constructed" slice of time and space that presents itself as an open window onto reality.[3] Media rhetorics sensationalized suffering, overwhelming audiences to the point of numbness, and implicitly framed that suffering as either rationalized and necessary or senselessly tragic. Taking up the frame as a formal technique made the implicit work of framing explicit, interrogating the common sense of media spectacle. This chapter explores how framing could be a rich aesthetic practice for giving shape to the structure of feeling emerging around state violence in the civil rights era. First, the chapter demonstrates how James Baldwin aestheticized suffering through the frame narrative in *Giovanni's Room*, then turns to Andy Warhol's reappropriation of mass media images of suffering in his *Death and Disaster* series. A form shared by textual and visual modes, the frame can deconstruct the clear-cut distinction between motivated and senseless violence, drawing attention to rhetorics of violence that rationalize law's force. In literature and art, the frame can also give form to the affective exchanges that often underwrite violent acts and their rationalization. As framing encloses and shapes a work's content, it also draws audiences into an encounter with the rhetorical work of form.

The Incoherence of Law and Order

In 1966, ten years after the publication of *Giovanni's Room*, Baldwin mapped a logic of the ostensibly "senseless" violence of the protests and riots that were by that time reaching a fever point in the United States. In *The Nation*, he contextualized the urban violence of the era through an extended explanation of the structural violence that placed Black Americans in positions of precarity: lack of union protection, increased automation that contributed to unemployment, segregated education, uneven infrastructure, biased textbooks, and racist hiring practices. People in this precarious position, Baldwin implies, are more likely to be pushed to the limit of violent action, not only because of the psychic damage of daily injustice, but also because they understand the government to be underwriting these injustices. Nowhere is this more apparent than in policing, carried out by those whom Baldwin describes as the "hired enemies" of the Black population, "present to keep the Negro in his place and to protect white business interests." In this context, argues Baldwin, calls to "respect the law" in times of social unrest are "obscene." "The law," he writes, "is meant to be my servant and not my master, still less my torturer and my murderer."[4]

Baldwin's experience in a Paris prison shaped his understanding of the law as a "master" that could lash out violently against Black, poor, and queer people. In 1949, not long after Baldwin arrived in Paris, he was arrested after a friend left a stolen sheet in his hotel room. Awaiting trial in a jail cell for eight days was one of the most harrowing times of Baldwin's life, which he describes in the essay "Equal in Paris," collected in *Notes of a Native Son*. After his release, Baldwin attempted suicide, failing only because the water pipe from which he tried to hang himself broke with the weight of his body. As D. Quentin Miller argues, prison links characters and figures throughout Baldwin's oeuvre and "focuses a theme that flourishes throughout his career" and helps him articulate "the reality of the law's power over lives like his."[5] Linking the social death of prison to the literal death of the guillotine through an articulation of the law as a violent master, Baldwin reconceptualizes the law's ostensibly rational violence as erratic, bloodthirsty, and misrecognizing. Drawing on the theories of Jacques Derrida and Saidiya Hartman in their reading of Baldwin's nonfiction, Jess A. Goldberg emphasizes how the law, as if by magic, converts unsanctioned violence into sanctioned violence rationalized as "necessary to maintain order."[6] As Goldberg argues, Baldwin theorizes law's force from the grounds of haptic encounter with the police to deconstruct the distinction between legitimate and illegitimate violence.[7] Through the body, people encounter the law's force not as maintaining social order, but as inflicting incoherent pain. As the anthropologist Anton Blok has put it, the law's monopoly on violence, legitimized through pervasive social narratives, stages the conditions for individuals to experience violence as senseless. Because "the dominant conception of violence in modern societies" is one in which violence has "long since been monopolized by the state," "people have developed strong feelings about using and witnessing violence. They are inclined to consider its unauthorized forms in particular as anomalous, irrational, senseless and disruptive—as the reverse of social order, as the antithesis of 'civilization,' as something that has to be brought under control."[8] Echoing points made by Stuart Hall in *Policing the Crisis*, Blok critiques media narratives for simplifying and sensationalizing violent acts, excluding context in ways that elide rationales or the relationship between means and ends, encouraging a view of these acts as senseless.[9] Baldwin's work reframes and questions this view, rhetorically reframing the exercise of state violence as incoherent and irrational.

In his essays, Baldwin traces those historical and cultural forces that mainstream American culture obscures, and one effect of his reframing is to reveal the motivations and rationales for the ostensibly senseless violence that erupts from marginalized people. In obscuring the historical forces that have produced social inequality, American narratives about its past have also invited citizens to imagine marginalized people—in this case, especially Black and queer people—as not only violent but as *senselessly* violent. In turn, the ostensibly necessary and rational use of authorized force is revealed, through haptic, terrifying encounter with its exercise, as arbitrary and excessive. "The law," writes Miller, "intended to be the most rational force holding together any society, becomes for Baldwin [while in prison] the most irrational force within society, one that would murder without remorse."[10] *Giovanni's Room* explores how this incoherent force is rationalized through mass media narratives that validate the state's exercise of violence to maintain white supremacy and heteronormativity. In his novel about a queer love affair that ends in two murders, Baldwin uses the frame narrative to highlight the forces of shame, whiteness, heteronormativity, and desire in facilitating violent encounters. Complicating notions of the antisocial, dangerous queer, the novel instead draws careful attention to the ways shame, a universal affect that undergirds identity, also activates violent encounters.

## Rhetorics of Violence in Giovanni's Room

*Giovanni's Room* received a "cautiously positive" critical reception upon its publication; though Baldwin's publishers warned him that publishing a novel with no Black characters that focused on homosexual desire would ruin his career, critics generally treated the novel as a "curious little detour" in his otherwise cogent oeuvre.[11] Later critical treatment, especially from Black queer studies, has recuperated his choice to write a novel with no Black characters by showing how this strategy allowed Baldwin to explore themes of queer desire and to theorize whiteness itself as a violent ideological structure.[12] Adopting the perspective of a white protagonist and narrator, the novel also uses a frame narrative to undercut the stability and reliability of its narrator. Frames mobilize perspective and are often visual forms; they can thus also index the question of the visual in literary representations of racial and sexual identity. Because literary imagery is not, after all, a mode for creating visual images, the novel can conceive of identity in ways that exceed the limitations of the visual regime. In light of the broader historical moment in which *Giovanni's Room* appears, the urgency of this move is clear: in a moment when the photojournalistic image held a privileged claim to truth, it also helped further naturalize categories of visible difference. As the rise of mass media reconfigured notions of personhood, the novel could address the role of imagery and affect in the world without reproducing visual images.

The novel's frame narrative takes place on the eve of Giovanni's execution for the murder of Guillaume, an older gay man. David, the novel's protagonist and Giovanni's former lover, recounts the story in flashbacks. David is a young, blond, and aimless white man who has emigrated to Paris from the United States and maintains an ambivalent romantic relationship with Hella. When Hella departs for Spain to consider her own feelings about their engagement, David meets the Italian émigré Giovanni and they begin a love affair. After David ends his relationship with Giovanni, in a seemingly unrelated sequence of events, Giovanni murders Guillaume in what may be a retributive act of violence after Guillaume sexually assaults him. Giovanni is soon arrested and sentenced to execution. David has abandoned Giovanni and will return to the United States, leaving Giovanni's ruined life in his wake. As David packs up his rented country house and prepares to return to the United States, he narrates their love affair and its dissolution, articulating a profound love for Giovanni that slowly becomes tinged with resentment, contempt, and disgust.

Henry James's influence on Baldwin is well-known, and *Giovanni's Room*, like many of James's novels, concerns an expatriate American in Europe.[13] It also mobilizes Jamesian framing devices in order to theorize an interlocking dynamic of identity, shame, and state violence. In her monograph about framing techniques in modernist fiction, Mary Ann Caws argues that "to frame in is also to frame out, so that the notions of grid and selection, or inclusion and exclusion, are constantly in play, as well as those of border and of centering or focus."[14] Frame narratives are only one of a variety of framing techniques in modernist fiction. Any of those techniques facilitate a heightened awareness of the question of attention itself: what do we see, and why? What is in frame, and what might lie just beyond? In *Giovanni's Room*, the frame narrative sets two models of cause and effect alongside one another, highlighting a dominant story in which the state distributes violence rationally only to set it against a competing narrative that surfaces how affects like desire, shame, and fear can move people to violent action. Framing techniques bring competing sense-making narratives into conflict, destabilizing perspective and epistemic certainty. In the case of *Giovanni's Room*, they also interrogate the commonsense beliefs that rationalize state violence.

Frame narratives have long been used to activate readers' engagement with plot, whether by providing orientation and justification for the narratives contained, as in *The Canterbury Tales*, or unsettling narrative certainty by offering multiple viewpoints on the events contained, as in *Frankenstein*. Framing *Giovanni's Room* through David's point of view on the eve of Giovanni's execution by guillotine positions the novel's protagonist in a melancholic, backward-glancing stance, one that shows how shame about his own sexual and racial identifications can be said to inaugurate a set of violent acts. The frame narrative indicts David for his treatment of Giovanni, suggesting that Giovanni's violent murder of Guillaume was at least partly a result of circumstances David caused. In turn, the novel suggests that state violence serves to maintain a violent white supremacy and heteropatriarchy, contesting its own narrative of itself as necessary to mete out justice or maintain safety.

Throughout the novel, David articulates shame about his queer desire and anxiety about his racial and class status, but in his framing narration he also seems to take responsibility for Giovanni's death. David's sense of responsibility might strike many readers as either an expression of guilt over his mistreatment of Giovanni or as a narcissistic symptom of a more general anguish. Yet the novel spins out an affective, rather than rational, logic of violence in which David is, in fact, to be held accountable for Giovanni's death. Soon after the first mention of Giovanni, in the frame story, David claims that, "when one begins to search for the crucial, the definitive moment, the moment which changed all others, one finds oneself pressing, in great pain, through a maze of false signals and abruptly locking doors."[15] He is speaking of his "flight" from America and from the truth of his desires. Associating this flight with his first homosexual experience as a young man in Brooklyn with a friend, Joey, he implicitly links the "definitive moment" of his shameful desire to the moment that ultimately causes Giovanni's death. Although David is an unreliable narrator, he does finally produce the "key" that unlocks the logical connections between his own behavior and Giovanni's death: "I was lying to myself," he claims near the end of the novel, at the beginning of a complex narrative chain I will discuss below.[16] This lie, David understands, has set in motion subsequent events that ultimately lead to the guillotine. Framed by the moment when Giovanni will be executed—framed, that is, by the specter of the guillotine—the novel also reframes a mass-mediated story about violence. The novel's form challenges familiar logics that authorize the state to mete out violence in the name of controlling racialized and queer people. *Giovanni's Room* heightens attention to perspective, framing scenes of suffering to multiply and ultimately destabilize familiar narratives about queerness and violence. The frame redirects attention to the ways homophobia, internalized shame, and racial anxieties authorize some forms of violence and frame others as inexplicable and in need of control.

The frame narrative reveals new ways of viewing overdetermined stories of suffering by juxtaposing competing narratives that remain in tension. As Mae G. Henderson argues, "the murder of Guillaume by Giovanni only appears to be the crime. The real crime, which leads to Giovanni's actions, and to the destruction of three lives, is David's deception and dishonesty. David, like Giovanni, is culpable; and, like Giovanni, he suffers for his offenses."[17] Whether or not Giovanni's attack on Guillaume is justified, it is not unmotivated: Guillaume sexually assaults Giovanni, insults him, and reminds him of his social power over Giovanni. In response, and in a fit of passion, Giovanni strangles Guillaume—at any rate, this is David's imagined reconstruction of events.[18] When Giovanni is discovered, he is tried. David relates newspaper descriptions, but not trial proceedings, when describing the case, emphasizing the media's role in shaping narratives of violence. Found guilty, Giovanni is led to the guillotine. In the French newspapers, Guillaume's death is reported as an act of senseless violence, one that is unmotivated and random. Yet David's account of the murder emphasizes Giovanni's motive, and moreover, the novel's plot maps a network of causal links that lead to Guillaume's death. As Stuart Hall has demonstrated in his work on the mugging discourse, the "senselessness" of a violent act is largely determined by the way it is framed in media narratives.[19] Similarly, the media account of Guillaume's murder produces a rhetoric of senseless violence that must be contained by the rational, ordering, and necessary violence of the state. Even David's counternarrative relies on a limited frame and offers a rationalizing logic for interpersonal violence. The novel, then, does not straightforwardly provide an explanation and motive for a sequence of violent events moving from rape to strangulation to guillotine, but instead confronts readers with competing frameworks for making sense of violent death. The frame cannot bring everything into focus; rather, it only enables multiple, but limited, views into events.

Immediately after David recounts Guillaume's murder, he describes the police roundups in the gay bars that follow, and the newspapers' reconstruction of the story that describes Guillaume as an honorable, kind man from a noble family who becomes a "symbol of French manhood." A silence surrounds the initial mention of Guillaume's murder: a chapter ends with the information that "Guillaume was found dead in the private quarters above his bar, strangled with the sash of his dressing gown," and the next chapter begins, "It was a terrific scandal."[20] Before narrating the details of Guillaume's murder in his own imaginative reconstruction, David notes its potential to "rock the very foundations of the state." Unpacking the state's logic of rational violence, David claims that "it is necessary to find an explanation, a solution, and a victim with the utmost possible speed," and in pursuit of this goal, "plainclothes policemen descended on the quarter, asking to see everyone's papers, and the bars were emptied of *tapettes* [derogatory term for homosexuals]," many of whom were arrested.[21] According to the novel, state violence appears to offer a necessary solution to the threat of violence against noble Frenchmen. Ultimately, however, this solution inflicts a great deal of arbitrary violence on poor, queer people and rationalizes that violence in the name of the nation. It is as if homosexuality itself threatens the well-being of the nation and its continuity into the future. In the normative story being told by the French media, Giovanni's execution will restore order to a disrupted social dynamic: violent and antisocial queers are policed, a patriarchal vision of family and genealogy is symbolically restored, and the state continues to operate rationally, offering justice and retribution to keep threat at bay and maintain social order.

However, the frame narrative subverts this logic by proliferating accounts of the event. Although the French media tell a story of a senseless act of violence that is finally resolved by the state's necessary violence, David offers a competing account in which he himself ultimately set in motion actions that would result in the death of both Guillaume and Giovanni. Early in the novel, David explicitly states that he is responsible for Giovanni's death. While pondering his earlier days, "before anything awful, irrevocable, had happened to me," David introduces Giovanni's character by stating, "people are too various to be treated so lightly. I am too various to be trusted." If this were not the case, he says, "Giovanni would not be about to perish, sometime between this night and this morning, on the guillotine."[22] Immediately linking Giovanni's death at the hands of the state to his own moral failings, David also sets up a major structuring conceit of the novel: he will explain exactly how he could be responsible for two deaths, neither of which he was present for. The frame narrative does the rhetorical work of orienting readers' attention toward some aspects of plot over others, manipulating available interpretive strategies. Indeed, the novel's framing perspective is that of its unreliable narrator, whose explanation of Giovanni's motive is ultimately just another frame that seems to make sense of Guillaume's death. Readers do not, ultimately, have access to a disinterested account of what transpired between Guillaume and Giovanni; the novel offers a French media narrative and David's competing, guilt-inflected narrative. As we will see when comparing the novel's frame narrative to Warhol's manipulation of framing at the end of this chapter, setting multiple frames alongside one another maintains a degree of hermeneutic openness, a gap in the meaning of Guillaume's death. In shaping how audiences can contextualize or interpret violence, the frame estranges the common sense of authorized and unauthorized force.

Aligning the frame narrative with the guillotine, the novel also situates its plot within the window of time when Giovanni's execution will take place. In the novel's last scene, as David prepares to return to America, he mentions a "small, blue envelope, [which is] the note from Jacques informing [him] of the date of Giovanni's execution."[23] On that date, David recounts the novel's plot from the vantage point of a state execution that may or may not have happened. Like Schrödinger's cat, Giovanni is both dead and alive. In this scene, Baldwin uses the frame narrative to imbricate his personal anguish with Giovanni's death, tracing a condensed and symbolic version of the affective logic of violence that structures the novel. Framed by two mentions of the blue envelope, David looks at himself in a mirror as he imagines Giovanni's death, solidifying the link between his feelings of shame and desire and Giovanni's ultimate death at the hands of the state. As he gazes at his own reflection, David begins to imagine Giovanni's slow walk to the guillotine. Paragraph by paragraph, Baldwin shifts between David's movements through the house and Giovanni's movements toward death, underscoring the similarities, and the intimacy, between the two men. As David moves to stand in front of a mirror, which he is "terribly aware of," "Giovanni's face swings before" him "like an unexpected lantern on a dark, dark night." Baldwin links the bodies of the two men in this section, thus reminding readers that the body is the site through which affect is felt and expressed, and on which the state inflicts violence. David "see[s]" Giovanni's "legs buckle, his thighs jelly, the buttocks quiver," and wonders whether Giovanni is "sweating" or "dry."[24] Soon after, David states that his "own hands are clammy, [his] body is dull and white and dry." Returning to Giovanni, David claims, "[Giovanni] wants to spit, but his mouth is dry. He cannot ask that they let him pause for a moment to urinate — all that, in a moment, will take care of itself." Shifting back to his reflection in the mirror, David looks at his own body, "which is under sentence of death. It is," he claims, "lean, hard, and cold, the incarnation of a mystery."[25] Legs, thighs, buttocks, sweat, spit, urine — it is through the body, finally, that David and Giovanni seem to become united in imminent death.

Giovanni's death, which may or may not have happened yet, is there at the beginning of the novel and at the end; it is a kind of threshold through which readers must pass in order to access the story that makes sense of it. This technique heightens the novel's "retrospective" mode, which Peter Brooks characterizes as the way plot works through and on discourse, with the novel driving toward a proper end, a kind of death.[26] The frame narrative that contains the story from the vantage point of imminent (or perhaps already past) death mobilizes this retrospective mode to unsettle interpretive approaches to seemingly senseless violence. Brooks's reading of narrative time is rooted in analysis of Stendhal's *The Red and the Black*, a novel that certainly appears to have influenced *Giovanni's Room*.[27] *The Red and the Black* is also structured around a death at the guillotine, but this death is the protagonist Julien's. Julien seems more like David than Giovanni, yet Baldwin has seemingly displaced his own "Julien" with Giovanni, whose death frames the novel but does not definitively *end* it. In Brooks's account, Julien "creates fictions" in which he is "the hero of his own text," and he "must unceasingly write and rewrite the narrative of a self defined in the dialectic of its past actions and its prospective fictions."[28] It is as though Baldwin has rewritten Julien but allowed him a scapegoat to send to the guillotine in his stead. The temporal dynamics of both Stendhal and James appear in Baldwin's frame narrative, where the narrator looks backward to his past self and forward to future readers, as *The Red and the Black* does. The frame narrative, in other words, produces a temporal collapse in the narrative, allowing readers to view the violent events in the novel from multiple points in time, producing a melancholic "binding"[29] that locks readers, with David, in the anguish of guilt, shame, and loss.

Drawing on the example of *The Red and the Black*, Brooks claims that plot seeks to contain story in a hermeneutic whole. Yet Stendhal disrupts this form of narrative closure with the protagonist's death by guillotine, near the end of the novel but with eleven chapters left to go. As in *Giovanni's Room*, the guillotine concludes a plot that involves a senseless act of violence: just as Giovanni kills Guillaume, Julien kills Madame Renard. This murder, according to Brooks, is senseless because it is not adequately explained or incorporated into a hermeneutic whole; while the violent act could potentially be made legible with interpretation, the novel withholds information that would facilitate such interpretation.[30] Brooks cautions that critics cannot fully account for Julien's motives, and any attempt to do so will "merely rationalize the threat of the irrational, which is not so importantly psychological as 'narratological'" because of how Julien's death disrupts the structure of the novel's plot.[31] This formal technique refuses hermeneutic protocols that would fit violent acts into a closed system of meaning.


## The Backward Glance of Shame

The blue envelope condenses the role David plays in Giovanni's ultimate death; it also indexes how reading and writing can modulate shame. Throughout the novel, David seems to confidently present a unified, heterosexual subjectivity to his father and fiancé through his written letters, while he consistently worries about his queer desire being "read" on his body and through his actions by other queer men.[32] As a first-person narrator speaking from the vantage point of the frame narrative, David mediates his own sense of shame through this dynamic of writing and reading: the written word is a kind of closeting, while embodied encounter exposes one to being read. The blue envelope will return in the novel's last paragraph, symbolically writing Giovanni's death on David's body. As he leaves the rental house, he tears the envelope "slowly into many pieces, watching them dance in the wind, watching the wind carry them away." However, they will not leave him: "Yet, as I turn and begin walking toward the waiting people, the wind blows some of them back on me."[33] Try as he might to take "flight"[34] from Giovanni's death, to discard the writing that marks his death in time and serves as an implicit request for David to finally return to Giovanni, David cannot escape the envelope's symbolic weight. Baldwin ultimately collapses David's perceived distinction between the self expressed in language and the embodied self, undermining David's command of this story as its first-person narrator. David imagines himself, throughout the novel, to maintain control of how he is perceived through his own writing, yet he consistently registers anxiety and shame about how his body might betray him. Framing the novel's last scene with a form of writing that confirms the truth of David's crimes against Giovanni, Baldwin undermines David's ostensible narrative control of his own story, drawing attention to David's embodied and emotional experience of looking back in shame at the story he has narrated.

David's shame sticks to him as he looks back on the narrative he has framed. The frame narrative also enfolds the novel's readers in the backward glance of shame. In a brief aside in their work on the affect theorist Silvan Tomkins, Eve Sedgwick and Adam Frank make a provocative suggestion:

> If, as Tomkins describes it, the lowering of the eyelids, the lowering of the eyes, the hanging of the head is the attitude of shame, it may also be that of reading: reading maps, magazines, novels, comics, and heavy volumes of psychology if not billboards and traffic signs. We (those of us for whom reading was or is a crucial form of interaction with the world) know the force-field creating power of this attitude, the kind of skin that sheer textual attention can weave around a reading body: a noisy bus station or airplane can be excluded from consciousness, an impossible ongoing scene refused, a dull classroom monologue ignored.[35]

To wrap oneself in the skin of textual attention is to enter into a different temporal relationship with the world, to occupy a novel's chronotope,[36] open oneself to the experience of affective response to the text, and at the same time to potentially become an object of affective attachment. The reader in public, like the ashamed person, can become a magnet for affective response: I see someone hang their head in shame and a wave of shame rushes over me; I watch someone read and echo their attention to the text with my attention to their comportment. Shame, that "peculiarly instrapsychic" affect that "exceeds the bodily vessel of its containment," shares with reading a phenomenological experience of being both hidden and exposed, bounded and porous.[37] Like reading, shame affords a shared experience and opens one up to the possibility of becoming infected with an affect.

The novel explores the relationship between reading and shame through narrative focalization that takes up the psychic character of whiteness, masculinity, and internalized homophobia from the inside and links acts of reading to the intrapsychic nature of shame. David's feelings of guilt and shame motivate his callous behavior while also obscuring his ability to truly see other people. In this way, Baldwin captures the sense in which shame becomes a "filter" through which we see the world.[38] As it becomes clear that something is happening between himself and Giovanni, David thinks, "I knew I could do nothing whatever to stop the ferocious excitement which had burst in me like a storm. I could only drink, in the faint hope that the storm might thus spend itself without doing any more damage to my land. But I was glad. I was only sorry that Jacques had been a witness. He made me ashamed. I hated him because he had now seen all that he had waited, often scarcely hoping, so many months to see."[39] Pleasure is imbricated with shame — David expresses not only shame here, but also giddiness and a kind of relief. David's turn of phrase in this passage emphasizes his perceived passivity. Affects act on David — excitement "bursts" in on him — and he understands other people as agents that cause affective response in him. Jacques "made" David ashamed: this statement is at once a desperate projection of feelings David is unable to take responsibility for and an insightful description of the way affect circulates between actors. The novel's affective logic of violence ties personal feelings of shame to larger social apparatuses by exploring how shame moves people to action. The novel tells a love story that makes the affective exchanges between lovers explicit and charts the development of love into feelings of resentment, disgust, and rage, or what Kathryn Bond Stockton calls "decomposition,"[40] ultimately supporting David's sense that his feelings of shame cause Giovanni's execution. The novel traces these feelings through its expression of desire and repulsion directed at Giovanni, and Giovanni's feelings of pain and anger in response.

The novel's language is compelling, reproducing in style the dynamic of decomposition it takes up as a theme. Formally as well as thematically, the text imbricates decay and beauty. Decomposition is "a sad epistemological force" of obsessive and painful thinking about one's own desires.[41] It manifests as a compulsive attempt to deconstruct or analyze one's desire, to decompose desire's object, the lover. The shame felt in cross-racial homosexual desire in the context of a homophobic and racist culture fueled this obsessive mode of thought. David's frame narrative structures the novel as a prolonged experience of looking obsessively backward at his own fixation on Giovanni. The novel's structure is that of "a blond narrator . . . whose only action is to think about attraction, obsessively think[ing] about a dark man's corpse." "To decompose attraction," Stockton writes, "is to break it down in thought" and "to think, with sorrow, of the relation of time to attraction."[42] The frame focalizes and distributes attention, replicating some of the pain felt in decomposition: a reader, like David, must obsessively unravel the contingent experiences that brought Giovanni to the guillotine. This impact on the reader demonstrates the frame's force as a kind of actor, and not just a choice with particular meaning-making effects in the narrative. Sedgwick's emphasis on the phenomenology of reading—and its intimacy with shame—highlights how forms enact a kind of force. The novel could hardly be said to violate or injure its readers, and indeed, its beautiful language cultivates aesthetic pleasure as well as emotional pain. Yet the force of its formal structure does draw readers into a kind of troubled alignment with David and into his obsessive, decomposing role in a broader network of affect and politics. These circuits of shame, violence, and desire also operate between the text and its readers, if only in the minor, fleeting, impressionistic way Sedgwick describes the echo between the stance of shame and the stance of reading.

Baldwin's frame narrative actualizes the phenomenological experience of looking back in shame—an affect that has been central to queer studies.[43] As Heather Love argues, queer time can be experienced as a mode of "feeling backward," of staying in a melancholic relationship to the losses and traumas of the past.[44] Queer history is, among other things, a history of suffering, and Love cautions queer theorists who are quick to declare this painful past over, having given way to a bright future of equality and pleasure.[45] The violence and pain of the past, argues Love, is often shameful to queer people in the present, and it is no surprise that some queer theorists have recuperated both the queer past and the experience of shame itself to resolve the bad feelings of the past, or at least to leave them behind. For Love, though, the bad feelings of the painful past remain, and we would lose a valuable historiographic approach to the past were we to set them aside or move beyond them. Elizabeth Freeman, seeking a queer historiography that recovers more positive experiences amid the painful past, has argued that subjects can be bound to one another across time even as they are bound in time. These bonds, she argues, can also reveal a queer history that is rooted in pleasure, and not merely loss or pain. This "erotohistoriography" identifies and draws out the ways pleasure can emerge through melancholic experiences. Remaining bound to an erotic moment in the past, for instance, can produce erotic charges in the present. Time "binds" us by creating connections to experiences of pleasure and pain out of time, "mak[ing] predicament into pleasure, fixity into a mode of travel across time as well as space."[46] The frame is a formal expression of how time binds, because the backward glance not only locks one in melancholia but also affords a view of the past as an encounter between history and affect. A view of the affective logic of violence reveals the senselessness of that violence: it could have been prevented, and now it cannot be escaped. Readers mourn what could have been, see the lost connections, and feel David's shame. One effect becomes clear when looking at the past through the lens of erotohistoriography: "historicity itself might appear as a structure of *tactile* feeling, a mode of touch, even a sexual practice."[47] Locking readers in a backward glance alongside him, David's frame narrative formalizes history as a mode of tactile, affective encounter.

The melancholic binding afforded by the frame thus offers insight into aesthetic experiences of violence that complicate mainstream discourses of suffering. Working across what Mikhail Bakhtin has called the chronotope of the novel, Baldwin's affective logic of violence draws readers into David's shameful feelings. Bakhtin's concept of the chronotope defines the meeting point of time and space in the novel. A novel necessarily unfolds in time, since it takes time to read, but time also spins out in the world of the novel in particular kinds of spaces, making time "palpable and visible."[48] As the driving force binding the novel together, the chronotope also indexes the enmeshed dynamic of fiction and life, work and world.[49] Heightening readers' sense of moving through the chronotope, the frame also modulates readers' sense of knowledge about the world and provides an experience of reading as melancholic binding.

The frame narrative thus also affords a queer reading practice that draws readers into a stance of melancholia and shame. As Marlon Ross has put it,

"Baldwin makes the central problem of the twentieth century the strange meaning of being white, as a structure of feeling within the self and within history—a structure of felt experience that motivates and is motivated by other denials."[50] The novel "posits the white man as a problem and then fantasizes what it might mean for a particular upper-class white man to become aware of the problematic nature of his desire."[51] Building on Ross's reading, I contend that Baldwin undertook a political project that was markedly different from that of protest fiction: imagining the subjectivity of an "ideal" subject—white, masculine, upper-class—in an attempt to reveal the shame, fragmentation, and violence of that subject position. The doubling effect of the frame also affords attention to multiple forms of suffering, and to their enmeshment: David's suffering is genuine in the novel, but it is a spiritual anguish that ultimately causes lethal harm to Giovanni, caught up not only in the affective logic of their decomposing love affair but also in the state's use of force. The frame narrative plays an important role in this broader aesthetic project; it allows Baldwin to focus readers' attention on how desire and affect are imbricated with historical forces, channels through which individuals come together in violent encounters.

*Giovanni's Room* mobilizes the frame narrative to create an affective map that reveals the relationship between shame, state violence, and the wider historical forces of racism and homophobia in midcentury culture. Jonathan Flatley characterizes affective mapping as the process of situating idiosyncratic, personal emotion in historical and social context. Literary writing, especially the novel, can portray this experience while also narrating it as an experience, showing readers their own affective maps. In this way, the modern novel can be a "mobile machine for self-estrangement," enabling readers to experience their own emotions from a remove, defamiliarized in order to be seen in a new light.[52] David's narration produces an experience like affective mapping, with David tracing the movement of shame in his own experiences to disambiguate the sequence of events that led to Giovanni at the guillotine. At the same time, David's own sense of shame and guilt limits his ability to be fully estranged from himself and to see himself clearly. Tied to the broader historical forces of European settler colonialism, David's shame might, however, illuminate an affective map for readers that enables them to see the logics of state-sanctioned violence as profoundly affective, bound up in experiences of shame that mobilize racist and homophobic animus. Invited to share the stance of shame with David, readers might become estranged from themselves. Additionally, attending to shame affords a view of the law's violence as incoherent—that is, as motivated by the morally irrational desire for white supremacy and heteropatriarchy.

Framing Systemic Violence

Framing formalizes the fundamentally rhetorical and contingent nature of violence, inviting attention to the relationship between affect and history that brings individuals into violent contact and unevenly subjects them to state violence. Given the rise of mass media spectacles of violence at this historical moment, it is no surprise that the frame—a formal feature that both constitutes a photograph and makes itself invisible through the photograph's claim to truth—could give shape to an emergent structure of feeling. To further explore the affordances of the frame, I now turn to Andy Warhol, whose *Death and Disaster* series multiplied frames and abstracted spectacles of violence to draw attention to the sensuous, violent meeting point of bodies and technologies of suffering. Theorizing the frame as a form of attention, I will argue that its aesthetic violence offered a counterpoint to the pervasive rhetoric of mass spectacle, which often naturalized the violences of modernity, even in attempts to witness or protest them. Susan Sontag dates the moment "when the power of photographs to define, not merely record, the most abominable realities trumped all the complex narratives" to 1945, when images of Nazi concentration camps and the aftermath of nuclear attacks on Japan began to circulate widely.[53] In other words, 1945 was a moment of convergence: cameras were able to get closer to death than ever before, and death was *mass-produced* in a new way thanks to the technological innovations of the death camp and the atom bomb. The photograph, Sontag contends, was understood to do what words could not: bring us face-to-face with death, articulate the shock of mass violence, and, most of all, give form to what is most abominable.[54] Yet like any other representation, photographs can also distort reality. Photographers can stage or restage a scene, and even candid images must always have a point of view, framing an observation for its audience and, in doing so, hiding what might be seen from other vantage points.

Warhol's *Death and Disaster* series engages the rhetorical work of framing and the questions raised by the ascendance of the violent photograph. Inspired by a newspaper headline and image proclaiming that "129 Die in Jet!," Warhol began appropriating news media images of disasters as subjects for his art. The *Death and Disaster* series that emerged includes images of contaminated tuna cans that killed housewives, car crashes, electric chairs, and white police officers attacking Black men. The *Death and Disaster* series reveals the relationship between mass subjectivity and death; like an iconic image of a celebrity, which can be reproduced and circulated to forge connections with large audiences, the anonymous image of the disaster victim can be circulated widely through mass media to represent the anonymity produced by death.[55] Disaster and death are important ways to articulate and construct the mass subject, because "in a spectacular society the mass subject often appears as an *effect* of the mass media (the newspaper, the radio), or of a catastrophic failure of technology (the plane crash), or, more precisely, of both (the *news* of such a catastrophic failure)."[56] The anonymous death is mediated, and the mediation is part of what produces our sense of the anonymous death. By silk-screening and repeating images of anonymous or iconic disasters, Warhol mobilizes the frame to draw attention to acts of violence while withholding narrative mechanisms that would explain or account for that violence.

In the same year that he started the *Death and Disaster* series, Warhol discovered the photo-silk-screen process that would become his signature method. Soon after, he created the *Suicide* silk screen, which appropriated a photograph of Evelyn McHale, who died by jumping from the Empire State Building. Inspired by the abstracting techniques that preceded pop art and by the theme of death, Warhol appropriated images from the news media and used repetition to render the images increasingly abstract. As Jonathan Flatley has noted, the black ink screened onto the photographic stencils also often blurred the images, further anonymizing them.[57] By heightening the anonymous and abstracted nature of the mass subject, the silk screens de-emphasize the narratives being told in mass media to invite alternate ways of experiencing represented violence. Bringing together a range of different deaths and disasters under the same aesthetic rubric, Warhol uses the frame to rhetorically position many kinds of violence as senseless: the accidental turn of the wheel that results in a gruesome car crash is framed as analogous to the intentional flip of the switch that produces an execution. This aesthetic strategy does not protest the forms of violence it represents, but it nevertheless brackets familiar logics of violence and helps focus audience attention on the rhetorical work of framing itself.

The effects of Warhol's framing techniques are on full display in his *Electric Chair* silk screens. Begun in 1963, "the same year Sing Sing State Penitentiary in New York carried out the state's last execution,"[58] the *Electric Chair* images are based on a photograph of an empty electric chair, purported to be the one in which Ethel Rosenberg was executed at Sing Sing in 1953.[59] Unlike other images in the *Death and Disaster* series, the *Electric Chair* images feature no people, only an instrument of state violence. Many of the silk screens in the series feature brightly painted backgrounds; pinks, purples, and teals contrast with the solitary, empty chair silk-screened in black ink. As a number of art historians have argued, the images largely refuse to make overt critiques about the politics of capital punishment; instead, "Warhol lays bare the aestheticism in executions."[60] The legal scholar Bennett Capers argues that Warhol's emphasis on the aesthetics of capital punishment seems to render the images inscrutable, but his choice of photograph, with the trace of its historical context, nevertheless raises questions about capital punishment: who is subject to it, who may mete it out, and who our culture is willing to imagine in the empty chair.[61] Without any people in the image, viewers must look at the machine itself, approaching the electric chair as an instrument of violence that is ultimately indifferent to the ethical or legal questions surrounding capital punishment. The hermeneutic openness of the *Electric Chair* images complicates the account of framing I have offered in my reading of *Giovanni's Room*. They extend the rhetorical work of framing, which in Baldwin's novel forecloses an objective account of the novel's story of interpersonal and state violence. The novel thus points to structures that authorize the force of law and the affective experiences that naturalize or rebel against that force. A Warholian approach to similar themes pushes the technique further, risking political agnosticism on the question of state violence. Warhol's work may not critique state violence, but it stages and estranges photography's role in shaping perspective and naturalizing violence.

Warhol's manipulation of the frame shapes how the photograph's broader context appears to viewers. The original photograph includes lighting and pipes that hang from the ceiling, a view of two walls in the room, and a sign above the execution room's door, which reads, "SILENCE." In many of Warhol's *Little Electric Chair* images, these elements are maintained in the silk screen. By contrast, in a work like the 1967 *Big Electric Chair*, the artist has cropped the photograph closer to produce the silk screen, cropping out the signage and many contours of the execution chamber. Viewers see the chair itself, slightly off-center in the painting, and the wall behind it with its horizontal line painted across the wall, bisecting the image just above the chair. *Big Electric Chair* was silk-screened onto a canvas painted in blue, spring green, and lavender, the blocks of color producing additional grids. The lines of the screened photograph and the paint on the canvas thus frame the chair itself within the frame of the painting, pulling the eye toward an even more closed-in view of the empty chair. The visual frame multiplies the painting's

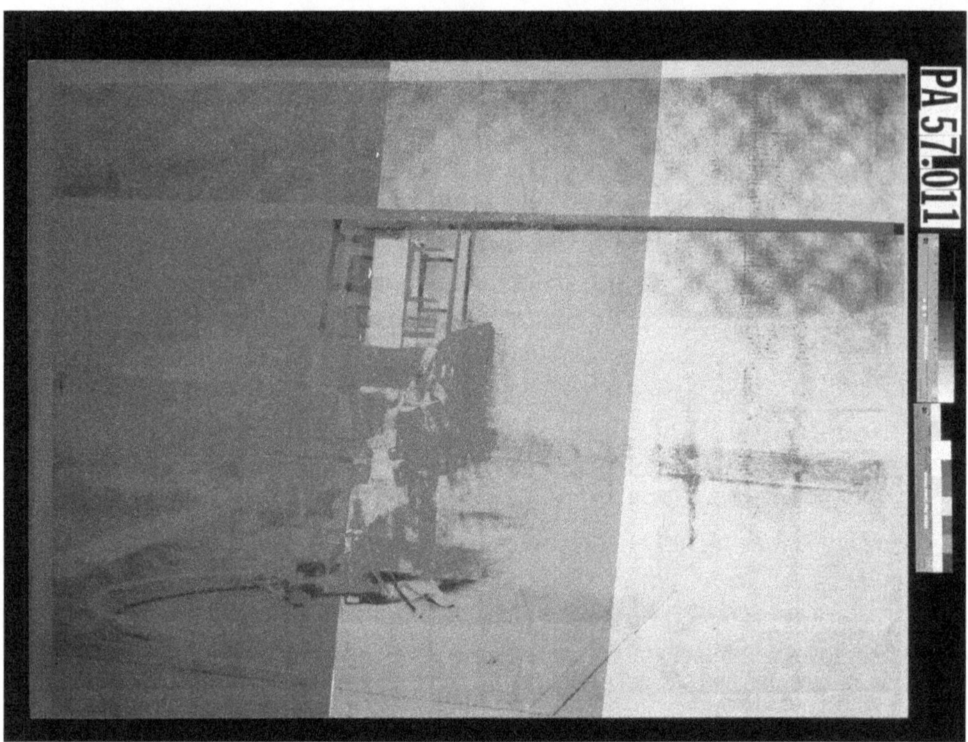

Andy Warhol, *Big Electric Chair*, 1967–68. Acrylic and silkscreen ink on linen. 54 × 74 inches, 137.2 × 188 cm. Image and Artwork © 2023 The Andy Warhol Foundation for the Visual Arts, Inc. / Licensed by Artists Rights Society (ARS), New York.

frame to further remove contextualizing details drawn from the source image. Within the painting's skewed frame, more "frames" appear: intersecting lines on the back of the chair form a series of squares, while the small table behind the electric chair and rug below it produce an effect of additional framing boxes. Through a formal strategy that encourages viewers to see the chair as a series of lines and imperfectly created squares, the *Electric Chair* images also encourage viewers to linger on the object that produces death. Delinked from narratives that lead a prisoner into the execution chamber, from legal discourses that rationalize the prisoner's execution, and even from counter-discourses that apply a structural critique to capital punishment, the machine remains. Viewers can still, of course, bring these associations to their viewing of the image, but the frame nevertheless encourages a view of the chair as a chair. Form slows perception and directs the eye, cultivating attention toward the technology of state violence while disrupting political or moral interpretations. Aesthetic violence in Warhol's work does not directly critique the law's force, but instead affords attention to its technologies and to the assumptions viewers bring to the images.

The *Electric Chair* images align the electric chair with the car, the skyscraper, the tuna can, the jet, the atom bomb: all are technologies that can kill, given the right set of circumstances. The series aligns tragedies of modernity—the cost we accept for the convenience of driving cars, for example—with larger social structures of the postwar period: Jim Crow violence, capital punishment, or nuclear attacks. Aligned under the rubric of "disaster," the events represented in the *Death and Disaster* series are framed in relation to time. Framing draws out the contingent nature of audience experience, soliciting a physical encounter with the abstracted images that is characterized by heightened attention. Warhol's use of repetition provokes viewers to look for differences among the copies, "thus trans*forming* a scene of death into a collection of formal elements. . . . Because repetition numbs you to similarity, it heightens your attention to difference."[62] The *Electric Chair* images aestheticize state violence, but just because they make state violence less gruesome and spectacular does not mean they lead viewers to accept or support that violence. Instead, they estrange state violence to enable new ways of engaging with images of suffering.

The images cultivate a sensory experience of violence that unsettles distinctions between victim, perpetrator, and witness. In his *Race Riot* images, Warhol appropriated photographs taken by Charles Moore of civil rights protests in Birmingham, Alabama that were originally published in *Life* magazine, applying his framing technique to a series of images designed to protest police brutality. Instead of reinforcing the claims of protest in the source images, Warhol uses the frame to abstract these images and invite other forms of affective engagement. Like many images in the *Death and Disaster* series, *Mustard Race Riot* (1963) emphasizes framing by repeating a silk-screened photograph on a single canvas and including a solid pane of color. In the left half of the frame, black ink is silk-screened using three photographs appropriated from the May 17, 1963, issue of *Life* magazine that depict white police officers and their dogs attacking Black men.[63] The right half of the image contains only background color, a mustard yellow. This flat, unmarked surface, which Warhol referred to as a "blank," not only draws attention to the function of the background surface, which often goes unnoticed as part of a painting's composition, but also echoes the open spread of a magazine. Unlike a magazine, however, the silk screens provide visual repetition and undifferentiated fields of color, rather than contextualizing information that would make sense of the attack on view.[64] By refusing to contextualize or narrate the images, *Mustard Race Riot* creates space for an aesthetic and affective experience of attending to the interpretive difficulty posed through form. Replacing the didactic framework of the source material with a much more abstracted form of represented violence, the painting produces an aesthetic experience characterized by an overwhelming proliferation of frames, a stuttering impulse toward narrative that is disrupted by the yellow blank. In an echo of the Assyrian relief sculptures discussed by Leo Bersani and Ulysse Dutoit, the movement of positive and negative space, of ink and paint, move the eye around the painting in an effort to apprehend what is being represented. At the same time, the repeated frame effects a feeling of stasis, which encourages audiences first to seek difference and development across each square and then to experience a sense of looking anew only to see the same violent act.

Interestingly, *Mustard Race Riot* is something of a critical anomaly and has been rarely discussed in the work on Warhol, "likely . . . because of its non-conformity to standard narratives about the politics of Warhol's art."[65] The few scholars who have analyzed the work, however, emphasize Warhol's interest in the narrative, history, and spectacle of anti-Black violence.[66] Moreover, they call into question a widespread assumption about the ethics of representing violence: we often assume that images should be as unmediated as possible if they are to make viewers feel ethically about suffering. They should shock or produce a similarly violent affective experience if they are to have an ethical relationship to violence. In an echo (or rather, an inversion) of critics' tendency to see *Giovanni's Room* as tangential to Baldwin's aesthetic and political project because there are no Black characters, it is as if critics avoid *Mustard Race Riot* because it challenges the critical consensus that Warhol's work is apolitical. The material history of the *Mustard Race Riot* further emphasizes its attention to the visual economy of race and racism; Warhol's drafts reveal that he had used the word "tan" to describe the color of the blank at one point, and he mixed the paint himself. Add to this the cultural associations that mustard and yellow bring to the piece, and we can see the blank on the right side as a kind of "mixed, indeterminate skin."[67] Functioning also as a "blank" that creates space for a sustained affective experience,[68] the diptych's mustard panel invites a sensory, almost tactile, engagement with the affective logics of white supremacist violence. It formalizes the incoherence Baldwin describes insofar as the blank panel refuses representation. The blanks also literalize racial mixing, recalling discourses of miscegenation that both reflect and are used to justify white supremacist

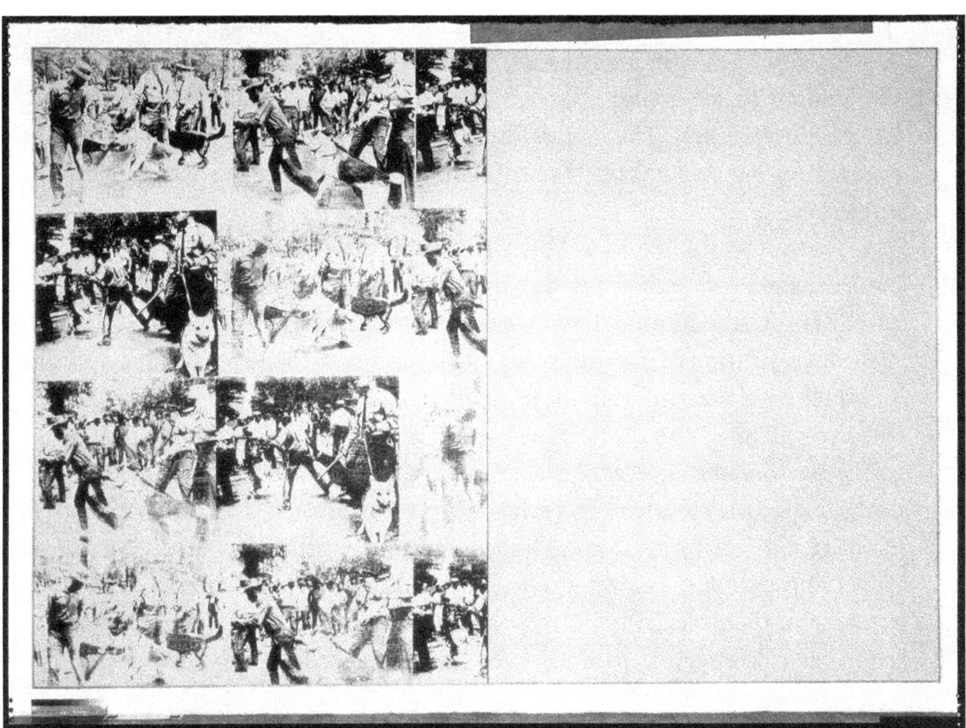

Andy Warhol, *Mustard Race Riot*, 1963. Silkscreen ink, acrylic and pencil on linen. 114 × 82 inches each (two panels), 289.6 × 208.3 cm each. Image and Artwork © 2023 The Andy Warhol Foundation for the Visual Arts, Inc. / Licensed by Artists Rights Society (ARS), New York.

violence. The blank formalizes affect's role in maintaining systemic violence. The repeated images set aside narratives of the protest sympathetic to the civil rights cause, but they also scramble and refuse the police narrative and logic of exercising violence to maintain white supremacy.

Warhol might be said to share David's shameful relationship to whiteness, his public persona informed by complex questions about "what it may mean to be a (white) queer in a queer-hating world, what it may mean to be a white (queer) in a white-supremacist world."[69] Warhol personally dealt with feelings of shame that emerged from his dislike of his own appearance and concerns about being liked by others. His sense of shame, however, energized his artistic practice as a way of engaging with his own "spoiled" identity.[70] In Baldwin's novel, the frame tracks the movement of affect, especially shame, in the workings of state-sanctioned violence. Similarly, in Warhol's work, framing techniques invite audiences into an affective engagement with violence that mass media typically forecloses. Though his oeuvre is often treated as politically indeterminate, if not troublingly apolitical, the *Death and Disaster* series invites affective engagements that might lead to new structures of feeling. The images thus do a kind of "protopolitical"[71] work by directing viewers' attention to defamiliarized images of overdetermined suffering.

Preceding Warhol's turn to film, the *Race Riot* silk screens also anticipate the artist's interest in the frame as a form that can freeze time (as in a photograph) or give the impression of a seamless flow of time (in a film). While Warhol's repetition of the frame can move viewers through a narrative moment, his emphasis on the frame itself also encourages viewers to pause and take in a still image, to see narrative as a fragmented sequence of nonnarrative, often violent impacts. The source images might encourage audiences to easily digest a narrative, feel affirmed in their outrage, and move on. By contrast, the jarring effect of seeing violence defamiliarized encourages a longer engagement, a closer attention. The frame's defamiliarizing impact emerges in the *Race Riot* paintings: recontextualizing mass media photographs as silk-screened paintings, Warhol introduces new frames around images laden with stereotypical meanings. My goal here is not to redeem Warhol as an antiracist artist whose work critiques white supremacist violence. After all, I believe an important part of what *Mustard Race Riot* is doing is to unsettle logics of violence that underwrite both racist *and* antiracist understandings of civil rights protest. That is, *Mustard Race Riot* resists both the white supremacist narrative of Black people as an unruly, senselessly violent mass that must be controlled by the state and the antiracist narrative of nonviolent protest captured in the *Life* magazine caption, "The Dogs' Attack is Negroes' Reward." But as Carmen Merport Quiñones puts it, "there are many ways of conceiving what an artistic intervention in the political might look like."[72]

By including the *Electric Chair* and *Race Riot* images in the series, Warhol challenges distinctions between the self-authorizing rationalizations of state violence and the senseless, eruptive disaster of a car crash or fatal experience of food poisoning. The authorized use of force and the accident are not totally distinct kinds of violence, since we could potentially trace a car crash or failure of the food production system to modern systems that, in prioritizing technological expediency or capitalist gain, make possible so-called random or senseless deaths. To extend this line of thinking, the visual alignment the series makes between these disparate forms of death and disaster also defamiliarizes state violence, enabling a view of capital punishment or police brutality that calls into question the underlying warrants authorizing state violence. While the *Race Riot* series might seem to use abstraction as a way of remaining oblivious to the logics of white supremacy that rationalize the violent suppression of the protestors, the works actually question those logics by aligning them with the stupid, tragic accidents of car crashes, or the never fully knowable suffering that might drive an individual to suicide. Taken as a collection that deploys appropriation, repetition, abstraction, and framing to unite these deaths in America, the *Death and Disaster* series invites sustained attention to the affective work of mass mediations of suffering.

When asked in a 1965 interview why he painted the electric chair, Warhol replied, in characteristic fashion, "I just think they're beautiful."[73] His reply deflects inquiry about the social meaning of the electric chair, implying a political agnosticism about capital punishment. But what if it is also true? The silk screens aestheticize the electric chair to help viewers feel "like" Warhol about its beauty,[74] and here their affective-political purchase coheres. It is a mistake to assume that seeing the chairs as beautiful means that one comes to share the state's perspective on violence. Indeed, the frame multiplies perspective and thus destabilizes or refuses to privilege and fix one point of view on capital punishment. An aesthetic approach to the electric chair, or a car crash, or even a violent political protest certainly can detach the viewer from the work's social context and invite a wide range of affective engagements with the work—engagements like absorption and pleasure rather than revulsion or outrage at injustice. However, the aesthetic also affords modes of attention that are otherwise short-circuited by feeling "right" about the suffering depicted.

Appropriating and reframing media images of suffering in highly aestheticized, multiplied frames, the silk screens emphasize the fundamental indeterminacy of photographs themselves and, moreover, engage that indeterminacy as a kind of ethical practice. Artist-critics David Campany and Stanley Wolukau-Wanambwa characterize this indeterminacy as a fundamental gap between what the photograph depicts and what it might mean—a gap that viewers fill in by drawing on "interpretive codes" "structured by racism and gender," among other contextual factors.[75] It is not just that a photograph's meaning is necessarily indeterminate—more fundamentally, what a photograph depicts or represents can never be fully determined or fixed. Precisely because the images purport to convey reality while also being, at heart, mediations, photographs should be approached from an ethical position that acknowledges their indeterminacy. To lose sight of this indeterminacy is to fall into familiar "reading practices steeped in deep disavowal of racial difference"[76] — a kind of willful unknowing that imaginatively fixes interpretation and occludes other contexts or truths the photograph might reveal. One way to resolve the photograph's indeterminacy is through the caption ("The Dogs' Attack is Negroes' Reward") or through critical context (the Rosenbergs were the last to sit in Warhol's electric chair). Another way is to move toward "an ethic of embracing indeterminacy."[77] I do not want to claim that the aesthetics of framing in Warhol's work unravel white supremacy or critique state violence, but they do formalize the indeterminacy of the photograph, forcing audiences toward an ethic of indeterminacy that lets them see the electric chair as beautiful.

Walter Benn Michaels might call this the beauty of a social problem. Drawing on Bertolt Brecht's concept of defamiliarization, he claims that "to feel the beauty of the problem is precisely not to feel the pathos of the suffering produced by the problem; it's instead to feel the structure that makes the problem."[78] For Michaels, an artwork's push toward autonomy through formal characteristics like abstraction is not a retreat from politics; instead, in its refusal to offer sympathetic identification with the victims of "social problems," the work may point viewers toward the structure that victimizes. As he puts it, "autonomy's indifference may be politically helpful" because artworks that formally separate themselves "from the world also declare[] the irrelevance of our feelings."[79] Also for Michaels, the most salient — the only salient — problem is that of class inequality. I agree with Michaels in his approach to formalism's politics, but we differ in the role affect and audience experience can play in this dynamic. Here we arrive at the question of identity, which Michaels rejects as distracting from both class politics and the act of interpretation. Apprehending the work of an aesthetic experience, however, would seem to demand some attention to the sensing body, a body that is also situated in history. *Giovanni's Room* makes identity strange by making its narrator white. And in focalizing a narrative in which seemingly senseless acts of interpersonal violence collide with policing and state execution through this narrator, the novel turns its audience, like Warhol does, toward the indeterminacies that remain in the act of framing.

This aspect of art's indeterminacy, as Campany and Walukau-Wanambwa claim, is inherent to the photograph as medium and form. I have been suggesting, in this chapter, that aesthetic violence responded to mass media images of suffering by heightening the latent indeterminacy in all photographs. Discourses about what violence means in this era were discourses, at least in part, about aesthetic experience. This is what *Giovanni's Room* explores by juxtaposing the "decomposition" process of a queer love affair with media discourses of so-called senseless violence. It is not that the novel seeks to produce an affective experience in readers that will motivate them toward a form of political activism. Instead, the novel limns the role of affect in the ongoing existence of the social problem. The formalizing act of framing, as many literary critics have put it, is what makes a work into a work of art and what makes the experience of the punctum possible.[80] The breakthrough of the world into the work is capacitated by the act of framing out the artwork as separate from the world. The circuitry of shame in *Giovanni's Room*, activated through its narrator, links work to world through shame's contagion, through the collapse of the stance of reading into the stance of shame. Readers may or may not feel shame as they read, but they can see shame as both form and feeling—as part of the structure of violence and its uneven, often incoherent, distribution.

## CHAPTER TWO

# Happening

## *On Being Collateral Damage*

In 2019, the Poetry Foundation staged an exhibit that displayed each page of Yoko Ono's 1964 book *Grapefruit,* inaugurating a critical turn toward approaching the intermedial artist as a poet.[1] A collection of drawings and instructions for enacting what she called events, *Grapefruit,* as the 2019 exhibit demonstrates, invites readings as a collection of poetry but also emblematizes the intermedial energies of the long 1960s counterculture. Defined by Ono's contemporary, Fluxus artist Dick Higgins, intermediality is a practice of artistic creation "between the arts," one that combines artistic media to create new forms.[2] Rather than fully assimilate art media into one new genre, however, Ono's work maintains the productive tension of different media alongside one another and demands active, embodied engagement to realize the work. Ono's intermedial poetics, as Keegan Cook Finberg has argued, resist the idea that "assimilation" of different artistic media in one work degrades those media. Instead, the intermedial encounter enables attention to the formal specificity of the different modes involved. The intermedial work of *Grapefruit* asks readers to engage its text as both poetry and procedural instruction; its form "makes reading central to her artwork: the process of combining art practices that also respects discrete identities — or sensations — happens best through reading instructions."[3] Amid critical reappraisal of Ono as a significant midcentury poet as well as a key figure of post-abstraction performance art, mainstream impressions of Ono still tend to erroneously reduce her to a Beatles accessory or avant-garde oddity. Overdetermined, dismissed, and misread throughout her long career, Ono's work is a key resource giving shape to structures of feeling in the postwar period.

The nascent intermedial forms of *Grapefruit* and her events also formalize changing experiences of contingency amid social systems increasingly conceived of as structures that might cause collateral damage. One approach to discourses of senseless violence in the long 1960s, as we have seen, was to defamiliarize the state's authority to delineate legitimate from senseless violence through techniques of framing. This chapter turns to more insistently countercultural responses to violence, connecting the invention of the performance art happening to discourses of senseless and systemic violence.

Exploring the development of the happening in the work of John Cage and Allan Kaprow, the chapter then focuses on Ono's work in *Grapefruit* and her 1965 performance of *Cut Piece* to show how the happening challenges commonsense notions of collateral damage. Concepts of collateral damage normalize Cold War neo-imperialism as well as systemic sexual violence facilitated and justified by war. Taking Ono as a key figure of the development of the happening, this chapter theorizes how intermedial, embodied aesthetic experiences responded to the pervasive possibility of being collateral damage. Working across text, image, and performance, Ono mobilizes experiences of happening to explore a suspensive structure of feeling characterizing this period. In particular, the happening's use of chance-based composing techniques and procedures also facilitated experiences of chance occurrence, experiences characterized by what Claire Seiler has termed "midcentury suspension," a complex phenomenological experience of looking back at the trauma of World War II and forward to the threat of a nuclear future.[4] Drawing together theories of suspension with those of race and gender, particularly theories of Asian inscrutability in the Cold War and neocolonial era, this chapter posits the happening as a structure of feeling.

Uses of chance in the happening formalize feelings of Cold War era suspension, a physical sense of stuckness that echoes the emotional and cognitive experiences of vulnerability to violence. Intermedial and performance-based art events that sought to bring embodiment back to the center of post-abstractionist aesthetics used chance to explore the experience of being in the wrong place at the wrong time, suffering the effects of intentional destruction that does not care who it targets. Since the advent of the Industrial Revolution, developments in technology made accidents more likely and wars more dangerous to soldiers and civilians.[5] Technological innovation also shaped beliefs about suffering. Innovation and efficiency become important values in themselves, such that "technological expediency often takes precedence over human convenience, and sometimes even human life."[6] The suffering of those called "collateral damage" is treated as the unavoidable effect of a logical system. The logic of collateral damage is a logic of expediency, which Steven Katz has linked to Aristotelian theories of rhetoric in which the purpose of argumentation is not to weigh the moral good of an end but simply to determine the best means to reach that end.[7] This "ethic of expediency," in which the central ethical value simply is the most efficient working of the system, Katz argues, formed a central "moral basis" of the Holocaust. It extends through much of contemporary culture, in which scientific and technological rationality fuels an ethical common sense in which "the only ethical criterion necessary is the perceptible movement toward the technical goal to be achieved."[8] The apotheosis of this expediency is the Holocaust, but the ethic of expediency underwrites many more quotidian aspects of contemporary life. Midcentury feelings of suspension were in part produced by the broader context of technological expediency; they also formed a resource for art that interrogated this logic.

The happening's aesthetic violence situates audiences between media and between moments of violent impact. The formal difficulty of orienting oneself in the chaotic unfolding of a happening cultivates feelings of suspension that can defamiliarize logics of collateral damage. The term "happening" names a new form of performance art that developed in the 1950s and '60s,[9] and I adopt this term to describe a broader aesthetic tendency arising in the era as well, one that heightens audience attention to the interplay of structure and randomness. In the multimodal performance artworks that came to be called happenings, an artist would determine rules or procedures for the event, then incorporate audience participation or other processes that introduced unanticipated or random elements into the work. Set in motion, the happening would exceed artistic intentionality, facilitating confusion, surprise, and feelings of suspendedness in audiences waiting for events they cannot fully anticipate. The happening's aesthetic violence engages epistemic crisis around violent events in the nuclear era, challenging the distinction between personal and political violence. Formalizing and producing the experience of waiting for an attack that may or may not come, the happening unsettles forms of patriarchal common sense that unevenly distribute bodily vulnerability—whether to sexual violation or to nuclear attack.

Postwar artistic and literary culture was shaped by a historical moment characterized by suspension. Seiler argues that the period between 1945 and 1955 was characterized by a feeling of being suspended between recent wartime violence and uncertain futures.[10] This "midcentury suspension" traversed Europe and the United States, extending to Asia as neocolonial US military expansion into Asia and the Pacific developed during the Cold War. In Japan, the recent memory of nuclear attack heightened such feelings of suspension. Even before the US atomic bombing of Japan, the Japanese term *bukimi* "spoke to the suspended question of whether Hiroshima and its inhabitants had been singled out for preservation or for annihilation."[11] Residents of Hiroshima described this feeling of *bukimi*, "an expectant, premonitory atmosphere . . . during the weeks before the bombing,"[12] a feeling fueled by rumors that the city had been spared from more conventional bombing, either because the city would remain safe or because it would undergo an even greater attack than had previously been seen. The sense of *bukimi* that suffused Hiroshima in the weeks before nuclear attack became, as Paul Saint-Amour has argued, a much broader condition of urban life during the Cold War. Still reckoning with the trauma of World War II and the Holocaust, Americans were also anticipating future violence in the form of nuclear attack as the Cold War began. In the wake of atomic bombing in Japan, the feeling of suspension also captured peoples' sense of being held within "the conditional space of catastrophe,"[13] a feeling of continual attunement to the possibility of annihilation that may yet not come to pass. Inhabitants of urban spaces in the Cold War came to feel this "eerie suspension" of the "nuclear uncanny" as "a structuring condition of everyday life."[14] Artists and writers of this period would explore and reproduce these feelings through formal techniques of chance and procedure. In the unsettled temporality of suspension—a conditional or subjunctive violence that reaches into the present from a possible violent future—knowing about violence became a problem. The happening formalizes this problem, troubling easy interpretations of a violent encounter and inviting sustained, suspensive, open attention to aspects of the encounter that might otherwise be overlooked.

While the rising tension and satisfying release of suspense plays out in the rise and fall of narrative action,[15] in multidisciplinary performance art, the "happening" of the happening suggests a resolution without a buildup, or a buildup without a resolution. This form of suspension, which has more to do with the taut and tense feeling of waiting and bracing oneself than with the cognitive and emotional journey from anticipation to resolution, enacts aesthetic violence on audiences. Suspension is cognitive and embodied, affecting audiences in the tensing and waiting of the body but also the paradoxical feeling of knowing and not knowing that something will happen. Suspension names an important structure of feeling that developed at midcentury, one that "pertains to both space, as in hanging or hovering, and to time, as in a pause or rest. Suspension suggests a holding pattern, a freezing or delay of action or progress, a deferral of decision, or a temporary revocation of a normal state of affairs. Distinct from paralysis, suspension effects a charged stillness, wherein a subject's cognitive or somatic movement is temporarily excepted from the imperative to decision or action, but within which the subject can move and be moved."[16] Midcentury suspension takes shape in recognition of bodily precarity, and theorizing violence via aesthetic strategies emerged as a way to help audiences confront the suspended position of vulnerability within broader systems that exercise biopower and mete out violence. Developing the sense of suspension as the midcentury moment turned into the 1960s, artists and writers responded to this zeitgeist with works that invited—and sometimes forced—a haptic, physical engagement with their texts, one that productively confounded attempts to fix the meaning of random or chance violent events.

## The Politics and Aesthetics of the Chance Procedure

The happening draws on a longer lineage of works that use chance or indeterminacy in their mode of composition or dissemination to audiences. Developing in Surrealist circles at the turn of the twentieth century, the chance procedure initially seemed to capture the feeling of limitless possibility, of truth gleaned through almost mystical chance occurrences.[17] The onset of World War II helped remake the chance procedure into a practice tied to much more violent dynamics of contingency and precarity, particularly the possibility of being rounded up by Nazis or bombed out in the war.[18] As Juno Jill Richards argues, "the chance procedure thus offers a conceptual language to map the uneven distribution of state violence upon raced and nonnormative sexual bodies."[19] In other words, as the rise of fascism redistributed power and remade the boundaries between full citizen and noncitizen according to hierarchies of race, gender, sexuality, and ability, daily life began to feel more subject to chance encounters with violence as well. The chance-based artwork, in this context, came to echo that sense of precarity.

A portable form, the chance procedure became a key element of American avant-garde movements of the 1950s, particularly those influenced by the composer John Cage. The chance procedure, in which an artist created a rule for enacting elements of chance within a work, became a foundation of the performance art happenings of this period. In the summer of 1952, Cage, choreographer Merce Cunningham, visual artist Robert Rauschenberg, and other faculty at the experimental school Black Mountain College staged a chance-based performance event in the campus dining hall. The event, which has been called the first happening,[20] included lectures by Cage, dancing by Cunningham, piano performance by David Tudor, readings by poets, images projected into the space by a projectionist, a staged phonograph incorporated into the work by Rauschenberg, and a suspended painting created by Franz Kline. Actions of the performers were determined by chance operations: using chance to determine when each performer would begin and cease their performance, the event's script enforced rules on the performers that were determined arbitrarily. Though little documentation of the event exists, a score for the projectionist was discovered in Cage's papers, and Cage recalls that each performer had notated times for performing and pausing, which were determined by chance.[21] The rich mix of art forms in the shared performance space, the seemingly random beginnings and endings to each performance, and the apparent disconnect between each element of the event presage the happenings that would become more widely known in the 1960s. While the effects produced through chance operations could certainly "make sense" to audiences, their unfolding in time, and in the context of the performance space, suspends those audience members in a cognitive and affective tension. As Allan Kaprow notes: "Chance then, rather than spontaneity, is a key term [for the happening], for it implies risk and fear (thus reestablishing that fine nervousness so pleasant when something is about to occur)."[22] In other words, the unpredictable experiences that take place during a happening are not generally the result of spontaneous actions—that is, of unplanned, unthought choices. Rather, they are the result of chance-based procedures, in which surprising events are the result of preplanned processes or scripts that allow for a range of possible events.

The happening's chance operations undercut the notion of the closed or completed artwork that is intentionally designed to convey particular meanings. Even in tightly scored events, where the basic action of the happening is predetermined, the form of the happening produces a multiplicity of texts that collapse or suspend time: the score itself is an indication of an event to come; the event is a belated and ephemeral enactment of the score. A score written by Yoko Ono in the spring of 1960, for example, directs its readers to:

> Use your blood to paint.
> Keep painting until you faint. (a)
> Keep painting until you die. (b)[23]

Depending on a reader's mood, these instructions might appear like a joke, a dire warning, or a clarion call to dedicate oneself to one's art. In the form of the event score, Ono is able to suggest an action that would kill the person enacting it. Ono's event instructions are subjunctive: they exist in a vexed temporal frame that is simultaneously present and future. The score is not the art object itself, but a means by which to arrive at the aesthetic experience, which is at once structured around a fixed endpoint (i.e., the piece ends when "you" die) and open-ended insofar as the *what* and *how* of the action "to paint" is left entirely up to the performer. While event scores are texts that can produce aesthetic experiences, they are not only texts. They are imbued with the subjunctive possibility of ephemeral action.

Ono's scores form a crucial part of the history of midcentury procedural aesthetics. Her Chambers Street Loft series would help inspire the Fluxus movement, featuring a number of artists who worked with John Cage at the New School.[24] Fluxus was founded by George Maciunas in 1962, and the first Fluxus publication appeared in 1964, the same year Ono's collection of scores, *Grapefruit*, was published, in a run of 500 copies, by Wunternaum Press in Tokyo.[25] Like *Blood Piece*, many of the scores in *Grapefruit* are difficult or impossible to perform in an art gallery or concert space, and are thus suited for print publication, indicating a "unique relationship between performance and publication . . . at heart in the history of Fluxus."[26] From its earliest publications, Fluxus tended to blur the lines between poetry, music, and dance. Especially for those Fluxus artists who were students of Cage at the New School, time was a key unifying element of poetry, music, dance, and hybrid works. The question of duration in time animated much of Cage's work, and Fluxus artists influenced by Cage also conceptualized their work in terms of how it unfolds in time.[27] Like Ono's instruction paintings, many Fluxus performances were grounded in a score, or a text that provides brief instructions for a sequence of actions. The relationship between score and enactment introduces epistemological dilemmas around what it means to perform or complete the work. Bringing awareness of its own limitations or impossibility into the work itself, this new aesthetic formation also engaged the body via intermediality, bringing a visceral sense of limitation into the work that makes it a rich resource for engaging violence.

Allan Kaprow traces the lineage of the happening backward through the action painting of the 1940s, Surrealism and Dada, and "all the way to medieval mystery plays and processions."[28] The prototypical happening is full of random, nonsensical, and shocking events strung together without seeming order, eliciting surprise in audiences. This is clear in Kaprow's opening segment of "Happenings in the New York Scene," when he goes on for more than a page describing what you might expect to see at a happening: "It's hot" and there are "cartons" that seem to move around on their own, "little blue lights" flashing all around, "loud breathing sounds" coming in over the loudspeakers, and "a hundred iron barrels and gallon wine jugs" that swing from the ceiling. There are "mushy shapes" that "pop up from the floor" and "a wall of trees" that "advances on the crowd." Among other events, "a nude girl runs after the racing pool of a searchlight, throwing spinach greens into it."[29] Throughout his page-long example, he ascribes feelings to the audience members, addressing them in the second person: "You come in as a spectator," he claims, but you cannot remain simply a spectator. "You're caught in it after all," afraid and claustrophobic but "all the time you're *there*, getting into the act."[30] This overwhelming, random-seeming series of events brings "you" *there*, to itself, catches you in the present of itself, a space full of action and sensation.

In waiting to be shocked or surprised, audiences are both more disoriented than usual and more attuned to their surroundings, taking in and trying to make sense of the zany flashes that appear, or might soon. This experience of waiting for what cannot be known recalls Karl Heinz Bohrer's theory of suddenness: a moment of aesthetic experience in which one encounters what is incomprehensible, and the very senselessness of what one encounters opens up a ground to imagine new possibilities and create new knowledge.[31] Seen in the form of the happening, an act of violence that is initially inscrutable might eventually come to make a kind of sense, but it is represented in such a way as to manipulate the interpretive possibilities accessible to audiences. Susan Sontag, who frequently attended happenings and wrote about them in 1962, provides an eyewitness account of the happening's suddenness. She compares them to "a firecracker going off dangerously close to one's face,"[32] emphasizing the ephemeral nature of the events and the central role of violence in them. Their "most striking feature" is their "abusive involvement of the audience."[33] Abuse manifests not only in the physical involvement of audience members, who may have objects thrown at them or undergo the sensory overload of extremely loud sounds, but also in the work's manipulation of time and withholding of narrative. The happening produces suddenness through its "asymmetrical network of surprises, without climax or consummation."[34] Situating the happening in the lineage of Artaud's theater of cruelty, Sontag emphasizes their formal techniques for aggressing against audiences by involving them in a work experienced as an ever-present sequence of surprising, embodied events. In the happening, dynamics of chance cultivate experiences of suddenness by introducing elements of randomness that suspend audiences in time, holding out new knowledge as a possibility but hardly promising it.

Though Kaprow's own writing attempts to make sense of the happenings by defining them as an aesthetic form and elaborating their art-historical and theoretical influences, he also emphasizes how happenings used the varied material of their creation to resist audience protocols for making sense. For Kaprow, the "sense" of language in the happening "is not part of the fabric of 'sense' that other nonverbal elements (noise, visual stuff, action) convey. Hence, [words] have a brief, emergent, and sometimes detached quality. If they do not make sense, then they are heard as the sound of words instead of the meaning conveyed by them."[35] Connecting the use of words to the chance operations of the happening, Kaprow also treats language as a material, like paint or an artist's body, that can be repurposed in the event. Random-seeming juxtaposition, nonsense language, and chance operations produce aesthetic gestures that may end up meaning things but do not initially appear to make sense. Here the modernist "shock of the new" is a shock of the senseless—it is not so much a work's novelty that makes it shocking as its incomprehensibility.[36] This form of senselessness, in which audiences cannot comprehend or make sense of the work of art, "does not disclose its potential meaning, thus depriving the recipient of the capacity to explain and thereby justify a work's creation."[37] The happening both activates and thwarts audiences' desire to puzzle out its meaning.

The happening thus affords aesthetic responses to the challenge of examining wide-scale structures of violence without losing sight of the individual experience of suffering within those systems. We can know that a violent system is in place yet not know who will experience the violating effects of that system; this is one important aspect of the feeling of *bukimi*, the nuclear uncanny experienced by those subject to possible attack. The disorienting attempt to keep multiple possibilities of future violence in one's view, or to attend simultaneously to the scale of the system and that of individual experience, is a nascent structure of feeling that gets articulated through the happening. As *Cut Piece* illustrates, this structure of feeling emerges in a postwar context concerned with bodily precarity. Indexing the bodily precarity that we are all subject to yet which, as disability scholars have suggested, our social commitment to the "normate" often overlooks,[38] the happening can also show that some groups are more precarious than others. In the United States and abroad, midcentury suspension was also an affective formation revolving around the ways violence could be meted out according to scripts that seemed logical from one vantage point and utterly senseless from another. Centering the experience of suspension offers an alternative to dominant ethics of expediency, not by overtly critiquing the war machine but by reworking time and aligning audiences' experiences with that of the nuclear uncanny. Happenings refuse to progress in time, affording a felt alternative to logics that see collateral damage as inevitable.

## Happening and the Limits of Interpretation

The chance procedure, characterized in Ono's work by the event score, took shape as an aesthetic strategy that placed audiences in a position of epistemic uncertainty by blending the fixed rules of the script with the random occurrences afforded, but not necessarily realized, through the performance. The epistemic crisis of the happening flourishes in Yoko Ono's work, which thematizes a number of broader social forces including the atomic age, neocolonialism, gender, and Asian identity. As it appears in Ono's *Cut Piece*, which she performed four times, in Kyoto, Tokyo, New York, and London between 1964 and 1966,[39] the happening both activates and thwarts the desire to interpret its moments of potential violence. By forcing this dual response, the happening places audience members in a precarious position, suspended between knowing and not knowing about a violent act. Moreover, audience members must occupy multiple positions vis-à-vis potential violence: they may find themselves perpetrating, witnessing, or even suffering forms of violation in the unfolding chance event.

Ono's poetics of chance mark an important departure from earlier abstractionist movements and the forms of indeterminacy employed most famously by John Cage. Ono's relationship to the aesthetics of chance operations was shaped by her experience fleeing firebombings in Tokyo before coming to the United States, a traumatic experience that registers how an accident of place and timing can render one the victim of intentional, politically rationalized violence. Critiquing her mentor John Cage's somewhat naive belief that chance operations rooted in East Asian philosophy could transcend the question of politics, Ono rooted her own use of chance in "a politics of practice responsive to mutually entangled histories of violence" across East and West.[40] Ono's use of chance, argues Brigid Cohen, pushed back against broader cultural narratives of neutral cultural exchange between East and West, and was rooted in her "experience of mass violence and betrayal perpetrated by each of her home nations, Japan and the United States, during and after World War II."[41] Tracing her work to its earliest roots, which often eschewed the score and its Cagean trappings, Cohen shows how "Ono's poetics [were] shaped by a specific, gendered history of displacement."[42] Her personal history, as the daughter of an elite Japanese banker who spent time in both Tokyo and San Francisco, informs her thinking about an aesthetics of chance and sheds light on her aesthetic violence. Living as a refugee near Nagano after the US firebombings in Tokyo in 1945, Ono would go on to study phenomenology at Gakushuin University, where she was the first woman to enter its philosophy department. Soon after her family moved to Scarsdale, New York, she left Gakushuin to study music and poetry at Sarah Lawrence. Instead of finishing her degree at Sarah Lawrence, however, she dropped out of school to marry the composer Toshi Ichiyanagi and begin her career as an artist. In 1961, she would begin to host art events in her Chambers Street loft in New York.[43] Drawing on her experiences of displacement as a refugee of US military attack and of marginalization as a woman in male-dominated intellectual and artistic spaces, Ono would go on to rework the chance procedure into a practice of *happening* that invited audiences to linger in the suspended place before applying any narrative coherence to a violent event.

Ono's transnational and gendered perspective informed an art practice that reproduced midcentury suspension as a feeling of being subject to the exercise of state power, recasting wide-scale geopolitical dynamics in the fine-grained interpersonal interactions of the happening. The postwar moment was also one of increased colonial presence in Asia and the Pacific, with the United States colonizing territory in the Pacific as well as using these sites as nuclear test grounds.[44] The moment of midcentury suspension, viewed in this light, is not only a time of reckoning with the past violence of the war and the imminent violence of the Cold War, but is also a moment of violent colonial expansion in Asia and the Pacific. As a key site for contestations between American and Soviet governments, including the Korean and Vietnam wars, Asia was also a locus of suspension, where "hardly war" characterized by small skirmishes, occupation, and nuclear testing made the boundary between war and peace difficult to discern.[45]

The Cold War in Asia was conceived as a "total war," one that was less a discrete arena of fighting than a quotidian experience of military occupation and intelligence, small skirmishes, and imperial institution-building.[46] The inscrutability of this war—the sense that it was not always present, not bounded in time, and "hardly intelligible"—poses an interpretive problem for historiographers and highlights new strategies of imperial violence in the period after 1945.[47] Taking shape as a diffuse and seemingly minor, unbounded set of experiences, the Cold War in Asia operated through and as an open question to be made sense of, an epistemic problem wherein the distinction between war and peace is not quite clear. Restaging this problem, the happening opens up space to experience the tensions and ambiguities of naming violence. When performing *Cut Piece,* Ono makes her embodiment present and available to her audience, making herself vulnerable not only to the actions of audience members but also to their reading of her embodiment, a reading that would likely be inflected with stereotypes about the passive, exotic, and above all inscrutable Asian woman.[48] This notion of the inscrutable Asian—whose affect is difficult to read, whose ethnic identity is not always legible, and whose status as friend or foe is unclear—reverberates in Cold War geopolitical dynamics of intelligence and ambiguity.[49] Reproducing the experience of inscrutability and discomfiting audience members, *Cut Piece* suspends audiences before the closure of judgment, keeping them attuned to the problem of inscrutable violence.

A formal exploration of what it means to know, the happening is well-suited to engagement with the politics of knowledge. Ono's work mobilizes these affordances to explore inscrutability and rework forms of "colonial unknowing," or a willful ignorance about colonial violences that simultaneously imagines itself to fully know and understand a colonial context. It is a "colonial insistence on epistemic mastery and [a] refusal of heterogeneous ways of knowing otherwise."[50] A colonial unknowing refuses to see dynamics of racialization and oppression, dynamics that play an important role in the colonial situation but are rendered unintelligible in this epistemic framework. Reworking dynamics of unknowing through the form of the happening, artists like Ono raised questions about what it means to know violence through the visceral experience of the performance art event. Instead of illuminating all that is unknown, we might "ruminat[e]" on the dynamic of known/unknown to see more clearly how epistemologies render some things clear and others opaque.[51] The happening's mixture of script and chance event formally echoes a relationship between "structure" and "event" that characterizes Cold War violence and neocolonialism in Asia and the Pacific. To apprehend colonialism as a "structure" risks making it eternal and timeless, and overlooks the violent confrontation, and the historical situatedness, of the "event," the moment of encounter.[52] At the same time, being structural, colonialism is a kind of long-unfolding event, suspending time because it is not yet fixed or completed, but ongoing. The happening reparatively takes up the relationship between structure and event to explore a number of questions: how do we think about structural forces in time, rather than as fixed? How do we acknowledge the overarching and wide-scale work of the structural dynamic without losing sight of the victim's particular, unstructured, and unanticipated experience of the event? In Ono's work, the happening intensifies feelings of suspension to explore the relationship between structure and event.

Reworking strategies of indeterminacy and the happening's script and score through a practice that is specifically informed by her experiences as a Japanese woman, Ono's work theorizes the difficulty of distinguishing between intentional and incidental suffering. Indeed, *Cut Piece* raises questions about the status of an act as violent at all. Because the work is realized through performance, its meaning is contingent on the actions of participants. In turn, the participatory, contingent nature of the work activates intense proprioception, involving audiences at the level of heightened bodily sensation and the experience of proximity. The work "consciously invokes the tangibility of affectively sensed proximal engagement."[53] Ono takes up the chance procedure as a strategy for creating experiences of radical contingency in her art without relinquishing full control over the structure and meaning of her work. *Cut Piece* is rooted in an event score, written as the following set of instructions in her *Script for Strip Tease* in 1966:

> Cut Piece First version for single performer: Performer sits on stage with a pair of scissors in front of him. It is announced that members of the audience may come on stage—one at a time—to cut a small piece of the performer's clothing to take with them. Performer remains motionless throughout the piece. Piece ends at the performer's option. Second version for audience: It is announced that members of the audience may cut each other's clothing. The audience may cut as long as they wish.[54]

*Cut Piece* was performed in 1965 in New York's Carnegie Hall, where documentary filmmakers Albert and David Maysles recorded the performance. As this fact should remind us, not only is Ono in control of the event—this score indicates that the event ends when the performer wishes it to—but there is a "third term" in the event's "viewer/object dyad. The eye of the camera, with its reassuring presence, not only acted as an extra witness to the audience participation, but also authorised the actions onstage."[55] As a mechanism that surveils, authorizes, and grants historical significance, the camera's presence imbues the performance with tension—about what will happen onstage, how far certain actions will be allowed to go, and what it means to participate.

In its multiplicity, the happening mobilizes indeterminacy and inscrutability to draw audience members toward attempts at meaning-making that will ultimately falter. The black-and-white film recording of the Carnegie Hall performance begins after the instructions have been expressed to the audience, with the camera looking at Ono and a participant from the perspective of an audience member. Viewers see the back of a man who is kneeling to cut a bit of Ono's clothing. For most of the eight-minute film, the camera captures participants approaching Ono and cutting off bits of clothing—a few inches from a sleeve, the hem of her skirt. Throughout, the camera captures close-ups of Ono's face, allowing viewers to see the increasing breakdown of Ono's attempt to be perfectly still. Although she does not move her body very much at all, she does increasingly move her eyes, and as more of her clothing is cut off, viewers can see the involuntary movements of her body more clearly. Like Ono's face, the pair of scissors onstage is occasionally viewed in close-up. Because the camera most frequently directs its gaze at Ono, usually in a medium-range shot but often in close-up, the film encourages careful attention to the performer and to the minuscule actions unfolding across her body.

Such an intense focus on Ono encourages viewers of the film to read the nonverbal communication she expresses, inciting attempts to interpret her expression and glean her thoughts. In this context, Ono plays on stereotypes about inscrutability, daring viewers to make sense of her expression. I have approached the film through this framework with undergraduate students, and as we viewed the film in 2015, we watched anxiously to glean what she might be thinking and feeling. Facial expressions, especially when they involuntarily leak through an attempt to remain perfectly still, pose a hermeneutic conundrum. They are at once truthful and unreliable. After watching the film, my students and I discussed our sense that Ono felt increasingly uncomfortable as the performance proceeded and she was increasingly exposed on the stage. We may not have been correct, but it is remarkable to note how easily we found a shared story to tell about the film we watched. Although I was quite familiar with the film when I screened it, my students were not. Encountering this new text, with only a minimal set of contexts for it, these students were positioned like the audiences of live happenings in the 1960s, at least insofar as they had little to no sense of how things might turn out. We were in a sterile classroom, not a buzzing concert hall, but we were drawn to attend to the event, expecting that something would happen, even if we could not predict it. As Kaprow writes in his overview of happenings, the open-ended nature of instruction-based events means that "almost anything can happen. And something always does, even things that are unpleasant."[56]

Indeed, something always does. At roughly its midpoint, the film cuts forward in time. Most of Ono's sweater has been cut away, the scraps taken as gifts to her audience members. She is left in a slip and her desiccated skirt. The camera pans up to rest on Ono's face, then as a man approaches her, it cuts to the audience and then once again to the man. This man, whom I will refer to as "the creep," goes too far, appearing to take too much enjoyment in transgressing the unspoken conventions that have been established at the performance. The creep seems to think *he's* the performer. As he walks up to Ono with scissors in hand, he looks out at the audience and says, laughing just a bit, "This is very delicate; might take some time," then kneels to begin cutting. Looking behind, perhaps to respond to a question from an interlocutor backstage, he says "I don't want to cut her."[57] He proceeds to cut much more of her clothing than other participants have to that point. The work enacts a slow approach to what might end up being a shocking or explicit image; as each audience member approaches the performer and picks up the scissors, a new possibility for violent exposure or physical violation flickers, then fades. As Ono continues to sit with her outfit increasingly taken apart, her body increasingly exposed, those viewing the piece are held in a suspensive moment of right before a shocking image that may come. The excessive actions of the creep register as violation, but they also engage audiences in continual anticipation of further violation.

The creep gets his name from a woman in the audience, who eventually calls to him, "stop being such a creep."[58] When he finally leaves the stage, other audience members boo and hiss. The creep has cut off Ono's slip and then snipped both of her bra straps, leaving her to cover her breasts by holding up her bra. Aside from the fact that the man does not take any of the clothing as a keepsake, he has followed the rules of the performance. His transgression is subtle, but it inflects the film with themes of gendered violence and violation. Indeed, his behavior offers evidence in support of Jack Halberstam's reading of the work, in which Ono "used her own body as a battleground to draw out the sadistic impulses that bourgeois audiences harbor toward the notion of woman."[59] Although Ono invites such an unpredictable form of participation, and does not stop the performance while the man is cutting away her clothing, this is the point at which Ono's stillness and composure begin to break, and viewers are drawn close to her vulnerability and embodiment. As the creep cuts off the strap of her slip, Ono briefly starts to move her arm, perhaps to hold her clothing, or help the creep, or get him to stop. She looks down at the scissors, then looks up, briefly opening and moving her mouth, as a still photographer takes a picture from behind her and the creep continues to cut. From the audience, a few phrases can be heard: a man says "expression on her face" and a woman says "carried away."[60] These audience members are observing her face too, and they think the man is going too far in his participation. Watching the film with my students in 2015, we too worried about the man getting carried away, and saw the first shimmer of panic on Ono's face.

The close-up sets in motion a frustrating and compelling dynamic between text and audience. Watching for a sign that will show them what Ono feels, viewers are placed in a position of trying to make sense of an "inscrutable" Asian woman and whether she is being violated. Ono's face is less and less

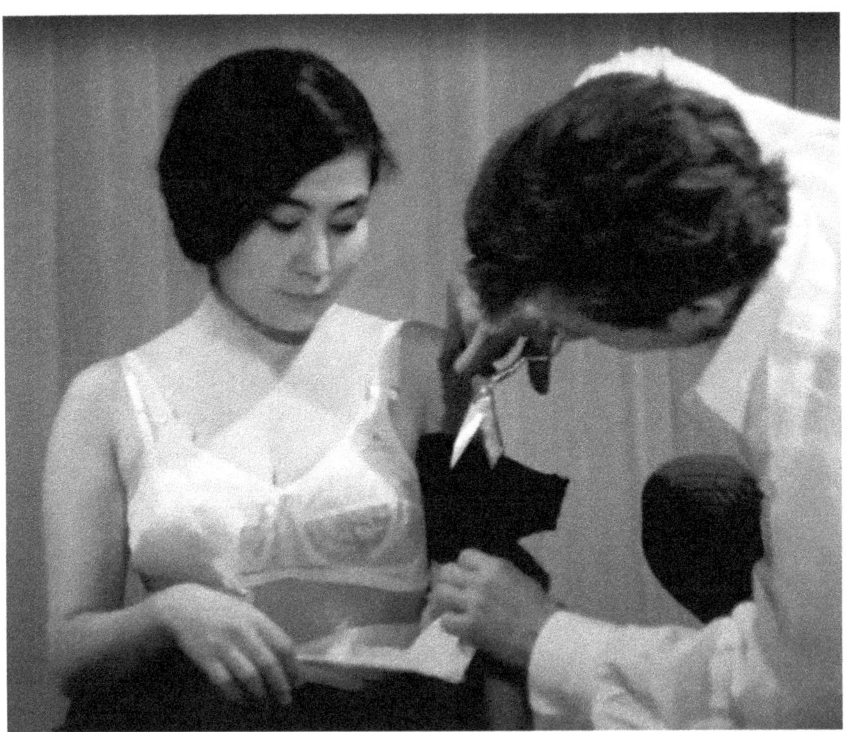

Yoko Ono, Albert Maysles, and David Maysles, *Cut Piece*, 1966, 8 minutes.
© Maysles Films, Inc. and Yoko Ono.

still as the performance continues, though it is still restrained. A few times she seems about to speak, and one additional time she moves her arm, then returns it to her side. Her eyes move more and more; as she keeps trying to look up and out into the middle distance, her eyes dart to the left and right. Finally, after cutting away her slip and cutting both bra straps, the creep sets the scissors down. As he begins to walk away, Ono looks upward in a distinctly visible way. Often, I read this moment as one in which she tries to regain her composure, looking upward to bring herself back from the mounting anxiety that the creep began to provoke in her. It was not until I viewed the film with a large audience at the Poetry Foundation in 2019 that I saw a different meaning in the movement of her eyes. Watching the film on a large screen as part of the opening event for their exhibit of Ono's instructions, I laughed along with the rest of the audience when Ono clearly rolled her eyes at this creepy, immature schmuck. Even a face can be a polysemic text: to me and my fellow 2019 viewers, Ono was not vulnerable to the

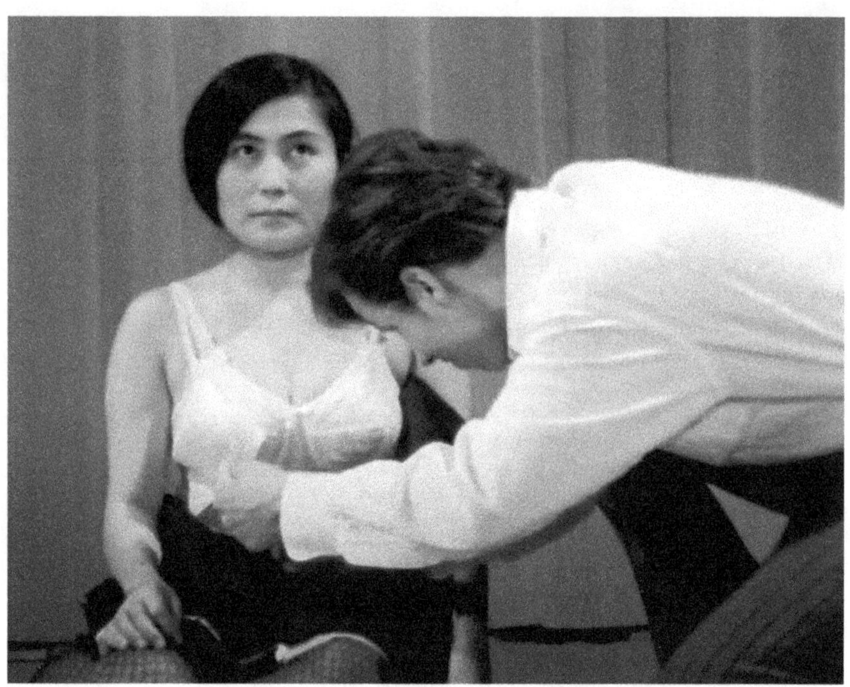

Yoko Ono, Albert Maysles, and David Maysles, *Cut Piece*, 1966, 8 minutes.
© Maysles Films, Inc. and Yoko Ono.

audience, but reacting along with them, rolling her eyes as the other participants and viewers of the event booed a sexist philistine. Shortly after the
creep leaves the stage, another man approaches and picks up the scissors.
Ono looks up toward the ceiling once again, the camera pans to the audience,
and the film ends. In control of the performance yet subject to the whims of
audience members, Ono facilitates a happening, wherein audience members
are drawn toward small signs that might reveal the nature of violence in the
artwork. The Carnegie Hall performance became about the creep's actions,
and audience response suggests that the overdetermined motivations driving his behavior was part of the work's themes: his Orientalist desire, his sexism, his sadism. Likewise, the audience response, which critiques and
polices his behavior, becomes a theme in the work. Yet these themes are not
scripted into the original score; they are simply enabled by its chance
operations.

As *Cut Piece* illustrates, the happening is a form of aesthetic violence that
draws audiences into a phenomenological engagement with the challenge of
recognizing violence. There may not be violence in the performance, but

there is always potential violence thanks to the hermeneutic suspension that shapes the performance event. In the Carnegie Hall performance, potential violence is symbolically realized through the behavior of the creep, whom members of the audience "read" as threatening and boorish. A contemporary viewer might also read into his actions a logic for his behavior: latent or overt sexism and racism; perhaps personal sadism. The formal structure of the event's score capacitates but does not guarantee the incorporation of these themes. In this way, the happening allegorizes complex dynamics of consent and violation: Ono's score makes many kinds of events possible, including those in which she may experience interactions that threaten her or test the boundaries of consent. The happening's intermediality—its multiple enactments of the textual score—formalizes feelings of suspension between consent and nonconsent.

The tactile, interpersonal dynamic inherent in *Cut Piece*, as in other famous touch-based performances, makes this art form uniquely suited for theorizing dynamics of violence. The potential for interpersonal violence that is latent in everyday interactions becomes manifest in the work. Indeed, it is an essential part of the work's realization in time. *Cut Piece* preceded more extreme "pain performances" like the work of Chris Burden and Marina Abramović in which "the artist deliberately places his or her body at risk" of "torment inflicted by the audience."[61] As Jennifer Fisher notes, the work's multiplicity and ongoing life in its performances has enabled the work to articulate with multiple contexts, taking on distinct valences and themes in those shifting contexts. The Carnegie Hall performance has circulated widely thanks to the Maysles brothers' film; its suspensive violence makes it an interesting case study for thinking about aesthetic violence, partly because it is in some ways less violent than other performances of the work in the period. In a 1964 performance in Kyoto, for example, one audience participant threateningly held the scissors over Ono's head.[62] The somewhat softer, subtler aggression of the Carnegie Hall performance, thought alongside these other iterations, queries the boundary between violence and nonviolence, asking what it means for art to be violent. In addition to exposing the performer to potential violence, and to representing and thematizing structures that produce collateral damage or unknown violation, the happening also inflicts aesthetic violence on audiences. It does this at the level of (thwarted) interpretation but also through the force of proprioception, the affective intensity of proximity and suspension. Even viewed on film, the work holds me in suspension, a holding that is a kind of pulling, and which does not resolve itself, but simply ends when the performance does.

*Cut Piece* does indeed *represent* real-world violence: the scissors symbolize more threatening weapons, and Ono's desiccated clothing visually echoes the ripped clothes of survivors from Hiroshima and Nagasaki.[63] In addition to themes of sexual violence or nuclear attack, *Cut Piece* has been understood to respond to "the war in Vietnam, riots, and the feeling of some of us against authority in society."[64] That said, *Cut Piece* does more than symbolically depict violence. The event incorporates the potentially violating act of cutting clothing to stage a scene of potential interpersonal violence, even inviting audiences to commit acts of violation. In its open-ended nature, the event introduces a kind of Chekhov's gun without the promise that it will eventually be fired. Moreover, even if the gun goes off, so to speak, it will not necessarily convey any fixed or clear meaning, given that the fulfillment of anticipated violence comes through the structure of chance. Blending fixity and chance through the score and its intermedial manifestations, *Cut Piece* involves history through the embodied presence of the performer. As Vivian Huang has put it, Ono's performance engages "a hegemonic discourse of hospitality" that sees Asian women as always available "to offer generosity to xenophobic systems that would normalize their labor of giving as complicity or aspirational assimilation."[65] Its deployment of chance, however, means the work does not straightforwardly display this discourse in order to critique it. Through her performance, Ono also "reconstruct[s] and trouble[s] the terms of [Asian feminine] legibility as such."[66] The unpredictable actions of the audience, facilitated through the chance procedure, opens the possibility for more expansive readings.

## Suspending Judgment

Violence is thus suspended in *Cut Piece*, and audiences are similarly suspended between anticipation and interpretation, waiting for what they are not sure will come. This suspended experience both invites resolution in the form of meaning-making and keeps in view the polysemic nature of the text itself—one that may be interpreted as a scene of misogynist violation or "a gift, a gesture of reparation, or a ritual of rememberance."[67] The threat of violence is coupled with the reparative act of gift-giving, producing multivalent tones and meanings. The formal inscrutability of *Cut Piece* explores what hospitality and gift-giving can look like when the host is a woman of Asian descent—a person who has been historically relegated to laboring, to being there for the taking, to "saying yes."[68] The aesthetics of inscrutability signal "the dawning articulation of a new form."[69] Drawing on Sianne Ngai's exploration of the "interesting" as an aesthetic category, Huang claims that, like what is interesting, what is inscrutable can "produce new knowledge."[70] The inscrutable, however, is more specifically in dialogue with "the Orientalist abjection of the Asian, the feminine, and the silent by quietly contorting its moves to uncertain social effects."[71] Framed through the lens of gender, racial, and national identity, *Cut Piece* is an inscrutable text that, precisely because it unsettles interpretative closure, produces new forms of knowledge about violence. The happening suspends audiences in the anticipatory stance of waiting for violence, using chance procedures to bring audiences to the frustrating limit point of interpretation. While interpretations of *Cut Piece* now proliferate, the phenomenological experience of the work is maintained because it can be restaged at any time, with unpredictable audience participants. The happening mobilizes indeterminacy, chance, and the contingency of meaning that manifests in each performance of the score to explore the experience of radical contingency within broader social systems.

In its subversion of fixed interpretations, the happening ultimately produces new knowledge about the relationship between structural and interpersonal violence, highlighting how social structures make some groups more vulnerable to collateral damage than others. The slowed, suspended feeling produced by the happening's aesthetic violence stands in contrast to a logic of expediency that helps to rationalize the violence of neo-imperialism. Its suspension disrupts the satisfying closure of narrative resolution, holding audiences back from hasty interpretation. Sontag observes that audiences are often not sure when a happening has ended, largely because the works have "no plot, no story, and therefore no element of suspense (which would then entail the satisfaction of suspense)."[72] Writing about suspense plots in Victorian literature, Caroline Levine has claimed that suspense fiction is more than a pleasurable plot formula; it is a significant epistemological formation that requires readers to suspend judgment about a situation. Suspense thus "performed a critical cultural role: narrative enigmas and delays could help to foster habits of hesitation and uncertainty."[73] Suspending judgment, according to many nineteenth-century thinkers, "was a necessary stage in the pursuit of knowledge."[74] Suspense was produced "as the consequence of a particular formal strategy."[75] Similarly, the formal strategy of the happening solicits audience interaction and rewards particular kinds of affective engagement. Instead of offering suspense, the happening provides suspension, the moment before judgment and clarity. The happening thus formalizes new epistemic problems related to the structure and scale of violence at midcentury. Instead of offering a claim or judgment about systems that produce violent collateral damage, the work invites audiences into the suspended feeling of *bukimi*, cultivating an aesthetic experience that contradicts logics of expediency, even as it echoes the feeling produced by those systems.

The happening, which seems to be all about chance, actually follows a tight script; moreover, it is the carefully controlled script that allows for chance events to happen within the performance. In fact, adhering to the rules of the performance leaves room for even more shocking contingencies to unfold. The creep, for example, could have cut away much more of Ono's clothing. In response, audience members could have left their seats and tackled the creep. Ono, according to the script, could end the performance at any point, but the potential for violence to spill out of the happening, to become irreparable or uncontrollable, is held out as a continual possibility at the level of form. The possibility of violation looms even as the work invites aesthetic engagement, highlighting the contingency of our bodies while offering gifts to the audience. As it manifests in the form of the happening, a midcentury concept of senseless violence is revealed as a problem of knowing in a moment when the boundary between war and peace, violation and intimacy, was particularly obscure. As a way of reckoning with the experience of being subject to violent geopolitical or social systems, the happening's aesthetic of suspension sustains attention to epistemic problems surrounding violence.

Like Austin Allen, I am reminded of Kurt Vonnegut's intermedial gestures when I read *Grapefruit*.[76] In addition to its incorporation of drawings, *Slaughterhouse-Five* shares with Ono's work a multivalent emotional response to the legacies and ongoing threat of war. Although Vonnegut does not employ chance-based procedures, as, for example, William S. Burroughs would, the novel produces an experience of the happening through its nonlinear chronology that seems to shift arbitrarily between different moments in the plot. These moments range from the protagonist, Billy Pilgrim's, experience as a prisoner of war in Dresden during the Allied bombing to scenes set in Tralfamadore, an alien planet where Billy lives in a zoo exhibit. Organizing his novel in this way, Vonnegut places readers "at the mercy of the 'Tralfamadorian' structure of the novel,"[77] which refuses linear time. Because Vonnegut's novel, unlike those of the Tralfamadorians, must still be read in linear time, readers experience the movement between disparate moments as a chance-based shift, reminiscent of a Cage score determined by chance operations. The reading experience can be disorienting, and it echoes the tense feeling of suspension. Billy Pilgrim becomes "unstuck in time,"[78] but readers are stuck in all times, suspended across the disparate scenes of the novel.

Likewise, the refrain of *Slaughterhouse-Five*, which punctuates any act of death, whether intentional or accidental, individual or mass, condenses the structure of feeling emerging in the long 1960s around concepts of violence: "So it goes." This refrain, repeated over one hundred times in the novel, appends to experiences as varied as the Dresden bombing, the destruction in the biblical story of Sodom and Gomorrah, and the "dead" Champagne Billy considers drinking in his home.[79] Partly reflecting the Tralfamadorian position that, because time is nonlinear, death cannot exist,[80] but largely pointing to a sense of overwhelming meaninglessness to death and suffering, "so it goes" also refuses distinctions between legitimate and senseless violence. Articulating a resignation to the inevitability of suffering, "so it goes" resonates in the formal structure of the chance procedure, an aesthetic gesture that, as we have seen in *Cut Piece*, opens the artist and audience to an unpredictable array of experiences. Published in 1969, *Slaughterhouse-Five* reflects on the trauma of World War II and critiques romanticized notions of war as necessary, heroic, and bounded in time—an ideology that underwrote US engagement in the Vietnam War and neo-imperial projects of the Cold War. Scrambling linear narrative to the degree that each shift in time happens as if by random chance, *Slaughterhouse-Five* also refuses a chronological approach to war that would "give a coherence to the totality of the experiences themselves and make[] sense of a series of occurrences that have no rational basis, as far as Vonnegut is concerned."[81] In Vonnegut's moral universe, the common sense that legitimates state violence is not valid because it causes suffering. When he collapses forms of death through the refrain of "so it goes," Vonnegut refuses that common sense. Refusing linear structures of time and challenging coherent reading experiences through intrusions of images throughout the novel, *Slaughterhouse-Five* protests war through the suspended, absurd set of narrative experiences it stages. It shares with the happenings a structure of feeling that attends not to the rationalizing logics of the military industrial complex and neo-imperialist ideology, but to the affective experience of senselessness and absurdity felt by those subject to military force.

The happening tends to refuse strategies of protest, but its aesthetic gestures may also be put to use for more straightforward social critique. *Slaughterhouse-Five*'s manipulation of time and narrative intentionality reflects one way to invoke the absurdity of suffering as a form of refusal.[82]

Yoko Ono's deployment of advertising art is another. Sharing with event scores like *Cut Piece* a formal strategy of suspension, one of her most famous protest works, created with John Lennon, was the series of "War is Over!" billboards and posters appearing the same year as *Slaughterhouse-Five*.[83] The joyous declaration that "War is Over!" appears in large font, followed below, in much smaller text, with the phrase "If You Want It." Manipulating typography also enables Ono and Lennon to manipulate the reader's experience in time. If the subjunctive experience of midcentury suspension was frequently characterized as waiting for an attack that may or may not happen, the slightly later protest work of "War is Over!" first seems to offer a conclusive statement, providing a sense of closure to readers that is then taken from them. Undercutting the feeling of closure, the poster flings readers back into a suspensive position and places responsibility for ending war on readers themselves. The billboards invert the affective structure of nuclear-age suspension to imagine that an end to war may potentially come. Once read, the billboard maintains the suspensive feeling of its subjunctive grammar. In an echo of the happening's aesthetic violence, it troubles audiences' experience of time, knowledge, and judgment to afford alternatives to the violent logic of expediency.

## CHAPTER THREE

# Grotesque

## *Epistemology of the Accident*

In the time of midcentury suspension, while the first happening was taking place at Black Mountain College and Yoko Ono was writing poetry as a student at Sarah Lawrence and beginning to draft event scores, Flannery O'Connor was writing the short stories that would soon be collected in *A Good Man Is Hard to Find*. Frequently characterized as grotesque, her fiction narrates scenes of random or accidental violation as they unfold within broader systems of oppression—not only the threat of nuclear attack and the recent memory of the Holocaust, but also the Jim Crow South. At a time when both avant-garde and mainstream writers and artists were exploring the ability of structure or form to produce particular audience responses, work in both registers was often simultaneously visible to mainstream audiences. In 1965, for example, *Time* magazine was reviewing O'Connor's fiction, which was marketed to a mainstream audience, in the same issue as a retrospective of the work of avant-garde artist Kurt Schwitters.[1] The author of this retrospective briefly mentions the "happenings" that were becoming more visible at this time. Four years later, the same magazine would review O'Connor's work in an issue that also discussed important figures associated with the happenings, including John Cage, Nam June Paik, and Charlotte Moorman,[2] all of whom were important interlocutors or colleagues of Ono.

A surprising number of her contemporary critics linked O'Connor to experimentalists of her era, in spite of her occasional dismissal of "experimental" writing of the time.[3] Although these critical approaches have largely been overshadowed by frameworks that emphasize her Southern, Catholic themes,[4] their existence in the critical record indicates a broader alignment with the aesthetics of the midcentury avant-garde, which sought to cultivate direct, physical engagement between art and audience. Literary critic and noted theorist of postmodernism Ihab Hassan, for example, grouped O'Connor with such experimental writers as John Hawkes and even William S. Burroughs.[5] Likewise, at a moment when she was securing her place in the canon, critics were analyzing her fiction "under the rubrics of southern literature, black humor, and experimental fiction."[6] As her reception history indicates, O'Connor has always been approached as a formal innovator, even while critical frameworks linked her to the Southern grotesque, to "local color" fiction, to the New Critical precision of her Iowa training, or to Catholic theology. Although she is rarely considered alongside the avant-garde movements of the 1950s and '60s, her poetics of violence is informed by similar commitments to a phenomenological engagement with art facilitated by formal constraints or rules. Her grotesque aesthetics emerge not only through what she depicts, but how: through the collision of form and deformation that characterizes the grotesque.

Nevertheless, O'Connor is perhaps an odd fit in this book, since her own minoritarian writing project is hardly equivalent to that of other, more politically progressive figures in this study. Indeed, one of the dominant questions scholars debate about O'Connor is the degree to which her racist beliefs shaped her fiction.[7] Her work's grotesque aesthetics, however, are important to explore in this book because they raise questions about the nature of suffering that point to the risks of seeing pain where it may not exist. O'Connor has often been associated with the grotesque, in terms that relate it to exaggerated depictions bordering on stereotypes.[8] This is the grotesque as it describes characters who exhibit bodily excess, exaggerated characteristics, or abject social positions—O'Connor's freaks and misfits. I would like to offer a different definition of O'Connor's grotesque aesthetics, one more related to form. Her formal techniques of narrating accidents and using third-person limited point of view shape her portrayal of grotesque themes to cultivate aesthetic violence. The form of the grotesque, which emphasizes contradiction and incommensurability, invites reflection on the boundaries between violence and nonviolence. Applying formal strategies of the grotesque to violent narratives that often feature disabled characters, O'Connor interrogates the kinds of knowledge we can glean from accidental suffering. The grotesque, in O'Connor's work, is a form that registers contingency through the ways it brings together contrasts. Her grotesque, I contend, is tied not only to the lineage of Southern fiction but also, and importantly, to the grotesque's association with the absurd and its avant-garde manifestations. Absurdism shares the grotesque's ambivalent mix of humor and horror, with incongruities and exaggerations that break a sense of realism.[9] Indeed, in the visual arts, the grotesque "plays a role in cubism and certain kinds of abstraction."[10] This formal grotesquerie cultivates ambiguity and multivalent meanings, unsettling fixed notions of meaning and identity.

Indebted not only to her experience as a visual artist and cartoonist but also to the street theater aesthetics of her friend, playwright Maryat Lee, this form of the grotesque inflicts aesthetic violence through the way it forms and deforms, blending constraints with exaggerations to engage audiences at the level of sensation. As Frances Connelly puts it in her overview of grotesque aesthetics in modern art, "grotesques are typically characterized by what they lack: fixity, stability, order. . . . the grotesque is a boundary creature and does not exist except in relation to a boundary, convention, or expectation."[11] The grotesque's aesthetic violence takes shape in the movement between forming and deforming, and it is made possible through the constraints artists placed on their composing process. O'Connor's key constraint is her consistent use of third-person limited narration, a constraint that cultivates irony and ambiguity around acts of violation. Lee's short street theater plays are shaped by a constraint of site-specificity, composed in collaboration with the community where they were staged and performed outside. Her plays also employ techniques of exaggeration and accident, sharing a grotesque aesthetic that, at the same time, challenges stereotypes of the grotesque that exclude people through racial or embodied difference. The constraint of her collaborative composing process gives voice to the subjects of her plays, such as the drug addicts in East Harlem who collaborated with her on her first show, *Dope!*. Lee, a liberal, queer, nonreligious feminist, saw the world quite differently than O'Connor. Their artistic practices were also distinct, but both artists used the form of the grotesque—a form that stages contingent events in an exaggerated snapshot—to unsettle ideologies of grotesqueness that dehumanize nonnormative embodiment. Grotesque aesthetics offer a partial portrait of an accident, raising questions about cause and effect that they also make difficult to answer. Tracing grotesque aesthetics in O'Connor's first short story collection and Maryat Lee's street theater, this chapter theorizes the aesthetic violence of the grotesque as an encounter with "contrastive structure" at the level of both form and content,[12] which cultivates ironic ambiguity around the status of a violent event.

O'Connor explores the contingency of random or accidental forms of suffering via "narrative chance," or depictions of chance events that also ultimately point to the design of the narrative itself[13]—in other words, to the impossibility of their randomness or non-intentionality. In contrast to the chance operation, in which a set of rules or procedures enables an artist to cede control over what the work will ultimately be, narrative chance is a technique for putting "cause-effect relations . . . under intense epistemological scrutiny."[14] Narrative fiction is a rich site for considering the role of contingency in life, since the novel in some sense aspires to a total world in which the randomness of life is reconfigured in a kind of order—even if that ordering force produces bewildering experiences for characters. At the same time, narrating the chance encounter remains an important motif through modernist and postmodern literature; it is a useful device for moving plot or developing character. Here, "the chance event is thus less a sign of universal contingency than an event that simultaneously emerges from this contingency and marks its transformation. It involves an element of ordinary reality that suddenly moves into the realm of the extraordinary through its impact on individual consciousness."[15] In shifting from the chance procedure at the root of the happening to the technique of narrative chance at the heart of O'Connor's grotesque aesthetics, this chapter also shifts attention from suspension—a feeling before the meaning or outcome of violence can be known—to contingency.

Suspension holds audiences between possible experiences, extending pauses before events are understood or judged. Contingency, though it produces feelings of suspension, describes how events unfold in time and gestures toward the complex, entangled nature of that unfolding. The "contingent event . . . is something that can happen, but that does not have to happen; if it does happen, then it could have happened differently, or not at all."[16] In his exploration of literary depictions of accidents, David Wylot, like other theorists of contingency in literature,[17] highlights the literary accident as a productive site for considering the relationship between a work and the world, since both real-world and literary accidents rest on narrative structures and invite interpretation.[18] Interpretations might seek to trace the specific cause of the accident, finding that the cause is a chance confluence of events. The accident invites retrospective understanding, an attempt to locate the specific turn of events, the one random moment in the chain that produced the outcome one now experiences. But the compulsion to understand will not undo or necessarily alleviate the suffering of the accident. If the chance operation is a formal technique for introducing contingency to the creation of a work, the use of self-imposed constraints exemplified by O'Connor's midcentury fiction is a technique for producing the feeling of contingency in audiences. Instead of suspending experience, the narrative accident multiplies possible events and produces the unsettling, dissatisfying experience of retrospection that does not alleviate suffering.

The grotesque is a form intimately connected to accidents and to irony. As a contrast to Kantian notions of the beautiful, the grotesque invokes not purposive purposelessness but the anarchy of chance.[19] In the long literary history of grotesque aesthetics, scholars debate the degree to which the grotesque constitutes a form.[20] It often manifests as a kind of deformation, a perversion or breakdown of form. The grotesque is difficult to define as a form, but one key characteristic is the way it brings together opposites or holds differences in tension. Across literary and visual media, "contrastive structure is not only a formal property but a persistent theme of the grotesque."[21] Such contrastive structure gives grotesque representations their strong or exaggerated character. The contrastive structure of the grotesque can manifest through depictions of transgression or excess, or by heightening visual contrasts, as in Diane Arbus's photographs, which used flash to heighten the contrast between light and shadow and sharpen the contours of her images. As James Goodwin puts it, the grotesque's "reductiveness" is "a radical procedure intended to disclose meanings otherwise obscured from apprehension in the phenomenal sense of the word."[22] The grotesque form is paradoxically characterized by its formlessness, but it is not so much that the grotesque lacks a form as that it draws attention to the shaping role of forms—and their ability to be transgressed. In this way, the concept of form's constraining or shaping properties illuminates grotesque aesthetics. Constraints are an essential part of a form: the constraint is the affordance's mirror image. At the same time, constraints afford. In other words, the constraint is a feature of an artwork that enables it to be one thing rather than another. We might even think of form itself as a kind of constraint. Indeed, the first of Caroline Levine's axioms in her work on form is this: "forms constrain."[23] The notion of form as constraining or limiting, according to Levine, has been one important reason literary critics have praised the breaking of form or the embrace of formlessness as politically liberating—liberation as struggle against constraint.

Yet the grotesque does not merely struggle against form; it takes form as well. Grotesque aesthetics thus offer "a perspective animated by incongruity."[24] The aesthetic violence of the grotesque manifests in the challenge of reconciling incongruities and confronting the ambiguities they produce. A mix of humor and terror, the grotesque also activates multiple, seemingly contradictory affective responses, produced through its combination of form and content. For O'Connor, the grotesque did not describe the abject or weird characters stereotypically imagined to populate the South; grotesquerie has a more positive connotation related to the fundamental spiritual mysteries fiction opens a view toward but cannot fully grasp. The grotesque manifests in "strange skips and gaps" that break realist representation such that "characters have an inner coherence, if not always a coherence to their social framework."[25] Volleying between coherence and incoherence, form and its lack, aesthetic perception of the grotesque feels violent not only because of what it might refer to or represent but because of the difficult engagement with form it poses. In his influential work on the grotesque, Geoffrey Harpham contends that the "form itself resists the interpretation that it necessitates."[26] Grotesques demand interpretation and subvert it.

## The Rule That Corrects Emotion

For O'Connor, the grotesque connects the concrete aspects of sensation and sensory perception to the unknown elements of mystery, which exceeds perception. Resisting sentimental approaches to grotesque imagery that link it to a "hazy compassion,"[27] she challenges glib models of reading as cultivating empathy with pitiful others. O'Connor criticizes this model of compassion because it short-circuits "intellectual and moral judgment" in favor of "feeling."[28] Easy feelings of "hazy compassion" are a problem for O'Connor because they produce bad fiction and bolster critical misrecognition of the South. Her critique also anticipates disability theorists' insight that sentimental approaches to disability can dehumanize actual disabled people by finding tragedy where there is merely accident, or by imagining a disabled individual's life as irredeemably tragic and thus not worth living. Likewise, the epistemology of the accident theorized in *A Good Man Is Hard to Find* anticipates disability theorist Ato Quayson's emphasis on the contingent nature of all embodiment. O'Connor's thoughts on the grotesque open up a critique of all manner of misrecognized violence. One of her favored quotations, for instance, came from the cubist painter Georges Braque: "I like the rule that corrects the emotion."[29] O'Connor was deeply invested in formal technique—rule—that cultivates multivalent affective responses rather than a straightforward dynamic of pity, sympathy, or catharsis—emotion. O'Connor's "aesthetic regime" was "extreme," with each story she wrote using "the same precisely calibrated mode of narration—the 'third person limited' form favored by Henry James and promoted by her mentors as the surest path to 'impersonality.'"[30] A perfectly disciplined creator of aesthetic experiences that were rooted in the creative pain of the Iowa Writers' Workshop,[31] O'Connor could deploy rules to correct emotion.

The grotesque is a form shared by textual and visual media, and O'Connor's abiding interest in the visual and performing arts shaped her grotesque aesthetics. O'Connor was an artist throughout her life and often drew on the visual arts to explain her writing process and beliefs about fiction.[32] O'Connor "identif[ied] herself as an artist" in high school,[33] was a cartoonist for her college newspaper, and painted throughout her life, even experimenting with abstract expressionist techniques in her youth. Undated sketches and paintings found in O'Connor's archives at Emory University demonstrate interest in, if not embrace of, abstract expressionist and even cubist aesthetics. In addition to experimenting with abstract painting, a sketchbook in her papers includes a series of figures rendered as composites of geometric shapes, suggesting interest in the aesthetic possibilities of modernism.[34] The influence of modernist art can be glimpsed in her published cartoons as well.[35] The constraint produced by her linocut cartooning process leaves rather straightforward, high-contrast prints of black ink and white space, without allowing for shading. The cartoons, as Kelly Gerald notes, demonstrate a strong command of form and the ability to render the human figure well within the crude constraints of the linocut, but they also demonstrate grotesque exaggeration and contrast. O'Connor's cartoons not only share some aesthetic influences of modernism, then, but also join the lineage of the caricature and its association with grotesque aesthetics, characterized by extreme pairings of contrasts, heightened features, and reductive typologies. As Rebecca Wanzo has observed, the "exaggerated, grotesque representations" of the caricature developed at the same time as "scientific racism," reflecting the influence of broader Enlightenment impulses toward taxonomy and racial categorization.[36] O'Connor published one cartoon depicting a minstrel performance in her career. The crude, binaristic depiction of blackface in the linocut technique exemplifies the morphological echoes between the cartoon and scientific racism's deployment of categories.[37] A grotesque aesthetics that focuses on the play of contrasts emerges in her cartoons, offering an early glimpse of how O'Connor would go on to mobilize constraints to produce experiences of grotesquerie in her fiction. Highlighting the cartoons' "planar opacity," Rebecca B. Clark also notes that modernist approaches to the grotesque resist or subvert the cathartic nature of more classically grotesque aesthetics.[38] For Clark, this modernist grotesque maintains an "ambivalent" affect through its formal imposition of "classificatory, diagrammatic" structure onto embodied, transgressive matter.[39] O'Connor's artistic practice as a cartoonist, then, was also a practice of developing rules that would structure unruly bodies and their affects.

Along with her interest in the visual arts, O'Connor's long friendship with the playwright Maryat Lee illuminates the uses of constraint for engaging audiences in violent aesthetics. Lee was a key figure in the development of community-based street theater, a movement adjacent to avant-garde theater of the midcentury that sought to collapse the distinctions between life and art. Lee worked with local members of her community, first in East Harlem and later in rural West Virginia, to conceptualize and write plays, which would be performed in public space on handcrafted, portable stages. In the vein of medieval mystery plays, Lee's street theater works were designed to offer a clear theme to audiences by developing character; with simple plots "built around a single, symbolic act," the plays facilitated contingent, often unpredictable aesthetic experiences for both performers and audiences.[40] As William French puts it, watching a performance of Lee's Soul and Latin Theater (SALT) "is unlike seeing a plotted play in a theater but more like viewing a painting in which the scene portrayed gradually reveals the essence of a person."[41] From Covington, Kentucky, Lee was also a Southerner, and she shares with O'Connor an aesthetic violence that cultivates grotesquerie through formal constraint and exploration of the accident. After meeting in Milledgeville in 1956, Lee and O'Connor wrote letters frequently for the rest of O'Connor's life. Scholarly attention to the Lee–O'Connor letters largely focuses on what they reveal about O'Connor's personal feelings of racist animus. Lee was liberal interlocutor to O'Connor's racist jokes and comments, language we would now call symbolic violence and which Angela O'Donnell distinguishes from the expressed, considered use of language (and therefore values) we see in O'Connor's fiction. The statements in O'Connor's letters to Lee reveal racist feeling but also adopt Southern personas that suggest an ironic tone.[42] Frequently cited are her comments about declining to meet James Baldwin in Georgia, an idea Lee introduced in a letter. O'Connor responded that it would be "nice" to meet him in New York, but not in Georgia, where the meeting would cause "the greatest trouble and disturbance and disunion."[43] As O'Donnell suggests, these statements could be protective of Baldwin as well as baldly racist, a reflection of personal distaste and bigotry or a sensitive assessment of the risks to Black people traveling in the South—or an ambivalent mix of both feelings.[44]

The Lee–O'Connor letters, however, also reveal an important aesthetic influence that places O'Connor in broader conversation with more avant-garde elements of midcentury culture and points toward the influence of visual and performing arts on O'Connor's writing practice. My intervention is to approach Lee as an aesthetic interlocutor, informed by evidence from the archive that shows how extensively O'Connor was in conversation with modernist and experimental aesthetics. O'Connor scholar Carole Harris has argued that Lee's feminism influenced O'Connor's thinking about gender as well as race.[45] Their correspondence history also strongly suggests mutual aesthetic influence between the two women writers, who exchanged drafts and discussed the writing life frequently. For example, O'Connor read Lee's work and was "fascinated" by her plays, claiming that she "was able to fancy myself hanging from one of those fire-escapes and watching it with complete absorption." Although the letter is dated 1957, O'Connor may be describing 1952's *Dope!,* calling it "a real morality play if ever I saw one and altogether powerful in spite of it."[46] Suggesting the street play's carnivalesque legacy in her mention of watching from the fire escape, O'Connor also gestures toward the importance of its location for cultivating its effects.

## The Street Scene

Lee's composing process was a carefully honed, collaborative experience in which she got to know local people, interviewed them, and asked them to improvise short performances drawn from their life experiences. From extensive notes on this process, she would compose plays that the local community would then perform. This well-developed set of rules enabled Lee to relinquish much control over what she would produce, drawing the lives and language of the local community into her work and distributing the author function like so many scraps of Ono's clothing. At the same time, however, constraints enabled Lee's control of the work; hers, after all, is the only name that appears on the published plays. With time spent in both commercial and avant-garde theater spaces and immersed in theories of the theater, Lee drew on extensive knowledge and experience to develop her own theory of an indigenous, community-based American theater, which she would explore in East Harlem in the mid-1960s and then in rural West Virginia for the remainder of her life. Although she was not a fan of Bertolt Brecht's writing on theater, his influence shaped her milieu, and the development of street theater calls to mind his influential notion of the street scene. For Brecht, the structural model for epic theater is the observer on the street reenacting an accident. This dynamic is shaped by perspective and the framing choices one must make in recounting an unanticipated, disruptive, and potentially violent event. The street scene invites attempts to understand and to judge; it is reenacted in order to determine what is meaningful about the scene.[47] Similarly, epic theater uses defamiliarization to invite reflection and judgment on social dynamics; its political critique manifests in how it invites audiences to connect representation to reality and to consider the relevant factors that shape an act of judgment. Lee diverged from Brechtian approaches, believing the influence of Brecht impeded the development of new forms of American theater.[48] She also ultimately resisted didactic or politically instrumental uses for theater after staging her first play, *Dope!*, in collaboration with the East Harlem Protestant Parish and Narcotics Anonymous. The play was staged to intervene in the drug crisis, but Lee ultimately felt that such instrumental uses of theater could not be ethical nor provide full aesthetic experiences.[49] Without adopting Brecht's approach to defamiliarization, her composing process nevertheless enfolds and is shaped by notions of the accidental—the contingent, yet potentially meaningful, experiences of the everyday lives of marginalized people shape what her plays are about and how they are written and performed. In form, her brief plays often crystallize an event. They are low on plot and emphasize characterization, placing audiences in the midst of a captured moment, one that has the potential to invite broader reflection on social circumstances or spiritual connection through the communal, self-actualizing work of theater.

Brecht's street scene evokes iconic imagery of the twentieth-century American grotesque as well, echoing the photographs of Weegee, a freelance press photographer whom James Goodwin calls "the first genuine adherent to a grotesque attitude" "in American photography."[50] Documenting the immediate aftermath of violent events like shootings and car accidents, Weegee would "conduct through the camera a visual postmortem."[51] Some of his most famous photographs document dead bodies and onlookers on the streets of New York at night, rendered grotesque not only due to the sensational subject matter but the techniques he employed. His technique heightened contrast between light and dark, effecting a grotesque aesthetic through form as well as the gruesome content of his images.[52] Likewise, the images' grotesque aesthetics were shaped partly by the play between control and accident of his photographic process, since the contingencies of light and shadow would frequently impact the image captured.[53] In a sense, Weegee's photographs capture the dynamic of the street scene, inviting attention to an accident during its aftermath. Yet the photograph is a postmortem; the eye of the camera arrives after the impact of the accident. The photograph can aestheticize the scene, rendering it grotesque, but it cannot narrate how the accident came to be. Like and unlike Brecht's street scene, then, Weegee's grotesque photographs index the dynamic of narrative sense-making entailed by the street scene yet freeze time to foreclose retrospection.

Similar grotesque aesthetics are explored in Maryat Lee's street theater. Like O'Connor, Lee is interested in representing lives often seen as grotesque. Lee's 1969 one-act play, *Four Men and a Monster*, explores the social conditions of these grotesque, abject others while also creating a grotesque depiction of accidental suffering. In one act, three itinerant Appalachian men who have migrated to a large city discuss a plan to escape poverty: they will deceive a "monster"—that is, an ugly prostitute—by seducing her, marrying her, killing her, and inheriting her money. The play takes place in a hotel room where the three men, Hal, Tot, and Upjohn, prepare to carry out their plan. The monster is staying in an adjacent room; at one point Hal, the leader of the group, drills a hole through the wall so he can see how she and Upjohn interact. Upjohn, who has suffered an injury that leaves him mentally impaired, falls in love with the woman in the process of seducing her. Hal becomes frustrated with this turn of events, and toward the end of the play he threatens Upjohn with a knife. When Tot tries to intervene, he and Hal fight; Hal accidentally stabs Tot, whose death ends the play in a "trio," described in the stage directions as an interwoven chorus between the three actors speaking lines, "providing an almost harmonic and rhythmic structure"[54] as they state impressionistic lines invoking the metaphor of a tree to describe Tot's death. A violent plan, overdetermined by the men's lives of poverty and hardship, is interrupted by a violent accident.

The grotesque "monster," who remains offstage throughout the performance, could certainly be said to demonstrate the violence of misogynistic representation. In a soliloquy reflecting on (or perhaps imagining) the experiences of the woman gleaned from her pimp, Hal claims that she has enjoyed prostitution because it makes her feel "useful," and after a number of years working, she's now "fat, warty, hairy, stinkin," and "lookin thataway pitiful, hairy, mountains of cheeze [*sic*] that no one on this ere earth ever wants to climb or cross."[55] She's "a cripple monstrosity" who would, Hal convinces himself, eventually be killed by someone if not him.[56] The visceral description of such "monstrosity," a sotto voce composite of attitudes Lee encountered growing up in Appalachian Kentucky, intersects with the structural violence that leaves these men desperate enough to commit murder, challenging audiences to disentangle structural forces from individual animus. Ultimately, though, the accidental stabbing interrupts the very interpretive act invited by the play's plot. In *Four Men and a Monster*, an accidental stabbing produces incongruity by interrupting plot. This grotesque form frames the accident as a scene of suffering onstage as well as an act of aggression against the audience. The play's ironic end allegorizes the role of constraint and contingency in Lee's street theater method. The self-imposed constraints of Lee's composing and staging techniques incorporate accidents and contingencies she cannot control. Inviting interpretation and judgment, the street theater scene, like Brecht's street scene, is grounded in the contingency of the accidental.

Grotesque Irony

O'Connor's work emerges in a Cold War moment of reckoning with "the violence of Dachau, Hiroshima, Mississippi."[57] While these phenomena of widespread political violence form an important backdrop to O'Connor's work, they have not always informed critical approaches to violence in her fiction. Because O'Connor herself discussed the violence of her stories as a mechanism for bringing characters to an experience of what she called grace,[58] critics have often explicated her scenes of interpersonal, often unmotivated violence through the lens of O'Connor's religious faith. As a devout Catholic writer, O'Connor could inflict extreme and apparently senseless violence on her characters, and that violence can be made sense of as an act of grace, a crisis point that invites spiritual awakening. Nevertheless, these violent scenes are often so extreme that it can be difficult to see any redemptive power in them—they are grotesquely exaggerated. While the very incomprehensibility of the workings of violent grace might, for O'Connor or some of her readers, only further indicate the metaphysical nature of such violence, for other readers the explanation of "grace" is insufficient.[59] Inviting multiple, often competing interpretations of the violence in her stories, O'Connor produces a second-order experience of the grotesque: the violent scenes are presented as controlled by chance, and their ambiguous framing makes them resistant to the kinds of interpretive impulses sparked by the accident.

Although she rejected didacticism and eschewed overt political commentary, O'Connor often thematized the experience of being implicated in a white supremacist, patriarchal, and ableist society where she both wielded and was subject to power. Although she refused to directly critique Jim Crow violence, her stories, as Patricia Yaeger argues, reproduce an "inchoate" response to the broader atmosphere and structure of Southern violence.[60] In stories that obliquely gesture toward this systemic violence while inflicting accidental forms of harm on her characters, O'Connor indexes the sadistic violence that threatened Black people in the Jim Crow South, a place "where terrible things happen, without rhyme or reason, to real human bodies."[61] O'Connor's use of constraint produces stories that represent, and often produce, the "inchoate" experience of living in a Jim Crow South characterized by its own overarching, if often unspoken, set of rules and social procedures, enforced by legal and extralegal violence. Her works cultivate a grotesque meeting of multiple registers of suffering that she refuses to bring into a unified logic.

Across the nine stories in *A Good Man Is Hard to Find*, violent accidents befall characters. Though these moments are often foreshadowed, they are also framed as random or chance-based within the plot, making them seem excessive or gratuitous. In the collection's widely anthologized title story, a murderer, introduced in the story's first paragraph, shoots a family after they have a car accident and the murderer happens to stop by their car. This story, threaded throughout with references to slavery and Jim Crow violence, juxtaposes two kinds of suffering—a structure of oppression and an accidental encounter with a murderer escaped from prison—without suggesting causal links between them. Throughout the stories in the collection, accidents cause irreparable harm and chance encounters turn violent: an old Civil War veteran dies suddenly onstage at his granddaughter's graduation; a young boy drowns in a river after being baptized; strangers come to the family home and end up committing arson. In the collection's last story, "The Displaced Person," a refugee from the violence of World War II has come to work on a farm in the South and is eventually killed by a jealous farmhand, who positions a tractor to roll over him as if by accident. These stories are grotesque not only because of the suffering they depict, but also because of the ways intention and randomness are drawn together in the narrative accidents. Readers experience a kind of aesthetic violence when they must engage the mix of humor and horror in depictions of accidental suffering.

The grotesque aesthetics arising from the accidental or chance events in O'Connor's stories emerges from the tightly controlled rules that governed her writing. In all of her published stories, O'Connor employs third-person limited narration, in which an anonymous narrator relates events in the third person, with access to the interiority of one character. This narrative style, also favored by Henry James, "stag[es] a *limitation* of knowledge"—the omniscient perspective that could always potentially be adopted by a fiction writer—in order to gain something else: an "'experiential intensity'" for the reader. Third-person limited narration juxtaposes a sense of real knowledge with an awareness of what cannot be known; the narrator, relating what a "character *really* feels," is also limited in their ability to know what all characters feel. Moreover, third-person limited also emphasizes "the limitedness of the central character's point of view."[62] This constraint facilitates both limitation and exaggeration, helping to shape O'Connor's grotesque aesthetics. As O'Connor suggests in her essay on the grotesque in Southern fiction, "the writer of grotesque fiction" is "looking for one image that will connect or combine or embody two points; one is a point in the concrete, and the other is a point not visible to the naked eye." For O'Connor, a grotesque aesthetics brings together sensation and mystery, producing "wild," "violent and comic" work "because of the discrepancies that it seeks to combine."[63] These multiple registers are connected but not fully congruent, producing a grotesque effect through form, as much as through the distinctive characters of O'Connor's work.

Her stories offer a grotesque blend of incongruous epistemologies of suffering, metabolizing discourses of the senseless and the systemic. "A Good Man Is Hard to Find" narrates a series of accidents that lead to a violent end and frames them in relationship to Southern violence writ large. The story forms a grotesque by inviting interpretation that links the direct violence of the Misfit to the implied violence of the story's setting. Although the series of choices made by the family, which bring them to the murderer, are largely random, they also signal the violent backdrop of white supremacy contextualizing the story as a whole. As the family drives from Atlanta toward Florida (and toward their death), they pass by a number of symbols that evoke white supremacy. They pass Stone Mountain, a large-scale monument celebrating the Confederacy that is literally carved into the landscape, overlooking the surrounding area. Soon after, the family drives past "a large cotton field with five or six graves fenced in the middle of it, like a small island," which the grandmother suggests is a family burial ground on a former plantation.[64] Throughout their trip, the grandmother makes a series of racist remarks and jokes. Focalized through the grandmother, an unappealing woman whose final encounter with the murderer concludes the story, "A Good Man Is Hard to Find" also ties the historic violence of the South to the localized violence of the family's unfortunate encounter with the Misfit.

It is the grandmother's desire to see an old plantation home, after all, that sets the family on its course toward the Misfit. After convincing her son, Bailey, to turn back on their journey toward a dirt road that the grandmother believes will lead to the plantation home, she has a terrible realization that causes her to disrupt the luggage at her feet in surprise, releasing her stowed-away cat, who jumps on Bailey's shoulder and causes him to crash the car. The grandmother's "horrible" realization that "the house she had remembered so vividly was not in Georgia [where they were] but in Tennessee" sets off a chain of events that culminates in the car accident.[65] Narrating the sequence of events but withholding the nature of the grandmother's realization until after the accident has taken place, the story shuffles elements of cause and effect, producing a disjointed sense of what has just happened, drawing out the desire to look back and piece together the sequence of events, to make sense of a disorienting and abrupt accident.

This epistemology of the accident, a grasping for causal linkages that, even once pieced together, will not fully explain or account for the violence that has taken place, is heightened by the story's foreshadowing. From the story's first paragraph, readers are primed to expect an encounter with the Misfit. A sense of inevitability shapes the story, but readers do not know what will unfold. The story memorably concludes with the Misfit and his two compatriots shooting the family, but acts of violence take place throughout. As the young daughter June Star says with glee after their car flips on the road, the family had "AN ACCIDENT!"[66] Indeed, the family's death will ultimately turn out to have been accidental: if they had not turned down the road they did, if they had not crashed the car, they would not have been shot by the Misfit and his compatriots. Readers must follow along as this series of "accidents" leads to the encounter with the Misfit, an encounter that was foreshadowed in the story's first paragraph.

Accidents are events that take place without intention; in order to establish "whether or not to call [an] event an accident," one must "interpret[] the relationship between intent and outcome."[67] While readers can track the chain of events that lead not only to the car accident but, subsequently, to the family's death, they also see that, within the world of the story, this death is arbitrary, accidental because it is an outcome different from what any character intended across the duration of these events. For Aristotle, making meaning from accidental occurrences is a necessary action for audiences to experience catharsis. The "shocking or surprising events" "that make up a tragic plot form a series of unexpected occurrences designed to compel the audience to perceive causal relationships between them."[68] A narrative structure would seem to foreclose the possibility of a meaningless accident, since any accidental occurrence within the story's diegesis could always potentially be interpreted, either as necessary to the story's plot or as conveying symbolic content. Interpreting accidents that befall characters enables the satisfying purgation of feeling by settling contingency and fixing accident within a broader, meaningful schema. Yet O'Connor's narrative constraints make situating the family's accidental death within a meaningful framework difficult, provoking emotional reaction but not necessarily cathartic resolution.

The grotesque death of the family in "A Good Man Is Hard to Find" emerges as the result of a narrative dynamic that ties arbitrary and localized acts of violence to the structural violence of the Jim Crow South while at the same time refusing to offer causal linkages that would illuminate that connection at the level of plot. Although the grandmother seems to experience what

O'Connor called grace when faced with imminent death, the story offers no suggestion that the grandmother's change of heart might have extended to her beliefs about the moonlight-and-magnolias South and the white supremacy that underwrites it. Near the story's end, when the Misfit's accomplices have taken all the family members except the grandmother into the woods and shot them, the Misfit and the grandmother have a conversation about faith, crime, and punishment. The grandmother seems to have a revelation, her tone shifts, and she murmurs that the Misfit is "one of my babies . . . one of my own children!" She then reaches toward the Misfit, who immediately shoots her.[69] The only murder readers witness appears provoked by the very moment of grace that later causes the Misfit to claim that the grandmother "would of been a good woman . . . if it had been somebody there to shoot her every minute of her life."[70] Perhaps he saw a glimpse of grace in this exchange and snuffed it out, retreating back toward his nihilistic view expressed in the story's last line: "It's no real pleasure in life."[71] At the same time, this final line undercuts an earlier claim, expressed by the Misfit and echoed by his accomplice Bobby Lee, that killing itself is the central pleasure one might draw from life.[72] Like other moments of grace in the story collection, it is unclear whether the revelatory moment upends or rests on characters' racist beliefs.

Like a number of O'Connor's other stories, "A Good Man Is Hard to Find" revolves around a fundamentally ambiguous climax, one that, in line with contemporaneous New Critical conceptions of irony, enacts a reading experience wherein two mutually exclusive interpretive conclusions are available to readers.[73] On the one hand, we might see the Misfit as symbolically punishing the grandmother for her thoroughgoing racism, seeing the family's journey toward their diegetically random yet narratively inevitable end as determined by the grandmother's racism. Her desire to nostalgically reclaim the Old South is a desire for her own destruction. On the other hand, the story offers no suggestion of a causal linkage between the grandmother's racism and her family's death, and readers might understandably find it difficult to see the random murder of an entire family as retribution for or resolution of the grandmother's racism. Setting these dynamics in play without clarifying their relationship to one another, O'Connor ironizes the senseless death that concludes her story, leaving readers ill-equipped to find a clear takeaway for the story's climactic murders. More than a mode of dramatic irony in which readers see what will befall characters before the characters themselves do, O'Connor's narration in "A Good Man Is Hard to Find" invites a form of readerly knowing that is continually undercut by doubt. The story's foreshadowing helps to produce the interpretive and affective incongruities of grotesquerie. Staging a kind of street scene and inviting readers to consider its relationship to the inchoate violence of the postbellum South, the story cultivates the grotesque through its use of narrative chance.

## Epistemology of the Accident

The narrative accident sparks a desire to determine cause, understand the sequence of events, and situate the accident in a broader framework. It also challenges this hermeneutic impulse through the sense that chance, and not only design, is at work. An often violent disruption, the accident is linked to the grotesque through the ways it deforms and challenges attempts at meaning-making. Like the accidental, the grotesque explores the contingency of meaning and the contingency of embodiment. To further explore how the grotesque formalizes contingency by constraining point of view, I turn to disability studies, which has much to say about the relationship between bodily contingency and the contingency of meaning. As Ato Quayson has pointed out, "corporeal difference is part of a structure of power," taking on cultural meaning and situating bodies within hierarchies of race, gender, size, ability, and other differences.[74] The impulse to hierarchize emerges from an impulse to categorize and impose order on the world, and disability can provoke the desire to contain difference by categorizing and imposing meaning, a reaction to an encounter with the question "of what it means to be human in a world governed by a radical contingency." The radical contingency that can produce the disabled body echoes the radical contingency of the accident. But all too often, "the recognition of this radical contingency produces features of a primal scene of extreme anxiety" in nondisabled people, rather than any sense of solidarity, shared humanity, or attention to the social construction of disability. Because this dynamic is "primarily emotional and affective,"[75] aesthetic experience offers generative grounds for encountering radical contingency and, perhaps, reconstructing this structure of feeling.

In Quayson's theory of "aesthetic nervousness," representations of disability short-circuit readers' typical aesthetic responses because disability is both overdetermined in literary representations and indexical of real disabled people out in the world. When disability appears in fiction, according to Quayson, it frequently short-circuits readers' typical interpretive approaches. Just as nondisabled people often falter when interacting with disabled people, becoming embarrassed or awkwardly trying to assist someone who has not asked for help, for example, so do nondisabled readers falter when confronted by disability in literature. Overdetermined and contrasted with the "normate," disability is rarely just an unremarkable trait of characters in literature. Rather, a character's disability often stands in for racial or social otherness, signifies extraordinary spiritual insight or incomprehensible tragedy, or acts as a metaphor for moral failing or evil.[76] In other words, disabled characters are overdetermined with meaning. For readers to work through their initial faltering in the face of a disability representation, they often rely on these overdetermined images to make sense of a text. As Quayson argues, disabled characters can also be repositories of "hermeneutical impasse," provoking a desire to understand the cause or nature of a disability without satisfying that desire.[77]

O'Connor's stories mobilize the ambiguities of grotesque form to interrogate aesthetic nervousness. Through her ironic portrayal of aesthetic nervousness and disability, the stories invite, yet ultimately foreclose attempts to make meaning of their central acts of violence. In a story less overtly focused on Jim Crow, but still quite interested in bodily contingency and the epistemic problem of the accident, readers follow a series of chance encounters to find themselves trapped with its protagonist in a hayloft, unsure about the nature of a violation that has just taken place. In this story, "Good Country People," readers follow Hulga Hopewell, who, like O'Connor herself, lives with her mother in Georgia, stuck there because she has a "weak heart."[78] Highly educated and resistant to the norms of femininity, Hulga is also, like O'Connor, physically disabled. Her leg was shot off in a hunting accident long before the story begins, and her prosthetic leg plays a central role in the story's plot. O'Connor herself used crutches, and as Jess Libow has argued, her use of assistive devices is an overlooked, but crucial, influence on her work. Nearly all of her stories feature an assistive or prosthetic device, and her letters evidence resistance to both the normalizing imperative of prosthesis use and stereotypes about disabled people.[79] Long approached as repositories of symbolic meaning, disabled characters are frequently overdetermined by stereotypes about disability readers bring to the work. By undermining such readings, O'Connor drew attention to bodily difference as a familiar part of a contingent world.

Foregrounding the contingent nature of the body, "Good Country People" also undercuts midcentury values that sought to erase bodily difference in the service of gender hierarchy and capitalist productivity. The postwar interest in rehabilitating disabled veterans became part of a broader approach to physical disability in which prostheses not only erased visible signs of bodily difference but also encouraged disabled people to return to highly gendered modes of productive labor.[80] Postwar rehabilitation focused on the effective use of prosthesis to enable men to "return to the workplace" and women to "increase [their] productivity in the home." As Libow puts it, "the value of prostheses thus lay in their capacity to achieve fantasies of gender and productivity."[81] O'Connor actively resisted such imperatives, and her stories often reworked prostheses and other adaptive technologies to resist or refuse gendered norms of productivity.[82] O'Connor's portrayal of disability in "Good Country People" combines with her use of third-person limited narration to cultivate aesthetic violence. The story's formal grotesquerie of ironic reversals foregrounds bodily difference while undercutting overdetermined readings of the disabled body.

O'Connor wrote "Good Country People" around the time she had a brief romantic relationship with a Danish book salesman, and some critics have claimed that the story was written in response to the pain of Erik Langkjaer returning to Denmark where, about a year later, he would propose to another woman.[83] Like Langkjaer, the story's antagonist, Manley Pointer, is a traveling book salesman—though he sells Bibles rather than textbooks. He is unlike Langkjaer in that he is a cruel fetishist who ultimately tricks Hulga into giving him her wooden leg, which he steals, leaving her trapped in the hayloft of a barn.[84] While the story's climax can be interpreted through this autobiographical lens to be seen as a metaphor for the emotional pain of unrequited love, its plot, like many of O'Connor's, is driven by chance encounters. Manley Pointer happens upon the Hopewell home, weaseling his way into dinner with Hulga and her mother and only then learning that Hulga has a wooden leg. Though Hulga believes herself to be manipulating the guileless rube Manley, it turns out that he is manipulating her, leading her to the barn's hayloft, where he talks her into taking off her prosthesis and then steals it from her. By withholding much of Manley Pointer's motivation for stealing Hulga's leg (and other prostheses that he carries with him in his suitcase), O'Connor encourages a kind of bewildered disgust at his behavior. At the same time, this scene reverses assumptions about Manley, inviting a mixed response of humor and disgust.

After following along with Hulga as she imagines Manley to be a simple, innocent boy who adores and truly sees her, readers might well share Hulga's pained bewilderment when, after he has convinced the reluctant but intrigued Hulga to let him take off her wooden leg, he sets it "out of her reach" and forcefully kisses her, then presents her with condoms, whiskey, and obscene playing cards. In an "almost pleading sound," she asks "aren't you . . . aren't you just good country people?" Focalized through Hulga, readers have shared her impression that he is "entirely reverent" when looking at her prosthesis, acting like a "delighted child" when he learns how it works. He is a person of "real innocence" who could "touch the truth about her" "with an instinct beyond wisdom."[85] As Hulga receives her comeuppance for mistakenly believing Manley is an innocent boy she can manipulate, readers likewise realize their error. The story's third-person limited narration encourages a dual response that characterizes the grotesque's deforming nature. Readers, sharing Hulga's viewpoint, are also likely to be complicit in her assumptions about Manley and her contempt for him. Narrating the negotiated removal of Hulga's prosthesis as a seduction scene and using third-person limited point of view to reveal Manley's true intentions to Hulga and the reader simultaneously, the scene portrays this moment as one of violation, even as the extent and degree of that violation is not fully legible. The scene allegorizes sexual assault and, at the same time, invites anticipation of an assault that does not end up happening. A grotesque blend of absurdity and violence is activated by Manley's dehumanizing behavior as well as Hulga's unkind and naive assumptions about him.

The story ultimately leaves key questions unresolved: to what extent does Hulga offer her wooden leg as a way to connect with Manley, and to what extent does he violently keep it from her? This dynamic raises the question of consent without resolving it; it is unclear when, exactly, Manley's violation begins. Is it when he coaxes Hulga to take the leg off? To hand it to him? Or when he refuses to give it back? The ironic reversal of knowledge and power depicted in the hayloft troubles readers' sense of how power is distributed in the story, cultivating a grotesque aesthetic characterized by the refusal of straightforward readings rather than the abjection or spectacle of the disabled body. By rendering the attack on Hulga aesthetic, O'Connor punishes not only her character, but also her readers who would make an easy kind of meaning from Hulga's form of bodily difference. The grotesque scene cultivates aesthetic violence not because of what it depicts, but through the rules determining its narration. Cultivated during her graduate training, one of O'Connor's aesthetic projects is "disciplining the egoic authorial self with the whip of impersonal narrative form."[86] Sharing some features with Hulga, the author masochistically punishes her for her arrogance. The mechanism of third-person limited narration also draws readers into a masochistic relationship with the story, a self-punishing attempt to locate, name, and draw boundaries around the question of violence in the text.

The experience of ambiguous, absurd violence produced by the grotesque is further facilitated by O'Connor's complex portrayal and deployment of disability. Disability and interpretation have long been tied to one another, and disability in O'Connor's work is a useful lens for bringing together the grotesque, the radical contingency of the body, and the limitations of interpretation explored through aesthetic violence. As Rosemarie Garland-Thomson's groundbreaking work in disability studies has explored, physical disability is overdetermined in representations and calls forth a desire to interpret. She claims that "the human variations we think of as disabilities have always been an occasion for interpretation, signs of an unsettling contingency or affirmations of an inscrutable design."[87] Disability, though it is connected to the material realities of embodiment, is a socially constructed identity whose representation can contain anxieties about bodily vulnerability and contingency by assuring "normate" readers that they are safe from "the vagaries and vulnerabilities of embodiment."[88] Like racial and gender difference, physical disability manifests in a visual regime, and the "visual difference" of disability is presumed to "signal[] meanings."[89] Such dynamics of interpretation are hardly neutral, and they imagine the disabled person as a repository of symbolic meaning or as a problem to explain and make sense of.[90] Though literary representations often mobilize the symbolic overdetermination of disability as an "opportunistic metaphorical device,"[91] they also have the potential to undo such a reductive approach rooted in the visual.

Though Garland-Thomson groups Hulga Hopewell with those characters who are overdetermined by the symbolic meanings of disability rather than fully realized characters, Hulga's experience of her disability in relationship to other characters also ironizes the dynamic critiqued in *Extraordinary Bodies*.[92] O'Connor repeatedly ironizes normate responses to Hulga's disability, highlighting their saccharine sympathy, morbid fascination, and stigmatization: Manley Pointer performs a reverent fascination with Hulga's "brave[ry]" as part of his strategy for appearing as a simple rube.[93] By the story's end, this fascination has turned to fetishization, another, crueler form of objectification. Hulga's neighbor Mrs. Freeman likewise participates in the visual regime of interpreting disability, with her interest in the accident where Hulga lost her leg as part of her broader fascination with "the details of secret infections, hidden deformities, assaults upon children."[94] Hulga's contemptible mother also embodies a normate approach to disability, one rooted in the stigmatization of physical difference and skewered by O'Connor's narrator. Mrs. Hopewell parrots ableist assumptions that Hulga's disability is "calamitous," a form of physical difference that removes her from the possibility of love, romance, or any other opportunity for "normal good times."[95] To the extent that O'Connor identified with Hulga, she also appears to cast her withering glance at these normate responses, unsettling reductive views of the physically disabled person. By emphasizing these characters' reading of Hulga's disability, O'Connor highlights the desire to interpret the disabled body and then short-circuits the sentimental or disgusted feelings that ground such interpretations through the story's grotesque end. In *A Good Man Is Hard to Find*, violence appears as a way of encountering this question: how do we acknowledge the inevitability of suffering without accepting the social systems that make some groups more vulnerable than others to certain kinds of suffering?

One lesson revealed by O'Connor's epistemology of the accident is this: misrecognizing violence can have negative, even violent, consequences. Throughout O'Connor's fiction, grotesque forms limn the idea of misrecognizing violence. Grotesque aesthetics are often treated as images of violence, as their exaggerated features of embodiment—stretched mouths, wide eyes, and other features of excess—can look painful. That is, these figures can look like they are in pain, and they can provoke a mirrored sense of pain in a viewer. Along with O'Connor, the photographer Diane Arbus is often mentioned in discussions about grotesque aesthetics in post-1945 US culture. Arbus developed an involved procedure for working with her subjects and creating her photographs, many of which feature people with exaggerated physical characteristics or nonnormative embodiment. Yet seeing disabled people as only repositories of pain is a kind of dehumanizing approach itself, a product of misrecognizing violence that is capacitated by the limited view of the normate. Arbus's work is controversial among disability scholars; additionally, critical response to her work largely treats it as depicting forms of violence.[96] As Rachel Adams has claimed, however, many of the images challenge ableist beliefs rooted in assumptions that physical difference is only experienced as pain or tragedy. Her portrait of Lauro Morales, titled *Mexican Dwarf in Hotel Room in NYC, 1970*, for example, "emphatically denies that only more conventionally proportioned bodies can be comfortable or sexually appealing in a state of undress."[97] Similarly, Adams reads her photographs of mentally disabled people in the *Untitled* series as a rejection of the tragic view of people with Down syndrome; instead, they show their subjects "in a state of contentment with the body and its capacity for play."[98] Many of her images of disability do not actually depict acts of violation or people who are in active experiences of suffering.

This dynamic points to the limits of empathy as a value cultivated by representation. Aesthetics of the grotesque offer a complicating alternative to the empathetic gaze that nevertheless maintains a boundary between self and other. In other words, the formal techniques of exaggeration and contradiction that characterize the grotesque are a "rule that corrects the emotion," to recall O'Connor's beloved statement from Braque. As Deborah Nelson puts it in her discussion of Arbus's photography, "Empathy for her seems to be a way not to see the other—a form of good intentions that collaborates in making the other invisible."[99] Arbus's photos of mentally disabled people in the *Untitled* series, for example, have widely "been received as painful images and images of pain," despite the fact that many of her subjects "look remarkably happy, even joyful."[100] In Nelson's reading, critics misrecognize these images as depictions of pain not because of what their subjects display but from the audience's own discomfort with the images, which they do not have familiar protocols for reading.[101] Arbus's photographs meditate on "pain that has no agency and no meaning," evoking something like the parenthetical mention of Hulga's hunting accident. This was a traumatic experience, to be sure, but it is not a repository of meaning or feeling in the story, except insofar as other characters dehumanize Hulga through their reading of her disability. In the story, Hulga's disability is not a source of suffering compared to the emotional pain of her encounter with Manley Pointer. It is the love affair gone awry, not the memory of the accident, that causes suffering in the grotesque reversal of the story's climax. Hulga's wooden leg is the product of an accident, but it takes on a different meaning in the story—it is a part of her, and not just a sign of trauma. Similarly, Arbus's aesthetic of pain attempts to "demystify or desacralize it."[102] For Nelson, it is important to desacralize the ordinary constraints on human agency that produce pain, not least because pain is an unavoidable part of life. Just as "the grotesque presents opposites without trying to reconcile them,"[103] the self-imposed constraints that shaped Arbus's, Lee's, and O'Connor's composing processes also produce ambiguous depictions of suffering, ones that maintain mutually contradictory interpretations without reconciling them.

At the risk of eliding social differences that circulate suffering and pain differently, this aesthetic violence also posits some aspects of suffering as meaningless because they are accidental or endemic to being alive. As Susannah Mintz has argued in a monograph on literature and pain, "pain is not only an inevitable component of human existence but also thoroughly entangled with our experiences of love, joy, humor, and intimacy."[104] This claim might sound like cliché. Worse, it recalls justifications of all kinds of suffering for a greater good or payoff—to suggest that love can hurt, for example, can excuse abuse. But in the context of represented suffering, Mintz's point is important. To take up the cultural study of structural violence is to identify many forms of suffering that could have been prevented, to highlight how unevenly pain is distributed across a culture. It is also to risk treating all suffering as preventable, in ways that can flatten approaches to both representations and lived experience.

The interpretive challenges posed by the modernist grotesque invite new ways of seeing that better accommodate the variability of human life. The modernist grotesque can thus be understood as a form of disability aesthetics, which rework conceptions of the beautiful. Attuning our sense of beauty to more kinds of embodiment, disability aesthetics undermine associations between "the healthy body" and concepts of beauty that are harmonious and whole.[105] The line between modernist aesthetic innovation and fascist kitsch, as Tobin Siebers shows, is a disability line: the efflorescence of modernist art that takes up the nonnormative body is precisely what the Nazis rejected and criminalized as degenerate.[106] These disability aesthetics challenge audiences who typically live within the normate to confront the insistent possibility of accident and contingency that can pull one out of the normate. Art that questions the status of pain through forms of contingency short-circuits dynamics of empathy that rest on a stable sense of the body. Indeed, grotesque aesthetics unsettle broader notions of bodily wholeness through their forming and deforming aesthetic techniques. Contra critical consensus that "takes empathy to be *the* ethical mode,"[107] the constraints that ground the aesthetic violence of the grotesque correct emotional responses of empathy to maintain the disorienting, internally contradictory sensation of contingency.

## CHAPTER FOUR

# Silhouette

## *The Art of Looking*

When news broke of Toni Morrison's death in August 2019, *The New Yorker's* art editor, Françoise Mouly, contacted contemporary artist Kara Walker to commission a cover paying tribute to the author. Conceptualizing and creating a memorial portrait in only a day, Walker experimented with a number of media before landing on her signature cut-paper silhouette. In an interview discussing the project, Walker notes: "I'm no portraitist, but I am a shadow maker."[1] Although Walker met Morrison only once,[2] she has long been inspired by Morrison, and the two figures share an aesthetic commitment to rendering anti-Black violence from across US history in forms that echo shadows and silences. These forms outline in order to make some elements of suffering ambiguous and challenge quotidian dynamics of looking at spectacular violence. Rendered as a silhouette, the shadow aesthetics of Walker and Morrison use its formal ambiguity to unsettle visual dynamics that underwrite discourses of race, gender, and violence in postwar America. Silhouettes can produce ambiguity by erasing facial expressions and relationships between actors, offering viewers a limited perspective on a violent encounter. Silhouettes thus provoke audiences' aesthetic interest in scenes of violence that remain fundamentally uncertain, inviting attention to what the silhouette reveals and what it hides. In provoking aesthetic interest, the silhouette also staves off the affect that breaks an aesthetic experience—disgust. With their ability to modulate disgust by leaving the "worse than the worst"[3] hidden, silhouettes are a particularly powerful form of portraying the suffering of Black people. Whether animating racist violence or antiracist social critique, representations of the suffering Black body have historically been expected to mobilize disgust for particular political ends. However, by erasing reliable signs of victims and perpetrators as well as the affective and visceral signs of bodies in pain, the silhouette both highlights and thwarts audiences' desire for spectacles of Black suffering. This aesthetic violence stages an ethical dilemma around familiar dynamics of looking at violence. The silhouette thus also aggresses against its audiences by pulling them toward a scene and ultimately pushing them away from it. Such an aesthetic experience—drawn toward; pushed back—engages senses of sight and spatial orientation. By moving audiences in this way, the silhouette's aesthetic violence interrogates naturalized dynamics of looking at suffering.

Emerging in the same Enlightenment moment when philosophers were both debating the role of disgust in aesthetic theory[4] and developing systems of taxonomy and morphology that reified racial hierarchy,[5] the silhouette "revealed a precise moment in western culture, when the highly individual nature of appearance was the subject of investigation, the body itself providing a focus for unprecedented study."[6] Understood as a quasi-scientific mode of portraying the "true" physiognomy of an individual without extraneous trappings,[7] the early silhouette aesthetic was aligned with broader ideological interest in categorizing individuals as types.[8] As the silhouette became more widespread in the nineteenth century, artists would often create tableaux, or scenes with a number of silhouetted figures interacting. Kara Walker's contemporary silhouette installations echo these tableaux, with scenes composed of antebellum-era iconography stretching across gallery walls without a clear beginning or end, like a cyclorama.[9] As a middle-class form of portraiture that was imagined to accurately and mechanically reproduce a true outline of the self, the silhouette reflected an emerging ideology of the individual as fully knowable and categorizable through careful examination of the body. The logic of racial difference reflected in silhouette aesthetics also helped naturalize racial hierarchy.

By contrast, Walker and Morrison use the silhouette to portray violent scenes, emphasizing what it cannot represent, rendering acts of violence ultimately ambiguous, and prompting a wide array of affective responses. Walker's visual silhouettes use color and shadow to outline a profile in precise detail while hiding what the profile contains, eliciting simultaneous experiences of seeing and not seeing. Similarly, Morrison's literary silhouettes use forms of erasure to cut away some aspects of representation that readers might use to interpret a scene of violence, such as refusing to provide key information about story events and characters' affective responses. By cutting away, erasing, covering, and outlining scenes of violence, Morrison's *Sula* proliferates possible meanings and affective responses that cannot be resolved. This postmodern exploration in perspective has little interest in addressing a white gaze, but it does invite reflection on how the gaze shapes concepts like disgust and empathy. In redefining the silhouette as a literary form—one central to Morrison's work—I want to frame embodiment in literature as a practiced, performative engagement between text and reader, whose embodied nature takes shape in the sensations of disgust, recognition, or anxiety that can be triggered by portrayals of violence. As a mode of simultaneously obscuring and emphasizing representations of suffering, the silhouette is deeply concerned with the circulation of affect that surrounds scenes of violence.

Whether animating racist violence or antiracist social critique, Black embodiment and anti-Black violence have been at the center of both post-Enlightenment aesthetic values and American social and political formations. From the spectacle of Sarah Baartman, whose body was studied as an object of sexual and scientific fascination on carnival stages and in scientific laboratories, to the circulation of lynching postcards displaying mutilated bodies, Black embodiment has been a site where fantasies of sexual and bodily excess, abjection, and extreme violence have played out since the nation's founding.[10] As scholars such as Robyn Wiegman, Ashraf Rushdy, Russ Castronovo, and Hazel Carby, among others, have shown, the lynched bodies of Black people held a peculiar fascination for white supremacist America at large: the lynch mob dehumanized, maimed, and tortured its victims, but it also consumed them as perversely aestheticized objects that reinforced "racial, sexual, national, psychological, biological, as well as gendered" borders.[11] The extralegal violence of lynching nevertheless drew on "rituals of public execution" and largely took place "with tacit or explicit state approval."[12] Like legal capital punishment, lynching is "part of the rhetorical ecology of 'punishment,'"[13] a state-sanctioned administration of violence designed to maintain social systems and communicate the message that white people can "kill with impunity" and Black people face "an irresolvable vulnerability to violence."[14]

While representations of "black bodies in pain"[15] have normalized and justified violence directed toward African Americans, they have also been mobilized to make antiracist appeals, and the history of lynching is accompanied by a robust counter-discourse. One such representation has been credited with igniting some of the action of the civil rights movement: the 1955 murder of Emmett Till, whose funeral was a major media event.[16] Till's murder coincided with a number of innovations in television and photojournalism to make the case "photogenic," that is, uniquely "pliable to visual mediation."[17] At the request of his mother, Mamie Till Mobley, Till's badly mutilated face and body were displayed in an open-casket funeral and in publications like *Jet* magazine.[18] By emphasizing the mutilation and decay of Till's body, the images draw on audiences' anxieties about death, the boundaries of the body, and "matter out of place."[19] Claudia Rankine suggests that in her "refusal to keep private grief private," Mamie Till Mobley "us[ed] the lynching tradition against itself."[20] "In her hands," Rankine continues, "the spectacle of the black body . . . publicized the injustice mapped onto her son's corpse."[21] Even when images of Emmett Till use the spectacular violence of lynching iconography against the lynching tradition, they draw on a nexus of embodiment, affect, and meaning that is presumed to be visible on the Black body in pain. Whether igniting or refuting racist beliefs, the violated African American body has been symbolically overdetermined, relentlessly put in the service of varying forms of social commentary.

This burden extends to ideas about what Black art should do and the politics of Black aesthetics. Nicole Fleetwood, along with other scholars of visual culture and race,[22] connects the question of Black suffering to the visual field as such, describing "weight placed on black cultural production to produce results, to do something to alter a history and system of racial inequality that is in part constituted through visual discourse. That something," Fleetwood continues, "is the desire to have the cultural product solve the very problem that it represents."[23] Though the affective formations that circulate around scenes of anti-Black violence are wide and varied, two key modes emerge: abjection, in which forms of embodiment are threatening to the point of becoming intolerable and thus expelled,[24] and sentimentality, in which the body in pain is understood to communicate profound meaning that will move observers into a proper feeling.[25] Framed through modes of abjection and sentimentality, the Black body in pain has historically been tied to excesses of affect and embodiment that needed to be either violently contained or properly performed. Whether abject or sentimental, anti-Black violence is, as Fleetwood, Hartman, Alexander, and others argue, spectacularly visual. The silhouette offers one way to negotiate the problem of the visual by reappropriating a form that shaped the common sense of white supremacist violence. Its aesthetic violence engages the bodies of looking audiences to refuse dynamics of spectacle and sentimentality.


## Kara Walker's Shadows

Kara Walker rose to prominence soon after graduating from the Rhode Island School of Design with her cut-paper silhouette installations, which populate large expanses of gallery space with antebellum-era characters in bizarre, fantastical, and violent scenes. Rabbits shoot guns, bodies seem to merge with boats, engorged genitalia seem to lift figures from the ground. Dense with iconography of antebellum culture, the silhouettes incorporate absurd juxtapositions to unsettle realist readings. Working from sketches in a notebook, Walker draws her figures on a black photographer's backdrop, hand cuts them, and adheres them to the gallery wall, creating tableaux some fifty feet long and thirteen feet high. Walker developed her signature silhouettes while in graduate school, drawing inspiration not only from Toni Morrison, but also bell hooks, Octavia Butler, and reference books on early American art. In an interview with Hilton Als, Walker recalls, "I had a catharsis looking at early American varieties of silhouette cuttings. . . . What I recognized, besides narrative and historicity and racism, was this very physical displacement: the paradox of removing a form from a blank surface that in turn creates a black hole. I was struck by the irony of so many of my concerns being addressed: blank/black, hole/whole, shadow/substance, etc."[26] At the time of its invention, a silhouette was imagined to produce a complete, precise portrait of an individual, where the outline conveyed the truth of the body. But Walker's interest in the silhouette arises from what it cannot convey, from the vast blankness within the outline. For the eighteenth-century "physiognomist" Johann Caspar Lavater, the silhouette "contained the key to a subject's character, one that might be gleaned more accurately from its essentially reportorial form than from the potentially obfuscating subjectivity of a painting."[27] In turn, the work of nineteenth-century mixed-race artist Moses Williams "provides another window onto the raced antebellum prehistory of Walker's silhouettes."[28] By making minor adjustments to his own profile in his silhouette art, Williams created a portrait of a non-white man that portrayed stereotypically white features, "signifying on a white method of image making" and "demonstrating his own agency in the visualization of his selfhood."[29] Similarly, the outline of Walker's silhouettes invites viewers to code each figure as Black or white, while their literally black interior unsettles fixed racial categories.[30]

The "blank" nature of the silhouette restricts Walker from depicting a number of features that would enable her images to tell coherent narratives: nuanced facial expression; the dynamics of encounter between figures, foreground, and background; and many aspects of visual perspective. Her silhouettes produce a powerful sense of being pulled or strung along through the gallery space, yet at the same time the tableaux use fantastical imagery and surprising juxtapositions to disrupt the familiar narratives audiences might project onto the gallery walls. Reworking imagery from popular culture including *Uncle Tom's Cabin*, *Gone with the Wind*, and other representations of the antebellum South, Walker uses the silhouette form to outline aspects of the body that identify her characters as raced, classed, and gendered types while erasing skin color and most aspects of facial expression.

The formal character of the silhouettes works against viewers' sense that they know what is happening in the tableaux: "Aside from the word or two we can put to the race, sex, age, prototype, social function, or symbology of any given element," claims Darby English, "everything that falls within the borders of this confabulation of silhouetted people, places, and things remains suspended somewhere between generated and projected meanings."[31] I take his argument further and suggest that even those minimal markers of racial, sexual, and temporal identification are in flux, ultimately inaccessible to audiences.

A detail from Walker's 1995 installation, *The End of Uncle Tom and the Grand Allegorical Tableau of Eva in Heaven*, demonstrates how the silhouette forecloses the very interpretive impulses it invites. The image appears to show a white man raping a young enslaved child while also impaling a baby with a spear. The viewer's first instinct is to read the image as a scene of brutality. Yet in this image, the silhouette obscures the boundaries of the body so that the narrative action is suggested, but actually indeterminate at the level of form. The silhouette prevents the viewer from determining foreground and background, undercutting audience assumptions about what is being portrayed. A viewer might at first assume they are witnessing sexual penetration and violent impalement, but the dynamic between the figures in the silhouette is rendered in shadow, erased by the black interior of the silhouette. Formally, the work is indeterminate, enacting aesthetic violence. As in Leo Bersani and Ulysse Dutoit's theory of aesthetic violence, developed from their reading of the Assyrian palace reliefs, "the force of this violent subject is, then, contravened by visual abstractions which disrupt the spectator's reading of the subject."[32] The extant cultural narratives surrounding the plantation, provoked by the iconography in this scene, compel viewers to make meaning from this silhouette, yet its form subverts this attempt as well. Disturbingly, the silhouette erases any sign of affect that might appear on the faces of these figures. The child, whose gender is ambiguous, looks back at the man's large gut, mouth open in an indeterminate expression—is it anguish? Shock? Surprise? Pleasure?

This image unsettles for a number of reasons. Chief among them is the ambiguity in the child's face, which suggests that the offensive transgression viewers witness may be bringing the child pleasure. The possibility of lighthearted surprise on the child's face recalls minstrel performance and suggests that the discomfiting nature of this image emerges from its reliance on older racist cultural production. In this scene, the silhouette's characteristic abstraction echoes the formal strategies of caricature that defined both the minstrel

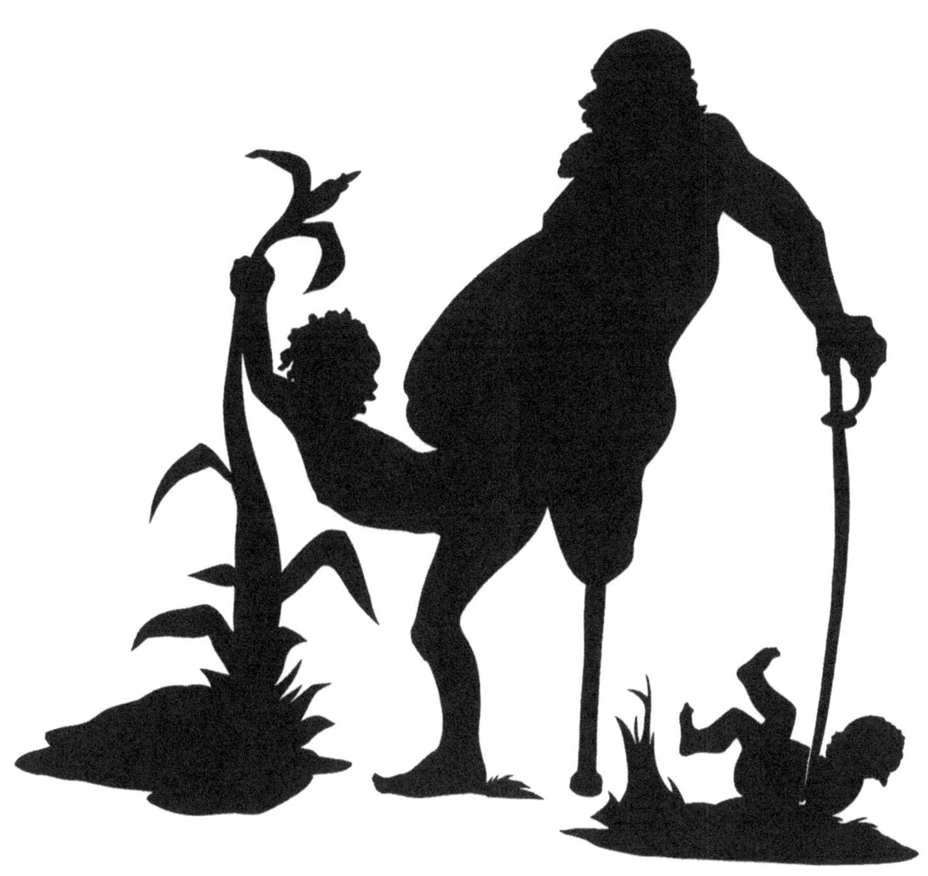

Kara Walker, detail of *The End of Uncle Tom and the Grand Allegorical Tableau of Eva in Heaven*, 1995. Wall installation, 156 × 420 inches (396.2 × 1066.8 cm). Artwork © Kara Walker, courtesy of Sikkema Malloy Jenkins and Sprüth Magers.

tradition and the cultural ephemera produced during the post-Reconstruction "nadir" of African American cultural history.[33] Simultaneously exaggerated and asserting the truth of its typology, the caricature paradoxically fixes the conventional "social significance" of anti-Black stereotypes.[34] In contrast, the silhouette invites viewers to draw on stereotypes and catches them in the act of doing so, denaturalizing those stereotypes and implicating viewers in their circulation.

Moreover, viewers cannot be sure they are actually witnessing a scene of violation at all. The ease with which viewers and critics identify and describe what is happening in the silhouettes — "a master is raping a slave girl" — is undermined by their very form. Even as it offers up what is, admittedly, most likely to be a disturbing scene of racial and sexual violence, the elision within the outline of the silhouette promotes the possibility that desire circulates in this scene. While it might be tempting to claim that this silhouette will horrify any viewer, the actions being depicted are too unstable to guarantee certain kinds of affective responses.[35] Within the black/blank space of the silhouettes, "the 'clearer picture' that might occupy this space has, in this instance, *failed to accomplish itself.*"[36] The formal properties of the silhouette invite the audience into a dynamic of determined looking, but they also explore that impulse—to look at and interpret violence—as a key theme. The failure English highlights as a formal property of the silhouette is also a refusal. In contrast to spectacular or sentimental "scenes" of subjection, which can just as easily "immure us to pain" as prompt "indignation,"[37] the silhouette refuses overdetermined readings of suffering Black bodies.[38]

Walker's highly aestheticized scenes of violence refuse dynamics of sentimentality while calling forth the aesthetic's "other," disgust. One among many affective responses a person might have to witnessing violence, disgust is closely tied to questions of the aesthetic as such.[39] To theorize the affective work of the silhouette, I adapt Eugenie Brinkema's formalist reading of disgust in film to show how the silhouette modulates a range of strong affective responses to violence, particularly disgust.[40] In her book on the "forms of the affects" in film, Brinkema claims that the close-up is a dominant strategy for portraying disgust because it allows filmmakers to manipulate the proximity to a disgusting object.[41] Instead of functioning "as a container for specific [disgusting] objects," the form of disgust is "a structure of the worse than the worst, an opening up through exclusion."[42] Like an inversion of the close-up, the silhouette both outlines and erases the scene of violence that could potentially disgust viewers. Erasing both the visceral details of the violence they depict and their characters' affective responses, Walker's silhouettes call to mind the "worse than the worst" while holding it in abeyance. As an act of erasure that modulates disgust, the silhouette not only critiques the emotional and political effects of staging scenes of anti-Black violence, it also explores the status of "reading" scenes of violence as an embodied, contingent practice.

In *Cut*, which has sometimes been understood as a self-portrait, a young woman in a full dress with two tight braids has slit her wrists with a large razor, which she still holds. Leaping in the air, perhaps clicking her heels together, she raises both arms above her head. Each wrist has split, emphasizing the fact that these wrists are not flesh but cut paper. Her wrists are opened up as if on hinges, and blood spurts from them in long, gently curling arcs reminiscent of paisleys. Below and to the left of the woman, the viewer sees two puddles that are probably blood, but, given their prevalence across Walker's oeuvre, could also be feces. *Cut* exemplifies the aesthetic violence that characterizes Walker's art. Her medium of cut-paper silhouettes prevents represented violence from mimetically reproducing real-world violence, highlighting the mediated distance between embodied violence and artistic representations. The piece reminds viewers that the woman they see before them has, in the work's narrative, slit her own wrists, while in fact it is the hand of the artist that has committed this violence. Indeed, the title, *Cut*, may describe the diegetic action of the piece, but it also describes the material process of its creation and characterizes Walker's method. *Cut's* playful approach to representing violence refuses "the imperative to make certain kinds of meaning" that has "burdened" Black literature and art throughout American history.[43] By insisting on its own status as an aesthetic object, the silhouette also insists on the aesthetic nature of any representation of suffering, from the mimetic to the abstract.

The silhouette foregrounds the ways in which representations of violence are inevitably aesthetic, even when they attempt to mediate real-world violence directly and viscerally. In other words, the very act of representing violence necessarily entails artistic choices about form. In turn, to view represented violence is to engage at the level of form as well as feeling or meaning, whether or not we realize we are doing so. Even the most realistic, gruesome, and powerfully affective depictions of violence are aesthetic constructs.[44] With her stylized, silhouetted depictions of bodily violation, Walker draws the eye to the form of violence, rather than its various meanings. The silhouette affords these varied responses because, paradoxically, it refuses to portray facial expressions that might signal what Walker's characters feel. In contrast to the notion that silhouettes provide stable and complete knowledge about the individuals they portray, Walker uses the silhouette to highlight what is not known. As Walker put it in an interview reflecting on the silhouettes, "it's not enough for me to just sort of say, you know, minstrelsy: bad," instead, the approach is "minstrelsy: complicated." Describing "interesting" approaches to iconography of blackface and other forms of symbolic violence, Walker also rejects the idea that the work is primarily about saying "no" to the politics of those representations.[45] Rather, interested approaches are attuned to the aesthetic work of these images and the way they keep the complexity of historical violence in view. Writing about her response to Hurricane Katrina in the catalogue *After the Deluge,* she laments the way events like Katrina pass into memory and narrative, becoming simplified and

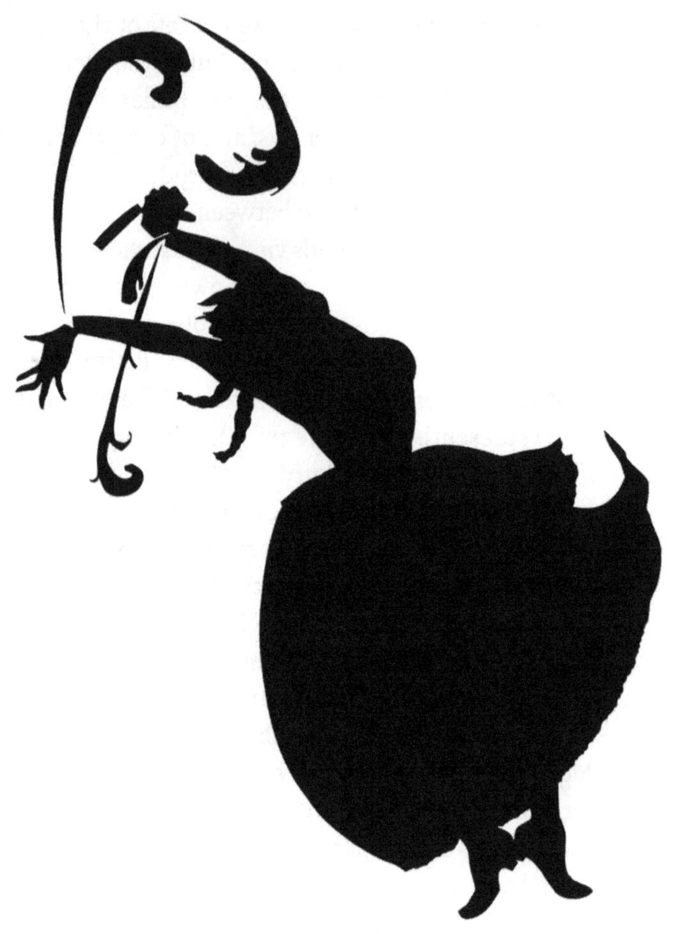
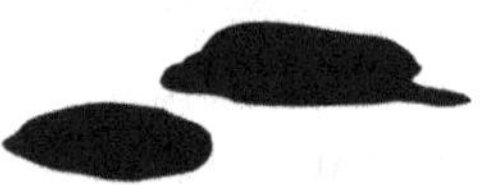

Kara Walker, *Cut,* 1998. Cut paper and adhesive on wall. 88 × 54 inches (223.5 × 137.2 cm). Artwork © Kara Walker, courtesy of Sikkema Malloy Jenkins and Sprüth Magers.

smoothed out into "a more assimilable legend." Even so, "always there is a puddle—a murky, unnavigable space that is overcrowded with intangibles: shame, remorse, vanity, morbidity, silence."[46] The silhouette contains this "puddle," drawing viewers toward a sustained engagement with the limits of their own ability to see what it might contain.

Walker's shadows contain and deflect dynamics of disgust that shape racialized perspectives on suffering. Many theorists of disgust agree that disgust plays a large role in attraction, aesthetic interest, and desire.[47] Walker's silhouettes suggest that the inverse is also true: desire and attraction may be present in the way audiences relate to the violence they witness in the gallery space. The silhouette, by outlining scenes of violence, eschews visceral or "core" disgust and simultaneously courts a form of moral disgust.[48] This dynamic makes Walker a politically troubling artist—she has been critiqued by prominent African American artists for "consciously or unconsciously . . . catering to the bestial fantasies about blacks created by white supremacy and racism."[49] Indeed, through an aesthetic of violence that encourages a wide range of emotional responses—disgust, sadness, or anger, certainly, but also laughter, delight, and pleasure in beauty—Walker courts the violent desire for Black suffering that runs through American history and culture.[50] Risking the possibility that her work will align with violent desires of the white gaze or self-destructive feelings of abjection in Black viewers, however, allows Walker to open up "shadowy" spaces for new and surprising emotional engagements with racial and sexual violence, ones that can imaginatively reconstruct the past and present of anti-Black violence in more complex ways.

Although the controversy surrounding Walker seems to have abated as she has gained further visibility and expanded her oeuvre beyond the silhouettes, it still illuminates the important role of disgust in debates about African American art and the politics of representation. Walker's often playful use of racist stereotypes and other vexed signifiers has made her work morally disgusting to her critics. I also want to make the case that the silhouettes have been controversial because they do not properly provoke core disgust. How can these violent scenes be so beautiful, so tidy, so stylized? Shouldn't they convey the horror of transatlantic slavery by forcing viewers to confront its violences in all their most repulsive details? These ambiguous images fly in the face of the assumption that ethical depictions of violence must convey stable messages. As Amy Tang has pointed out, critics who understand Walker's art as either rehearsing the trauma of chattel slavery and white supremacy or masterfully deconstructing racist ideology through parody can only make such claims by assuming that artistic agency "functions as a zero-sum game" in which Walker "either . . . defeats the forces of racism or . . . is defeated by them."[51] Instead of worrying over the seemingly irresolvable question of whether Walker's silhouettes are fundamentally racist or antiracist, critics might understand Walker's work as precisely *about* the impulse to read depictions of Blackness according to this binary. Arlene Keizer reminds us that Black viewers can have "multiple nontraumatic responses" to seeing Walker's work.[52] Her silhouettes can, for example, "dare to imagine that enslaved black women may have experienced sexual desire for the white men who dominated them."[53] Restaging scenes of violence in silhouette deflects some overdetermined readings to facilitate a wider array of affective responses to the work, refusing dynamics of "melancholy historicism"[54] in favor of expansive aesthetic and critical engagement with the as-yet-unknown and unpredictable affective dynamics of these images.

## Toni Morrison's Silhouette Aesthetic

*Sula* takes place in a small Black community in Ohio known as the Bottom between the years 1919 and 1965. Although Sula shares her name with the novel's title, she disappears for large stretches of the book, a phenomenon that Deborah McDowell has linked to the novel's radical decentering of its own formal conventions.[55] Examining those formal conventions alongside Kara Walker's visual aesthetics, however, reframes this decentering not merely as a disruption but as part of a broader pattern of silences and erasures Morrison deploys to create literary silhouettes. While the term "silhouette" is often used as a synonym for "character sketch" or "literary portrait," Morrison's silhouette aesthetic capitalizes on the fundamental gap between signifier and signified in language to provoke an irresolvable desire to affix meaning to events. Just as Walker uses the silhouette to hide many aspects of her characters and the violent interactions between them, Morrison uses strategic forms of erasure to portray violent action in silhouette, producing a form of uncertainty that prompts attention to the aesthetic shape, rather than the social meaning, of violence.[56] The uncertainty of the silhouette simultaneously invites and prevents the familiar dynamic of looking at "scenes of subjection"[57] as either abject or sentimental.

Although Morrison deploys forms of the silhouette across her oeuvre, her silhouette aesthetic is most explicitly rendered in her only published short story, "Recitatif," which she characterizes as "an experiment in the removal of all racial codes from a narrative about two characters of different races for whom racial identity is crucial."[58] The story follows two friends, Roberta and

Twyla, as they drift in and out of one another's lives from their childhood in the 1950s through the social changes of the civil rights era, the "Black is beautiful" movement, and the desegregation busing controversies of the 1970s. Mobilizing the fundamental representational gaps of language, Morrison portrays one character as white and one as Black, but she never reveals which is which. Narrated by Twyla, the story illustrates the postmodern notion that race manifests through linguistic categories of difference and calls forth audiences' own awareness of racist stereotypes by daring them to determine which character is white and which is Black. For Elizabeth Abel, the story activates her own awareness of her own "white critical fantasies" when reading "black women's texts" when she realizes how she has unintentionally relied on both racist stereotypes and interpretive methods that emphasize psychology over politics in her reading.[59] The characters have racial difference without race; racial identity motivates much of the story's characterization, but the characters, like Walker's, are silhouetted, forcing audiences to look for racial identity everywhere but on the body.

The language play of racial difference without racial identity is one form of silhouette in "Recitatif"; another is the unresolvable narrative gap at the heart of the story. The story's last line is spoken by Roberta, who asks Twyla: "what the hell happened to Maggie?"[60] Throughout the story, Roberta recalls fragmented memories of Maggie, a mute woman who worked at St. Bonaventure, the girls' home where Roberta and Twyla spent their childhood. Something violent befell Maggie: Twyla marks time by referring to "the day before Maggie fell down."[61] During one of their encounters, Roberta tries to convince Twyla that Maggie did not just fall; she was knocked down by some of the older girls in the home, who also "tore her clothes."[62] In a later encounter, while Roberta and Twyla argue about busing policies during a protest, Twyla insists that Roberta not only saw Maggie being pushed down, but that she also kicked Maggie herself. She also claims that Maggie was Black.[63] In contrast to Roberta and Twyla, who have racial identity only through difference from one another, Maggie's skin is described as "sandy-colored."[64] Maggie embodies a diegetic form of the racial ambiguity that structures the whole story. Indeed, Maggie, "the kitchen woman with legs like parentheses,"[65] carries forms of indeterminacy on her body, functioning as a corollary to the pair of Roberta and Twyla. The racial indeterminacy of Maggie's "sandy-colored" skin, I argue, is linked to the narrative indeterminacy in the "parentheses" of her body that outline and contain something unspoken. In "Recitatif," withheld information functions like a visual silhouette to make racial identity indeterminate through Roberta and Twyla and to outline an unknowable violence through Maggie. Although contested stories about what happened to Maggie build across each of Roberta and Twyla's encounters, the true story is never revealed. Echoing the outline of a visual silhouette, the "parentheses" used to describe Maggie's legs suggest an unknowable interior, an unspoken violence that can be read for, but never fully realized. What do these parentheses enclose, and what the hell happened to Maggie?

"Recitatif" incorporates two forms of silhouette: the language game of racial difference and the narrative erasure of the violence inflicted on Maggie. The story illustrates how a silhouetting function is embedded in language as such, but Morrison's silhouette aesthetic also extends to a stylistic and narrative strategy of removing information to produce uncertainty about why a violent act occurs and what it means. Sula's disappearance in the middle of the novel bearing her name echoes the disappearance of key narrative elements in the novel's scenes of violence, producing a narrative form of the visual silhouette that asks viewers to "fill in" the shadows Walker places on the wall. Morrison's elisions and erasures provoke forms of uncertainty about the social position of characters and the meaning of their violated embodiment.

The silhouetting in "Recitatif," which anticipates some elements of Walker's aesthetic of ambiguity by making race fundamentally unknowable, reappears in Morrison's approach to violence in *Sula*. Throughout the novel, readers are confronted with violence inflicted on numerous characters. Sula's grandmother Eva kills her son by setting him on fire, and she may have lost her own leg by allowing it to be run over by a train; Sula slices her fingertip off in the middle of the street; a large group of townspeople die in a march toward an unfinished tunnel. One could look to sociological reasons to explain much of this violence: Eva needs insurance money, so she injures herself. Her son is suffering from drug addiction resulting in part from the trauma he experienced in World War I, so she puts him out of his misery. Sula cuts her own fingertip to show local white boys they cannot intimidate her. The townspeople die in an impromptu protest of the racist hiring practices for building the tunnel. Clearly, the suffering of the Black characters is soaked through and through with social meanings.

Yet much of the novel's violence cannot be assimilated into a commentary on injustice. When Chicken Little drowns, for instance, the novel renders his death as accidental, unnecessary, bizarre, and disorienting through narrative gaps and an image of aporia—a "closed place"[66] that echoes Walker's use of the silhouette. While young Sula and Nel are playing by the river, Chicken Little approaches them and Sula begins to swing him around playfully. She loses her grip and sends the boy sailing into the water, which "darkened and closed quickly over the place where Chicken Little sank."[67] Echoes of Emmett Till emerge in the novel's explanation that Chicken was missing for three days before his body went to the embalmer. Like Till, "he was unrecognizable to almost everybody who once knew him."[68] Unlike Till, Chicken would not have an open casket at his funeral. This information is conveyed in its own, abrupt paragraph: "So the coffin was closed."[69] Instead of accruing moral weight, Chicken Little's death is senselessly tragic, and the framing Morrison uses to signal Chicken's aporetic, senseless death—a single sentence bracketed by the white space of paragraph breaks—highlights the limitations she places on readers' access to a visceral, emotional experience of represented violence. Chuck Jackson notes that *Sula* "borrows from and rearranges objects and actions typically found in lynching narratives" and is set during a period of rampant lynchings.[70] By creating a silhouetted version of the lynching of Emmett Till, the novel short-circuits readers' attempt to find a social payoff for this fictional death. Instead, readers are encouraged to apprehend Chicken's death as *aesthetic*, with attention to form and sensation.

In Chicken Little's fictional death, the echo of Emmett Till is also an echo of the spectacle of Black suffering and the complex nexus of grief, disgust, fascination, and horror that attached to images of Till. The aftermath of this scene highlights the reflexive disgust that underwrites white supremacy through the figure of a white bargeman who finds Chicken Little's body, who "[shakes] his head in disgust at the kind of parents who would drown their own children."[71] He also anticipates a visceral disgust response at Chicken's body: "Later, sitting down to smoke on an empty lard tin, still bemused by God's curse and the terrible burden his own kind had of elevating Ham's sons, he suddenly became alarmed by the thought that the corpse in this heat would have a terrible odor, which might get into the fabric of his woolen cloth."[72] Aligning with Carolyn Korsmeyer's definitions of "core" or visceral disgust and "moral" disgust, the bargeman's two disgust reactions also illustrate the ways in which affect attaches unevenly to raced and gendered bodies.[73] The novel highlights racist assumptions rooted in and routed through feelings of disgust, assumptions tinged with abjection and sentimentality.

While Chicken's body might elicit disgust in other characters, Morrison suggests these affects only through elision, closing the coffin that Mamie Till Mobley left open. Chicken's death reminds readers of the antiracist work disgust can perform, and, indeed, of the way grief and mourning can insist upon Black humanity. At the same time, however, the scene emphasizes a remainder that accompanies spectacular Black suffering: absurdity, senselessness, tragedy, and numbing shock. As Fred Moten explains, the photographs of Till's mutilated body do more than stand as evidence of the horror of Jim Crow violence. They also challenge broader assumptions about the ontological status of visual experience. For Moten, images of Till encourage viewers to engage Black suffering "in terms of a kind of beauty, a kind of detachment, independence, autonomy, that holds open the question of what looking might mean in general."[74] In this encounter with a photograph that portrays suffering to make moral and political claims, "the looker is in danger of slipping, not away, but into something less comfortable than horror—aesthetic judgment, denial, laughter, some out and unprecedented reflection, movement murder, song."[75] Looking at Chicken Little, readers slip comfortably into the kaleidoscope of responses Moten identifies. This violent scene reorients dynamics of looking at Black suffering to proliferate possible meanings and emphasize the tenuousness and danger of expecting scenes of violence to do predictable political work. In simultaneously suggesting and preventing strong affective responses, particularly disgust, the silhouette brings together visceral and aesthetic responses to represented violence.[76]

Like Walker's silhouettes, Morrison's second novel has prompted debates about whether it "defeats the forces of racism or is defeated by them."[77] Sula herself is a confounding character—admired by many readers for her independence and reviled by others for her selfishness. Namwali Serpell includes Morrison's *Beloved* in her discussion of novels that afford productive ethical challenges through "uncertainty,"[78] and Yung-Hsing Wu cites *Beloved* and *Sula* as texts that "compel reading upon reading of ethics."[79] What kinds of ethical judgments are afforded by *Sula,* and how do ethical questions meet up with the forms of represented violence and the feelings that imbue the reading experience? Wu faults critics for assuming that the ethics of Morrison's novels must lie in readers' judgments of characters' behavior. Instead, the act of reading itself prompts ethical questions that can never be resolved, but instead must be asked again and again.[80] Morrison's novels refuse to allow readers to reach either "a definitive and comfortable ethical stand" about the transgressions of her characters, or "a resolution to the problems posed by the novels' ethical dilemmas."[81] The difficult reading experience staged by the silhouette not only gives shape to a structure of feeling in the aftermath of Jim Crow but also invites reflection on the role of aesthetic experience in making ethical judgments. Manipulating dynamics of disgust and desire, the novel explores how those affects function as a kind of common sense, naturalized because they are strongly felt. Ultimately, the novel also defamiliarizes this common sense through its silhouette aesthetic.

Morrison draws on "modernist convention[s]" like the fragmented narrative of World War I veterans including Shadrack and Plum.[82] Along with formal innovations like fragmented narrative or thematic boundary-pushing that seeks to shock audiences, modernist writers provoke disgust to transgress social boundaries and articulate truths about the human experience.[83] Indeed, disgust has enjoyed a kind of vogue in artistic and critical circles.[84] Narrative silhouettes allow Morrison to register disgust without necessarily provoking it. Although disgust is often thought to demarcate the limit of aesthetic experience and shut down any experience of desire, in fact, disgust and desire are deeply enmeshed. Abjection pushes repellent objects outside the boundaries of the self, but it is prompted by the canny fear that what is abject inhabits the self. The disgusting object is repellent in part because, at the same time, it "seems to say, 'you want me,' imposing itself on the subject as something to be mingled with and perhaps even enjoyed."[85] Disgust, in other words, does not merely repel; it also draws us in. Disgust and desire are imbricated; what disgusts us does so precisely because of the possibility that it may infect us, and because we may want it to.

Disgust is also shaped by—and used to reinforce—social hierarchies, a phenomenon the novel thematizes even as it formally manipulates audience disgust responses. Throughout *Sula*, townspeople in the Bottom are collectively repulsed by behavior that falls outside social mores. After Sula sleeps with her best friend's husband and institutionalizes her grandmother, the townspeople speak of her as "a roach" and "a bitch." Moreover, the men in the town "gave her the final label, [and] fingerprinted her for all time. They were the ones who said she was guilty of the unforgivable thing . . . the dirt that could not ever be washed away. They said Sula slept with white men."[86] Disgust is prompted by Sula's promiscuity and cruel behavior, but what truly taints her is the claim (unfounded, Morrison goes on to note) that Sula has betrayed her racial identification and slept with white men. These men betray an ethics of disgust that is grounded in cruel, violent desire. Although Sula disgusts the men because her desires fall outside moral or political correctness, Morrison carefully describes their disgust in violent, misogynistic terms. The rumor about Sula makes "young men fantasize elaborate torture for her—just to get the saliva back in their mouths when they saw her."[87] Like other examples of disgust in the novel, this one draws violence and desire into the affective movement of disgust. The narrator reports that all the men in the town imagined Sula "underneath some white man," "each according to his own predilections." Although these imaginations "filled them with choking disgust," we also learn that they are specific to each man's "predilections." This description suggests that desire is sparked by Sula's transgression, even though there is "nothing lower she could do, nothing filthier."[88] By linking the men's metaphorical disgust to their ethical judgment of Sula, Morrison reveals the ways an ethics of disgust has been shaped by racist and sexist notions of Black female sexual excess and availability.

The visceral strength of affective responses imbues them with a sense of truth. And in theorizing affect, many scholars invoke its precognitive flow, framing affect as a force that exceeds language and culture, part of a "primary motivational system."[89] However, that force cannot be disentangled from the social.[90] Audre Lorde offers a vivid illustration of the social mechanisms of affect in "Eye to Eye: Black Women, Hatred, and Anger." As a small child on the subway, she sat down beside a white woman who immediately pulled her coat away from Lorde's "little snowsuited body." The woman's "mouth twitches as she stares and then her gaze drops down, taking mine with it." Lorde continues, "I do not see whatever terrible thing she is seeing on the seat between us—probably a roach. But she has communicated her horror to me. It must be something very bad from the way she is looking, so I pull my snowsuit closer to me away from it, too. When I look up the woman is still staring at me, her nose holes and eyes huge. And suddenly I realize there is nothing crawling up the seat between us; it is me she doesn't want her coat to touch."[91] Here, Lorde makes three points about disgust: it is expressed as a desire to distance the self from the disgusting object, it is partly an anxiety about proximity, and it plays a role in maintaining racial hierarchy by attaching, in the context of white supremacy, to Black embodiment. In the context of the essay, Lorde also links this phenomenon of racist disgust to Black women's politically directed rage, drawing out the complex circuits of affective exchange that are constantly playing out in the terrain of social and political life. Clare Hemmings points to this example to remind us that "only for certain subjects can affect be thought of as attaching in an open way."[92] Morrison echoes this argument in her treatment of disgust as a theme and a feeling expressed by characters. *Sula* explores how disgust can help to police racial and gender hierarchies and to naturalize forms of community common sense through shared affective experience.


## Disgust in Silhouette

Although disgust is typically linked to a transgressive, modernist aesthetic, *Sula* routes disgust through the form of the silhouette, a form that also invites aesthetic absorption and can render even the most violent scenes beautiful. If "the boundary of the self is manned at its most crucial and vulnerable points by disgust,"[93] then aesthetic violence troubles the naturalized, felt experience of disgust through formal foreclosures. As a form of portraying violence that indexes bodily violation while withholding disgusting details, the silhouette draws readers into a key tension in the novel between *aesthetic* and *rapport*. Barbara Johnson uses these terms to distinguish the solitary, removed experience of an aesthetic observer from the visceral, embodied experience of the world that brings individuals into the Bottom's community. Johnson adapts these terms from Nel, who thinks of them when she catches Sula sleeping with her husband.[94] Johnson characterizes "aesthetic" as "the domain of the contemplation of forms, implying detachment and distance," and "rapport" as "the dynamics of connectedness."[95] Arguing that the novel is about the tension between these two modes, Johnson frames *Sula*'s ethical questions not in terms of "who was good," but in terms of the problems that arise when depictions of suffering fail to provoke rapport, and instead function mainly as aesthetic phenomena.

The tension between aesthetic and rapport is best demonstrated in a scene that marks Sula as the Bottom's pariah. The third-person narrator is following Eva, Sula's grandmother and Hannah's mother, as she searches for a comb in her bedroom. Eva glances out the window to see Hannah trying to light a fire in the yard, then continues to search for her comb. When she finds it, she looks out the window again and sees Hannah on fire, the flames "making her dance."[96] Eva's first impulse is to "cover her daughter's body with her own," and she attempts this by jumping out the window. Eva cannot save Hannah, and a neighboring couple pours a bucket of water on her in an effort to stop the flames, "sear[ing] to sealing all that was left of the beautiful Hannah Peace."[97] Although she is taken to the hospital, "she had already begun to bubble and blister so badly that the coffin had to be kept closed at the funeral"[98]—another hidden, mutilated body. The chapter ends with Eva's thoughts about Sula, who watched the burning from the porch:

> Try as [Eva] might to deny it, she knew that as she lay on the ground
> trying to drag herself through the sweet peas and clover to get to
> Hannah, she had seen Sula standing on the back porch *just looking*.
> When Eva, who was never one to hide the faults of her children,
> mentioned what she thought she'd seen to a few friends, they said it
> was natural. Sula was probably struck *dumb*, as anybody would be who
> saw her own mamma burn up. Eva said yes, but inside she disagreed

and remained convinced that Sula had watched Hannah burn not because she was *paralyzed*, but because she was *interested*.[99]

Sula's response contrasts importantly with that of another young girl on the scene, whose vomiting "finally broke the profound silence and caused the women to talk to each other and to God."[100] The young girl's reaction of extreme disgust provides a counterpoint to Sula's aesthetic response to violence.

Rendering Hannah's death in silhouette erases aspects of embodiment that are hinted at through the reactions of other characters, and diegetic responses of disgust, somewhat paradoxically, point our attention to what the silhouette eliminates in its shadows. The girl's vomiting highlights the distance between a visceral, embodied engagement with violence and Sula's aesthetic engagement with silhouetted violence. To vomit is to exclude, and just as the young girl vomits in response to the gruesome scene, the silhouette excludes aspects of the violent scene that could trigger disgust. According to Brinkema, "the form of [disgust] is . . . a structure organized around a process of exclusion and not a content that fills it in or gives it definition, shape, coherence, substance."[101] Precisely by foreclosing a disgusted response, the silhouette is thus a *form* of disgust. This formal disgust aligns reader with Sula, inflicting aesthetic violence by making readers interested, too.

If disgust, for the vomiting girl, binds her to the Bottom's community, then Sula's aesthetic response excludes her from it. Instead of pushing away the violent image of Hannah's burning body, Sula draws closer in a position of interest. And in watching Sula watch, readers are forced into a phenomenological position vis-à-vis Hannah's gruesomely burnt body that echoes Sula's own. It is certainly possible that readers might vomit when they read about a woman being burned alive. It is more likely, however, that readers' reactions to Hannah's immolation will be more like Sula's than the little girl's. Like Walker's silhouettes, which erase aspects of the self to proliferate narrative possibilities, Sula becomes a focalizing structure through which multiple social and emotional meanings of violence proliferate but cannot be resolved. The silhouette aesthetic shared by Walker and Morrison enacts a push–pull of absorption and repulsion, and the silhouette expels—we might even say that it vomits—the anti-Black violence that is intimately tied up in the history of American visual culture.

Although Houston Baker compellingly argues that *Sula* paints a clear and cohesive picture of Black community,[102] its protagonist is excluded from that community because of her aesthetic disposition and concomitant failure of rapport. In distinguishing between Sula and the young girl, disgust also distinguishes between diegetic and non-diegetic responses to scenes of violence, as if the characters in *Sula* can see the full picture of what Morrison outlines for the reader in silhouette. Readers experience the violence inflicted on Hannah, focalized through Eva, primarily as a scene of Sula looking. Morrison uses perspective to render Hannah's death in silhouette. Its cause is never explained in the novel, but moreover, her death is experienced as aesthetic by Sula. Although the reading experience, with its repeated description of Hannah's "hot, bubbling flesh," might provoke disgust and engage rapport, it is also inevitably aesthetic. Like Sula, then, readers look on this scene of violence because they are interested. The tension between aesthetic and rapport thus extends to the reader's experience of represented violence. In the face of "horrible images, painful truths, [and] excruciating losses," Johnson asks, "do we just sit back and watch? What is the nature of our pleasure in contemplating trauma? What would be a response that would embody rapport rather than aesthetics? Is this what Toni Morrison is challenging us to consider? Or is she merely trying to make us less innocent in our contemplation, our analysis, our 'interest'?"[103] Johnson's questions, I think, are central to understanding Morrison's silhouette aesthetic and, by extension, her practices for engaging readers bodily. While an aesthetic engagement with Black suffering forecloses a kind of community-building rapport, it also disturbs familiar dynamics of looking characterized by abjection and sentimentality. As Moten argues, scenes of subjection engage audiences in a multisensory way through form as well as content—they demand aesthetic engagement. *Sula* frames aesthetic and rapport as in tension with one another, with silhouetted scenes of violence acting as a kind of threshold between the two modes of engagement.

Like Walker's visual silhouettes, which erase signs of emotion from characters' faces and render what may be horrific acts of violation narratively ambiguous and aesthetically pleasurable, *Sula*'s narrative silhouettes highlight the constricted ability of scenes of subjection to produce moral or political knowledge. Depending on the observer, looking at Black suffering has provoked for some visceral disgust and moral outrage, but for others it has provoked callous delight, indifference, or aesthetic absorption. For white participants, for example, a lynching was a moment of affective connection and community-building: lynching postcards circulated affect to reinforce communal bonds.[104] The phenomenon of the lynching picnic exemplifies how the meaning of violence is profoundly shaped by racialized perception. Morrison has spoken about refusing to write for the white gaze.[105] This refusal extends beyond subject matter to a formal commitment manifested in the silhouette's erasures and refusals, and it is also a refusal of didacticism and protest. An aesthetic commitment that produces ambiguities, Morrison's silhouetted violence also risks facilitating ethically ambiguous representations, though these ambiguities also point back to the perspective of audiences and the limitations of their perspective. When readers pick up Morrison's novel, they risk, like the character Sula, the possibility of being absorbed in, rather than repulsed by, racialized and gendered suffering.

Yet the silhouette can also register the limits of rapport—a mode of community engagement that relies on specific, limited affective responses to violence. Invoking *Sula*, Sandy Alexandre suggests that aesthetic approaches to violence can query the assumed moral goodness of rapport, or common sense grounded in shared affective experience. In her writing about *Without Sanctuary: Lynching Photography in America*, an exhibit of lynching photographs displayed in galleries in New York and Atlanta in 2000, Alexandre advocates a focus on "the *form* of these politically charged images."[106] As she demonstrates, the formal structure of the images mirrors and gives shape to the placelessness of Black people in the Reconstruction and Jim Crow era United States. If lynching was motivated in large part by anxieties about Black property ownership, as Ida B. Wells contended, then the iconography of lynching displaces Black people from the land, making the land itself, once again, white property. Just as the novel's setting, "the Bottom," is high above the central, white-occupied town of Medallion, so is the lynched body over and above the white lynch mob.[107] The white lynch mob is "landed" while the Black victim is "suspended"—"its hanging . . . a posture affirming its homelessness, its being un-propertied and ungrounded—its being out of *site*."[108] Alexandre's attention to the form of lynching violence allows her to "look beyond the hanging black body as a spectacular sight"[109] that many scholars approach in psychosexual terms and to return to our sight the contestation over property that fueled lynching violence.

Implicitly taking up the tension between aesthetic and rapport, Alexandre explores critical responses to *Without Sanctuary*, further illustrating the potential value of formalist approaches to images of racial terror. She characterizes Hilton Als's response to *Without Sanctuary* as "aesthetic" rather than "historical."[110] While Als worries about his inability to look "past" the pictures to their historical context, Alexandre suggests that his aesthetic response of looking "at" the images themselves facilitates a disturbing impasse. The formal impasse invites an experience of the *punctum* and reveals other kinds of knowledge made visible through formal arrangement. Similarly, Walker's silhouettes use a symbolic vocabulary that at first encourages "looking past" to historical origins and yet also prevents "looking past" the indeterminate arrangements of the silhouettes. Like Als at *Without Sanctuary*, then, viewers of Walker's silhouettes are forced to look *at* the images on the wall. This aesthetic response, produced by looking "at" an image rather than "past" it, unsettles calcified narratives about violence that are felt as common sense. A silhouette aesthetic engages embodiment not by representing bodies in a way that draws viewers closer or elicits empathy. Instead, its erasures and foreclosures invite attention, an aesthetic engagement that is affective and sensory, but purposefully circumscribed. The form excludes mimetic representations of affect, but in doing so it highlights and defamiliarizes overdetermined modes of reading the body in pain. While the historical silhouette was presumed to stabilize knowledge about the body, Morrison and Walker reimagine the silhouette form to create uncertainty. This aesthetic violence shifts audience attention from the overdetermined embodiment conveyed in scenes of subjection to the embodied aspects of looking at violence.

A form that resonates with the epistemological violence of modern racialization, the silhouette gives shape to the senselessness of lynching in the Jim Crow era, a form of violence that could collapse distinctions between legality and illegality, spectacle and secret.[111] From the perspective of the white gaze, lynching could hardly be more logical: it is a naturalized response to naturalized feelings of racial animus. It is a community picnic. It responds to the mythical threat of Black violence. It maintains white supremacy. Our understanding of lynching remains limited, however, if we only critique the logics of white supremacy. Reorienting perspective away from the white gaze, silhouette aesthetics also refuse forms of sensus communis that rationalize lynching. Instead, this aesthetic of violence renders some aspects opaque or ambiguous to stage the feeling of senselessness, formalizing the moral illogic of white supremacy from the perspective of its victims. The postmodern silhouette of the long 1960s redirects dynamics of looking that uphold the racial, gender, and class hierarchies that lynching polices. Yet the silhouette also refuses clear-cut narratives of sentimentality or protest, inviting instead a sustained engagement with dynamics of disgust and desire that can emerge in aesthetic experience. Risking ethically ambiguous representations, the silhouette nevertheless affords a range of affective experiences that might ground other ways of encountering and theorizing violence and power. By letting shadows be shadows,[112] the silhouette pushes and pulls audiences in sustained engagement with the limits of their own looking.

## CHAPTER FIVE

# Collage

## *Rewriting Grammars of Violence*

In the acknowledgments to her 2005 book *Jane: A Murder*, Maggie Nelson thanks the literary critic Mary Ann Caws for teaching Nelson "that pain has, or can at least sometimes find, form."[1] In this instance, Nelson's pain finds the form of a collage text, a book-length work of Nelson's original poetry interwoven with excerpts from the childhood diaries and college journals of her aunt, who was murdered in Ann Arbor, Michigan, in 1969.[2] Nelson additionally incorporates language from news reporting about Jane's murder and what were likely related murders committed by a serial killer at the time—though Jane's murder officially remains unsolved. Whose pain takes form in the collage, and why is the collage an apt form for giving shape to the pain of murder and loss, especially a form of loss that feels senseless? Just as the Manson murders pulse through Joan Didion's "The White Album" as an emblem of the discourse of senseless violence, so is Jane's death a thread stitching together dynamics of misogyny, technological change, and discursive formations of the long 1960s. The collage gives shape to the pain that can be named but not known—Jane's pain—as well as the unfurling, intergenerational pain of her loss. The spectacular, aberrant violence of Jane's murder, when articulated through the collage form, also hooks up to more quotidian experiences of violation and suffering. In this way, a book focused on making a kind of sense from a senseless murder draws on a feminist lineage of collage that, in an echo of the broader cultural formation of serial killing, draws together "our most basic sense of the body and society, identity and desire, violence and intimacy."[3] Reworking discourses of serial killing in collage form, *Jane* illustrates the paradox of so-called senseless violence: serial killing is figured as senseless, yet is explicable through social critique, especially attention to misogyny. For its victims, however, serial killing is experienced as arbitrary. To formalize this paradox through the collage is to maintain it, facilitating an aesthetic experience of violence as unanticipated and contingent.

Collage becomes a formal response to discourses of senselessness embodied by the serial killer, discourses overdetermined by cultural constructs about violence, race, and gender. The serial killer's most sympathetic, prototypical victim, after all, is the beautiful young white woman. As Nelson implies, the collage form complicates these discourses and reworks the feeling of senselessness to imagine new ways of understanding misogynist violence. The serial killer blends public and private by making sexualized crimes hypervisible, opening the body for the public to see, and refusing to be an individuated person with a private interiority—he is "the mass in [a] person."[4] In spite of the fact that he (and it is pretty much always he) proliferates written explanations for his crimes,[5] the serial killer is framed as an incomprehensible figure, made comprehensible when we situate him in the context of what Mark Seltzer has called our broader "wound culture."[6] Sensational discourses of serial killing also obfuscate more quotidian forms of violence that police gendered identity while affirming a commonsense notion that young, often beautiful white women are both particularly vulnerable to senseless violence and socially valuable as victims of that violence. The collage is an apt form for the senseless pain of serial murder in part because it juxtaposes found text from the real world—personal writing from Jane, media reporting on the Michigan murders—with imaginative writing by Nelson to explore the relationship between representation and reality, between the personal and the political. The collage is a form, then, that can accommodate the fragmentation of experience produced by suffering and intervene in a media environment that collapses representation and reality.

As we have seen in the examples of the frame, the happening, the grotesque, and the silhouette, postwar aesthetics are shaped by sociocultural dynamics that raise questions about the nature and quality of violation. A key concept for answering these questions will be the subject of this chapter, which explores feminist theories of consent that arise through collaged representations of senseless violence. Consent is a way of demarcating violence from nonviolence, one that focuses not only on the way force might affect a body, but also on the way an individual feels about the action taken. It is also a concept that indicates changing understandings of sexual violence, a new chapter in a long discourse about rape. In the long 1960s, second-wave feminists developed a new understanding of rape grounded in the notion of "breaking the silence," rejecting the widespread assumption that rape was rare and exceptional and countering a long history in which rape was conceived as a violation of another man's property, rather than as an act of violence against women.[7] Breaking the silence is an epistemic as well as political intervention, a claim about the nature of violence that seeks to revise commonsense definitions of violation. The long feminist history of collage aesthetics became an important site for theorizing these political and epistemic claims as well as giving form to pain that has historically been silenced or disavowed. Having traced aesthetic violence as responses to the nuclear age, the state violence of policing, and the state-sanctioned violence of lynching and Jim Crow, the book now turns to the sex wars of the 1980s, a moment that saw new discourses of sexual violence taking shape in both courtrooms and radical feminist spaces.

As Edgar Allan Poe's infamous line that nothing is more poetic than "the death of a beautiful woman" indicates,[8] violence and gender have long been intertwined in the American imaginary, with the category "woman" containing a dense collection of ideology and overdetermined meanings. Indeed, Nelson's collage text critically engages this notion, citing Poe's "Philosophy of Composition" twice in *Jane* and insisting "that Jane was not beautiful."[9] Violence against women has a long history in art and literature, with images of sexual violence, in particular, appearing throughout literary history. Representations of sexual violence are called on to do different kinds of work in the long 1960s, however, as feminists were rewriting rape as a crime explained by misogyny and patriarchal power dynamics, rather than an unavoidable, naturalized crime of passion or as theft and destruction of another man's property. Sexual violence is significantly bound up in "epistemological questions about the nature of experience formation and the role that experience plays in our formation of knowledge."[10] One way to reckon with these questions, as we will see, is through the fragmented and recombinatory formal properties of collage, an aesthetic that links consent in the reading experience to consent in sexual encounters.

A key concept for distinguishing sex from rape, consent more broadly helps to determine the status of an act as violent or nonviolent. Consent is not, however, a term typically applied to the reading experience. Yet as an important concept for theorizing sexual violence and cultural responses to it, consent also shapes the dynamics of representations of violence. And no writer challenged readers' experience of consent quite like Kathy Acker. A post-punk experimental writer publishing from the late 1960s until her death in the 1990s, Acker is an iconic figure of the postmodern American canon. Her collage novel *Blood and Guts in High School*, which was copyrighted in 1978 and published by Grove Press in 1984, blends text and image to raise the question of consent in the reading experience. In turn, some of Acker's readers went on to use a similar collage practice as riot grrrl artists, constructing zines built of found and original images and text that portrayed sexual violence as senseless violence. This aesthetic approach could condemn rape without also making sentimental appeals based on images of ideal victims, rejecting the misogynistic demand that rape victims perform a particular and tightly demarcated set of emotional responses and social behaviors in order to have their experience viewed as violating. The collage was an important aesthetic strategy that could interpellate readers into a contested dynamic of consent and elicit a wide range of emotional responses.

## Collage and Consent

Collage is often considered one of the most important artistic innovations of the twentieth century, influencing subsequent artistic movements including abstract expressionism and pop art.[11] Its blend of verbal and visual modes renders collage at once unified and unstable; thanks to its combination of image and word, "the *mise en question* of representation" is "inherent" to the form.[12] As the practice rose to prominence in the art world in the first half of the twentieth century, it also inspired mimicry by writers and musicians.[13] Notably, in the 1950s and '60s, William S. Burroughs and Brion Gysin collaborated on "cut up" texts composed by cutting and ordering preexisting writing. Burroughs noted that in creating cut ups he would "apply the painter's technique to writing; things as simple and immediate as collage or montage."[14] Acker was directly inspired by this technique, and she would often lightly revise her collaged texts to amplify their aggressive tone. For example, when working on an early text called *Politics*, Acker revised fragments from her notebooks, "cutting up" her own work to transform "I'm sick of fucking and not knowing who I am" to "I'm sick of fucking not knowing who I am."[15] While this example largely maintains grammatical coherence, it also collapses multiple statements into one, hiding the "seams"[16] of collage and layering statements on top of one another.

Across European avant-garde movements of the twentieth century, including Dada, Surrealism, and Futurism, collage was understood to tear at the relationship between representation and reality and to aggress against audiences.[17] As it migrated from Europe to the United States, reaching a kind of saturation point with the 1948 Museum of Modern Art exhibit entitled *Collage*, the politics of collage were reimagined in a new context of postwar immigration from war-torn Europe and the increasingly visible civil rights movement.[18] Like the performance work of Fluxus, collage also intervenes in politics by inviting physical participation and a heightened awareness of embodiment vis-à-vis artworks.[19] It unsettles the distinction between life and art by incorporating found material and invites a phenomenological engagement with the work by drawing viewers physically toward the site of the cut, the seams that bring together disparate objects.

Understood as political from its beginnings, collage is also intimately tied to legal questions, which open out onto concerns about ownership and property, theft and consent. Like the Dadaists who appropriated text from newspapers in order to render reports of war nonsensical, the later Situationist practice of *détournement*—or recontextualizing slogans or logos to turn consumerist texts into critiques of consumerism—used collage for subversion and critique.[20] Given its use of the work of others, collage is also bound to questions of originality, theft, and legality.[21] A collage work nearly always infringes on copyright. For Acker, this was part of the appeal. She described her writing style as "piracy"; she would purposely steal with little regard for hiding her thievery. Paige Sweet argues that Acker's piratic technique challenged "the legal categories that protect and even sanction one kind of thievery (that which operates on behalf of capitalist accumulation) while criminalizing another (such as copyright infringement)."[22] As an artistic practice of taking without asking, collage challenges notions of ownership and private property. It also raises dynamics of consent from their typically subterranean role in art-making.

Collage is a form of stealing that can potentially injure the creator of the copyrighted material, although that creator often holds more power than the collage artist. Whether they hold the cultural capital of a Walt Whitman poem or the *capital*-capital of the Disney corporation, the victims of copyright infringement are often more secure than the perpetrators. And in turn, the injury of the collage work does not extend in the same way to its consumer. The collage form, by drawing on extant works, may spark recognition in an audience, but such recognition can work in different affective registers. A reader may experience the pleasure of "oh, I know that!" or the discomfort of seeing a familiar text or image warped and rearticulated. Such recognition can unfold in multiple directions, reinscribing the original work for audiences. I, for example, knew Acker's writing before the Marquis de Sade's, and I only recognized Acker's borrowing from *The 120 Days of Sodom* long after being affected by her appropriation of the language. To encounter Sade's language was thus, for me, an experience of recognizing Acker's writing, not the other way around. The words became hers, were marked by her, even in their original context. As an "aconsensual" form,[23] collage relies on dynamics of consent and nonconsent for its social subversion and critique of capitalism. Even its aesthetic force depends in part on underlying dynamics of legal transgression and assumed nonconsent. With questions of legality and harm inherent to its formal and material practice, collage is a particularly resonant form for theorizing notions of consent and harm in other contexts, even when those contexts are shaped by quite different power dynamics.

Collage is also integral to feminist avant-garde practices.[24] The "radical juxtapositions of collage" have been mobilized by feminist avant-garde artists to raise questions about the gap between representation and reality, especially as representation is informed by and reproduces sexist assumptions.[25] While theorists of the avant-garde have typically viewed collaged representations of the female form as straightforwardly misogynistic, "it is also possible to see, in the experiments of what will come to be called the avant-garde, the recombinant possibilities of collage form as a template upon which to imagine new forms of personhood."[26] Collage facilitated feminist critique and the reimagining of avant-garde coteries themselves, disrupting assumptions about the neutrality of the authentic experiences that avant-gardes sought to cultivate. Denaturalizing assumptions about the nude body and revealing the sexist and racist primitivism of avant-garde practices, feminist collage also deconstructed the notion of the found object so central to collage aesthetics. Rather than a neutral artifact of the everyday, the found object is frequently "shaded with repressive gendered sensibilities."[27] In other words, a feminist avant-garde is attuned to the social conditions that determine artistic meaning, and this extends beyond a collage practice of making new meanings and into the ostensibly neutral materials used in such a practice.

Though collage can consist of only visual or only textual media, the works in this chapter use collage to blend image and text, heightening the jarring effects of their compositions. Acker's collage practice incorporates images into the novel to undermine readers' sense that they are in control of their own reading experience, raising the concept of consent. In feminist avant-garde hands, collage produces an experience of senseless violence that troubles simplistic notions of consent by disrupting narrative cohesion and thwarting audiences' interpretive protocols. Such fragmentation not only echoes or represents the fragmentary experiences of sexual trauma, but also also affords a reading experience of shock that could facilitate a wider range of emotional experiences. While this shock effect depended on transgressing against readerly consent, it also built feminist affective communities. In these writers' hands, shock provides an entry point into multiple responses, which can include recognition, joy, and love.


## Kathy Acker's Cruelty

The manuscript of *Blood and Guts in High School* was delivered to Grove Press in a Citadel notebook, with its contents literally cut and pasted onto the ruled pages. Even some of Acker's editorial markings were transposed into the printed version of the text, and the notebook includes instructions titled "Dummy for Blood and Guts," accompanied by a page that reads "Instructions for Putting This Damn Book Together."[28] The instructions provide detailed guidance for formatting the book—for translating the collage work into a printed codex.[29] The printed novel thus elides some aspects of the work's material history as a cut-up assemblage that incorporates rewritings of nineteenth-century poetry, excerpts from Acker's diaries, her drawings, and handwritten Persian grammar exercises. The novel is "A visual and verbal collage that blurs the boundaries between art object and book."[30] Though in its printed version *Blood and Guts* hides the seams of its collage aesthetic, its disjunctive, recombinant effect remains, inviting a modified form of Artaudian cruelty that centers on the question of consent in the aesthetics of shocking violence. By foregrounding the complicated question of consent, the novel creates a discursive space for readers to experience the conflicting emotions that are frequently elided in debates about sexual violence.

The novel follows ten-year-old Janey through the remaining four years of her life. She lives with her father in Merida, Mexico, but leaves him early on to move to New York City. Janey and her father have an incestuous relationship, with much of their dialogue lifted from Acker's diary entries detailing her own (adult) relationship with Peter Gordon.[31] This collage of life-writing and fiction produces a dual effect: because Janey and her father interact like adult lovers, their interaction does not register as violating in the same way that a realist representation of incest might. At the same time, the uncanny effect of this collage disturbs precisely by collapsing a violent sexual relationship into a nonviolent one; that is, a relationship of statutory rape and one between consenting adults. Throughout the novel, Janey's experiences provoke questions about the possibility and nature of consent. She joins a street gang, is enslaved, and enters into sadomasochistic relationships with both Jean Genet and President Jimmy Carter. Riffing on Genet's *Thief's Journal* to describe how she feels about such relationships, Janey claims: "I want the textures of your lives, the complexities set up by betrayals and danger—I like men who hurt me because I don't always see myself, I have my egotism cut up. I love this: I love to be beaten up and hurt and taken on a joy ride. This SEX—what I call SEX—guides my life."[32] By raising the issue of love and desire in considerations of sexual violence, Acker situates Janey in a tension that has been central to feminist debates: on the one hand, the concept of personal autonomy protects the choice of women to engage in violent encounters; on the other hand, the notion of gender performativity and cultural contingency suggests limits on subjects' ability to self-determine or have anything like true autonomy. At the time Acker was writing, anti-pornography feminists like Catharine MacKinnon and Andrea Dworkin were also claiming that, in the context of a patriarchal culture and its long legacy of power imbalance between men and women, it is not possible for women to fully consent at all.[33] Janey's masochistic relationships with other characters raise questions about which subjects can consent, and who decides whether their consent is valid, while Acker's aggressive form suggests that representations have the power to violate terms of consent as well.

Acker's involvement in sadomasochism provides a context for her treatment of consent as well as her relationship to the sex wars that were reaching a fever pitch around the time of the novel's publication. Acker was briefly a member of the lesbian sadomasochism organization Samois.[34] As another Samois member, feminist and queer theorist Gayle Rubin, has explained, sadomasochistic pornography was used as evidence that porn is inherently violent and misogynistic—the images of violation ostensibly speak for themselves.[35] Acker's redeployment in *Blood and Guts*, however, emphasizes the inherent complexity of representation, image, and reception. Acker aestheticizes sexual violence to destabilize the systems of meaning that the anti-porn movement took to be self-evident. For feminists, sadomasochism has been understood as either a troubling symptom of gender oppression or a playful reappropriation of female submissiveness.[36] For Acker, however, sadomasochism stems from an approach to subjectivity that imagines it as always already fragmented and traumatized; instead of shattering the self, sadomasochism psychically reorganizes a self that is grounded in sexual trauma.[37] Like Acker, Michel Foucault would reject out of hand the notion that sadomasochism is a straightforward symptom of sexual trauma. Instead, it is a socially contingent formation—a creation of sexuality, rather than an expression of anything inherent.[38] It is also, as Gilles Deleuze claims, a dynamic of sexual pleasure that is "structured around the logic of the contract."[39] Masochism's contractual nature relies, of course, on consent—contracts both express the consent of involved parties and performatively create those parties and their ability to consent.

Although Acker's approach to sexuality contrasts sharply with the anti-pornography feminist ethos, her approach to consent, I argue, wrestles with the same impasse that Catharine MacKinnon highlights when she rejects the notion that consent is fully available to women as free and equal subjects.[40] Anti-pornography activist Diana Russell offers an illustrative example of the movement's treatment of consent vis-à-vis representations of suffering. She writes of a pornographic film: "boiling candle wax was dripped onto a bound woman's breasts. Had she consented beforehand? Even if she had, this is a violent act."[41] Russell suggests that the injury or pain inflicted on a body obviates questions of consent of the subject inhabiting that body. And if we do not like the kind of violence inflicted, then her consent is impossible. Further, Russell suggests that naivete, ignorance, or false consciousness must have informed this consent, and thus, her consent is no consent at all: "even where models have consented to participate, they don't necessarily know what they're in for, and often they are in no position to maintain control."[42] While this line of thinking may be partly informed by a disgust at sex in general,[43] it also emerges out of a sense that both nonviolent sex and the fully consenting woman are myths. Yet while this awareness leads anti-pornography feminists to reject sadomasochism and, crucially, representations of violent sex, Acker draws the opposite conclusion. She layers multiple representations of violence on top of one another through the tactic of collage to materialize the notion that our experiences are multilayered and complex. Violence and pleasure can be difficult to disentangle, but just because sexual pleasure might be tinged with danger, constraint, or violation, it does not follow that feminist politics must unilaterally condemn these experiences.

Acker's involvement in sadomasochism indicates some of the sexual politics that infused her work. But the politics of her work are affective, with the formal qualities of *Blood and Guts* facilitating modes of textual engagement that are felt in the body. Indeed, Acker's collage aesthetic invites—or perhaps forces—an "opening to sensation."[44] Collage enacts violence on language, but in Acker's hands it also inflicts senseless violence on readers, drawing them into sensory engagement with the novel's multimodal form and forcing new modes of perceptive engagement with the text. *Blood and Guts* disrupts "normative structures of perception and representation," which both "reveals their limits or crisis points" and makes "extreme demands on readers,"[45] short-circuiting narrative causality and refusing familiar modes of expressing sexual trauma. By forcing encounters with shocking images, the novel's collage aesthetics violate the implicit terms of consent between reader and text. As Georgina Colby puts it, Acker struggles "against the imposition to make sense."[46] Instead, affect is a new site of meaning-making in *Blood and Guts*.[47] The novel represents certain negative affects, but it also provokes a whiplash effect that provokes responses of shock and stuplimity[48] but also, perhaps, laughter or shame—responses that saturate the perceptual experience of the reading event. Perceived as a visual field, and not just a linguistic sign system, the novel keeps readers in a dynamic of tensions between visual and textual modes, facilitating different kinds of meaning-making grounded in affect.

More than representing violence, the novel enacts it through formal strategies of disjuncture and parataxis.[49] Acker's signature is her "terrorist style," which works with her violent subject matter to "exacerbate and exploit" the potent intersection of art and violence.[50] On one level, this terrorist style is a form of extralegal warfare waged against source texts, literary conventions, and notions of copyright and intellectual property, yet such an attack extends to readers as well. Acker's drawings, for instance, leap into a reader's field of vision as she turns the page, breaking novelistic convention. Imagine reading the novel in a coffee shop, feeling marked by the book in your hand, which is open to a full-page spread of a hand-drawn vagina captioned, "My cunt red ugh."[51] While this image does not depict a violent act, it stages a potentially violent dynamic between novel and reader, a terroristic attack that is likely to shock. Acker's instructions in "Dummy for Blood and Guts" direct the press to "insert 'my cunt red ugh' picture as soon as possible after same phrase on p. 21 xerox," suggesting Acker's intention to attack readers with the drawing.[52] The novel, as if wearing a trench coat with nothing underneath, shows readers something shocking, which they cannot unsee.

Expressed through a practice of collage, violence in *Blood and Guts* is shocking not only because it calls up images of real-world violation, but also because it often appears unmotivated, random, or heedless of generic convention. Late in the novel, for example, while its protagonist is in jail in Tangier, form and content merge, with Janey locked in a cell next to Jean Genet while the text is increasingly borrowed from Genet's *The Screens*. In the midst of their conversation about war and suffering, an unexplained eruption of violence intrudes in the form of what appears to be an italicized stage direction:

GENET: Look . . .

>*Dim light has gathered through a tiny hole high up in the wall. Suddenly it goes black. In this blackness, caused by a power blow-out, the upper-middle class women and the cops smash store windows, beat up bums with chains, and wander about. A young black man sticks his hand under a ten-year-old girl's tight yellow sweater.*

JANEY: Let us pray to madness and suffering and horror.[53]

Readers are prevented from making sense of this passage at multiple sites: the characteristic dialogue in the novel, which mimics the form of a play and emerges without warning in the text, disrupts traditional genre conventions. This echo of the theater also reminds readers that a play, unlike a novel, is brought to life through human actors. When the stage directions in the passage appear, the novel's generic features are further blurred. With these stage directions, however, we can see the ways a novel can access modes of representation unavailable to a play. Readers are pointed to "a tiny hole high up in the wall," through which characters can see rioting. Yet all this action takes place, of course, in "blackness." If we were watching a play, we might hear screams and the sound of glass breaking. We could not, however, see that "a young black man sticks his hand under a ten-year-old girl's tight yellow sweater." In this form, readers are encouraged to notice that the blackness of the street is echoed in the Blackness of the man, and language functions differently in the new context of a novel than it would in a play. Racial signifiers shift, leaving readers to wonder about what, exactly, the language in this novel is depicting.

On one level, the passage disrupts readers' sensemaking capability by stealing and mangling generic conventions, yet it also introduces brutality that seems not to have any reason to exist in the novel. Readers can entertain a number of possibilities: the riot sheds light on the unrest that is merely the background to Janey's and Genet's own experiences, perhaps. As McKenzie Wark notes, Acker's interest in anticolonial struggles, "in Algeria and elsewhere," inform her aesthetics of revolution, and her interest in the postcolonial African novel is an understudied influence on her writing.[54] While the scene with Genet may thematize anticolonial struggles in Algeria, Acker's collage poetics interrupt or make difficult interpretive reading strategies that would situate the eruption of violence in a legible, real-world social context. Alternately, it might allegorically depict hierarchies of racial and gendered violence, drawing on the way her source texts flatten kinds of "cultural difference" to articulate a feminist critique of how those writers "ignore the problem of gender difference."[55] Yet the text's collaged structure disrupts the forms of hermeneutic closure theorized by Roland Barthes. If, as Barthes claims, any element of a novel must necessarily make meaning, fit into a closed system of interpretation, then even the most unmotivated plot points can be worked into an interpretation of the novel: "everything has a meaning, or nothing has."[56] Acker's collage novel, however, challenges this notion of hermeneutic closure by incorporating found materials that point toward the source texts from which they have been wrenched. The juxtaposition of the stage-direction interjection with the emplotted events befalling Janey and Jean Genet suggests a relationship, yet for many readers, it is difficult to see how the violence on the other side of the "tiny hole high up in the wall" can shed light on what is happening in Janey's cell. Instead, meaning comes through the affective and perceptual difficulty of the work's seeming arbitrariness.

Collage thus affords a kind of masochistic reading experience, raising the question of consent in the context of a reader's engagement with a text. Collage enacts aconsensual pairings of source texts and, in turn, stages an aconsensual encounter between a reader, who brings to the reading experience expectations for form, genre, and the affective contours of reading, and a novel that is violent on the levels of form and content. Evocative of Antonin Artaud's theater of cruelty, *Blood and Guts* deploys a prose style that "violates the implicit contract between author and reader that forms the basis of the novel as a genre."[57] The novel-as-collage aims to make reading itself a violent, risky interaction. And in embracing this masochistic, vulnerable, aconsensual relationship to the text, readers also open themselves up to the possibility of feeling a whole range of responses to representations of violence. This openness to feeling might hurt, but it might also become a resource for readers when reckoning with their own beliefs about and experiences with violence.

Violating implicit dynamics of consent between reader and text, Acker's work capacitates a wide range of responses to sexual violence, including those that break taboos. Instead of exploring Janey's inner world, *Blood and Guts* turns toward the reader to explore the emotional valences of masochism and consent. The novel imagines an alternative to representations of sexual violation that rely on and bolster constricted frameworks of the "good" victim — one who is chaste, passive, and properly traumatized. It is not exactly the case that readers will feel like Janey, treated poorly by the novel itself in an analogous way to Janey's treatment by her father, President Carter, and Jean Genet. Instead, readers experience the violent emotional encounter of shock, which, as Rita Felski explains, "tells us less about the specific content of an affective state than about the qualitative impact of a text or object on the psyche."[58] Shock can "unravel the certainty of one's own convictions."[59] Rather than providing life lessons, a window onto the world, or clear-cut social protest, literary "shock invades consciousness and broaches the reader's or viewer's defenses."[60] As readers follow the series of violations inflicted on Janey, they open themselves up to the possibility of having their "convictions" about the nature of consent and sexual violence "unravel[ed]." In baiting readers to see Janey as a flat, one-dimensional character who is difficult to identify or empathize with, the novel opens up the possibility of responding to her violation with a much wider range of emotions "than self-righteous anger or hushed tones of sympathy or respectful silence."[61] The novel thus also critiques the overdetermined notion of the sexual assault victim—passive, clearly nonconsenting, broken, and traumatized—for reinforcing patriarchal ideologies of sexuality and reducing women to less than full human beings with a complete range of capacities and emotions. In offering a more complex dynamic of consent, one that is both thematized and enacted in the relationship between reader and text, *Blood and Guts* foregrounds a flawed assumption that often underwrites discourses of consent—the notion that we are always able to predict our future emotions about an experience, or even fully account for our feelings about an experience as it unfolds.

In addition to engaging a masochistic relationship with the novel, readers also open themselves up to the possibility of gaining discomfiting self-knowledge, learning, perhaps, that they have the capacity to laugh at violation or be bored by it. While in principle one can set a book down at any time, the compulsions of narrative often pull a reader across pages that make them wince, tie their stomachs in knots, and call up their bile. Karin Littau reminds us that books are physical objects that engage readers' bodies, sensations, and affective responses. Pointing out a tendency in critical theory to imagine reading as purely cognitive that dates at least since William K. Wimsatt and Monroe C. Beardsley decried the "affective fallacy," Littau points out that "reading is historically variable and physically conditioned."[62] Heightening bodily engagement, the novel thus raises questions about the relation between violence and consent inside the text and outside the text.

When readers are deeply affected by shocking scenes of violence, they register an empathetic, almost ghostly impression of the violation that is located in our own bodies. We could say that a text reaches out and touches us—or even slaps us. "Like trauma," suggests Ann Cvetkovich, "touch is a term that has both physical and emotional, both material and immaterial, connotations. To be emotionally touched, like being traumatized, is to be affected in a way that *feels* physical even if it is also a psychic state."[63] Indeed, when compared with visual art or film, literature can extend the experience of shock: while I am making a split-second decision about when to turn my eyes away from a scene of torture in a Michael Haneke film, the mode by which language mediates violence protracts my engagement with it, as I more slowly decide when I have reached the limit of the violence I can stand. *Blood and Guts* is a haptic text, one that returns readers to the felt experience of shock and the physiological aspects of aesthetic engagement.

Its haptic nature also illuminates the role consent plays in the epistemic conundrums of violence.

This dynamic leads us to ask how literature can manufacture or override consent. What does it mean to consent to an action taken by a text? Is it possible to withhold consent from certain kinds of reading experiences? Like sadomasochism, perhaps, the reading experience can demand continual negotiation of consent.[64] And as with sadomasochism, a collage text offers unpredictable experiences, wherein readers may consent to painful or unanticipated experiences. Confronting audiences with collaged representations of violation, the text theorizes concepts of senselessness shaped by changing discourses around rape and responsive to the problems of interpretation, experience, and self-understanding that swirl around sexual violation. Writing against the anti-pornography concept of sexual violation, which came to echo puritanical constraints on acceptable forms of sexual encounter, Acker's avant-garde approach to sexuality and violence emphasizes the complicated nature of understanding our own experiences and challenges conventional notions of "consent" as an agreement between informed subjects to engage in a particular relationship. Once you consent to, say, being slapped in the face, the terms of injury or violation operate differently—because you have consented to being hit, you were not violated in the same way (if indeed you were violated at all) as someone who did not consent to such an assault. In violent sex acts, arousal or desire may come into play, and in consensual sex acts, pain and power imbalances may also emerges. Therefore, consent, while a crucial concept for understanding sexual violation, is not the ultimate arbiter of whether a relationship will be harmful or safe, pleasurable or dangerous.

One's sense of one's own experience, as feminist theory has suggested, is profoundly enmeshed in ideology, meaning that we cannot make straightforward claims about the truth of how an event unfolded simply through recourse to our own experience of the event. As Linda Martín Alcoff has argued, an individual's experience, particularly if she is socialized as a woman, can "be subject to the weight of ideological socializations" that manifest "at the deepest levels of feeling and response."[65] Experience can certainly tell us something about the nature of sexual violation or violence, but it cannot tell us everything; it is so thoroughly directed and shaped by ideology. This raises a number of problems, but one has to do with our ability to recognize sexual violation and demarcate it from noncoercive sexual experience. This problem runs in two directions, as Alcoff notes. Both "the *denial* of abuse" and "the *positive identification* of abuse" can be "subject to problematic processes of interpretation."[66] Although I would venture that in a patriarchal society, we are more likely to misrecognize abuse as noncoercive or justified, rather than to see abuse where it does not really exist, her point is significant. As she notes, "the process of defining and demarcating the boundaries of those domains we generally want to put in the nonbenign category of sexual experience—harassment, sexual coercion, sexual abuse, even sexual violence, all of which [belong] in the category of *sexual violation*—is an interpretive process."[67] Staging this problem as part of the reading experience, *Blood and Guts* enables additional experiences of considering these interpretive problems, of attending to the complicated question of experience. Developing a counter-discourse that rejects the assumptions of anti-pornography feminists, *Blood and Guts* also rejects the ways anti-pornography discourse reduces women's ability to claim complex or multivalent experiences as something more than totalizing, traumatizing violation. The material practice of collage, which produces a palimpsestic novel that layers diaristic writing, plagiarized material, and images, then further recombines these elements to blur the boundaries between found and original material, reproduces the multivalence of experience, mobilizing a feminist shock aesthetic that welcomes the wide range of feelings that arise around sexual violation.

## Riot Grrrls as Readers

Riot grrrl artists not only inherited Acker's punk feminist avant-garde legacy, they also used collage aesthetics to provoke and theorize the connected experiences of shock and consent. Kathleen Hanna is perhaps the most famous of the early-generation riot grrrls who came together around 1989 at Evergreen State College in Olympia, Washington. She is also an important reader of Acker's writing, and her relationship to Acker's work demonstrates how aesthetics of violence can draw readers into experiences of recognition, identification, and love. In *Girls to the Front*, Sara Marcus's cultural history of riot grrrl, Hanna discusses her experience of reading *Blood and Guts* for the first time, saying, "I was just writing all this crazy shit and I thought I was totally insane . . . And I got *Blood and Guts in High School* from one of my photo teachers, and I totally felt like, Oh, I'm not crazy! It was such a confidence builder for me. I wasn't even sure what kind of artist I was going to be, like if I was a writer or a photographer or what. But it made me feel like these other women had done this amazing shit and I could too."[68] Hanna describes a sense of recognition, specifically along the lines of being "crazy" and "insane." A tic of contemporary speech, these references to mental illness nevertheless point toward the way *Blood and Guts* approaches narrative, sexual violence, and the phenomenological experience of being a young woman. Through an aesthetic mode that would be seen through a more normative lens as "insane," *Blood and Guts* depicts the conflicting, surprising, or incoherent ways an individual might respond to violence. In doing so, the novel also took Hanna out of isolation and pointed her toward a model for feminist art-making.

Acker was a literal influence on Hanna, but this lineage also points toward more general thematic and formal linkages between Acker's punk feminism of the 1970s and riot grrrl aesthetics of the 1990s. In 1974, four years before the publication of *Blood and Guts*, Acker was performing in the underground poetry scene in New York and publishing her work as the "Black Tarantula." Combining her own writing with the appropriated work of other authors, she mimeographed documents and circulated them through a subscription service to interested readers.[69] Her method of dispersal anticipates modes of zine production and circulation. For girls in the 1990s, zine exchange helped constitute what Alison Piepmeier calls "embodied community," a sense of material connection between writers and readers who may never encounter one another in shared physical space.[70] For Piepmeier, the experience of embodied community is rooted in the pleasure of zine writing, reading, and exchange. The "materiality" of zines "functions not simply as another component of their meaning but also as a means of linking creator and reader, creating a particular kind of community," one that "is embodied because it activates bodily experiences such as pleasure, affection, allegiance, and vulnerability."[71] Yet the aesthetics of riot grrrl zines productively complicate this notion of pleasure: even emotionally and aesthetically difficult reading experiences, provoked by discussion of violence but also through the fragmenting reading experience of the collage-based zine text, play a role in the pleasure Piepmeier identifies.

Acker's influence, as well as the continuing resonance of Poe's quip, is evident in Hanna's 1992 zine, *The Most Beautiful Girl Is a Dead Girl*. Like Acker, Hanna writes sexual violence in ways that make violation explicit while also withholding displays of suffering that would affirm typical characterizations of "good" and "bad" victims, even in a genre characterized by emotional disclosure and vulnerability. *The Most Beautiful Girl* follows the teenage years of a female narrator who undergoes a series of violent encounters, much as Janey does. Composed primarily of typed text, the zine is also interspersed with cut-and-pasted images of medical professionals, their cheerful, children's-book aesthetic contrasting sharply with the sexually explicit and violent content of the zine.[72] Collaging together moments of sexual pleasure and sexual danger, the zine rewrites what Sharon Marcus has called the "grammar" of sexual violence.[73] Arguing that rape must be understood as a language, enmeshed in cultural scripts about gender that imagine men as active agents of violence and women as passive victims of violence who are "always either already raped or already rapeable,"[74] Marcus deconstructs the grammar of violence to show how we might rewrite the scripts of rape.[75] Published in 1992, Marcus's discussion of sexual violence echoes the theories developed at the same time in riot grrrl zines. In advocating for "a politics of fantasy and representation," Marcus claims that "New cultural productions and reinscriptions of our bodies and our geographies can help us begin to revise the grammar of violence and to represent ourselves in militant new ways. In the place of a tremulous female body or the female self as an immobilized cavity, we can begin to imagine the female body as subject to change, as a potential object of fear and agent of violence."[76] Rewriting this script by articulating women's "capacity for violence"[77] in general would help to unsettle a pervasive "gendered grammar of violence" that "predicates white men as legitimate subjects of violence between all men and as subjects of legitimate sexual violence against all women [and] portrays men of color as ever-threatening subjects of illegitimate violence against white men and illegitimate violence against white women. In an intraracial context, this grammar generically predicates men as legitimate perpetrators of sexual violence against women."[78] Marcus argues that even feminist theorists of sexual violence, notably Susan Brownmiller, naturalize this grammar.[79] Artworks that articulate women's capacity for violence, then, offer a resource for rewriting these cultural scripts. Feminist collage aesthetics imagine new arrangements of pleasure and danger, creating new kinds of representations of girls—violent girls who fight back; free girls who are not afraid. These representations are unlikely to convey an immediately legible politics thanks to the disjuncture of collage, however, but instead mobilize aesthetics to build new structures of feeling amid changing conceptualizations of sexual violence.

In her 1993 zine *My Life with Evan Dando, Popstar*, Hanna continues to use collage to scramble stereotypical representational protocols. An ambivalently violent extended love letter to the Lemonheads's lead singer, *My Life* consists of collages made with confessional letters, nude drawings, and images of Dando covered with cutout lines of text that ironically explore her parasocial, ambivalent desire for him.[80] Like this collage, which fragments the background image of Dando by overlaying it with cutout text, other pages in the zine overlay lines of text on drawings of women performing in strip clubs, drawing formal connections between the gendered power dynamics of fandom and of the strip bar.[81] The disjointed, aggressive form of the zine works in tandem with its content to surface the ambivalent, aggressive responses young women have to objectification and sexual violence. The zine's use of collage enacts a palimpsestic layering of experience and emotions, a formal expression of the ways identity and emotion can be fragmented and incongruous. Its author fantasizes about objectifying Dando as she has been objectified, while also expressing desire to be like him and critiquing the cultural fetish for the young, sensitive male genius.[82] Echoing this formal strategy, the zine's content refuses cohesive expressions of emotion or identity that would align with the "gendered grammar[s] of violence"[83] that enforce women's fear, passivity, and self-concept as powerless.

Zines offered a powerful textual space for readers to consider their own relationship to bodily vulnerability and violation, as well as their own capacity to enact violence. The music of riot grrrl likewise offered aesthetic, embodied experiences for reimagining one's relationship to embodiment and vulnerability. When riot grrrl bands played in clubs and basements around Olympia, New York, Washington, DC, and elsewhere, the mosh pit was a place for young women to make themselves vulnerable to the violent dancing of the crowd. Zines and other material covered strategies for safety in the mosh pit,[84] helping girls understand how to protect their bodies by following the unpredictable flow of the crowd and giving themselves over to unpredictability. The inclusion of safety strategies demonstrates one of the central, if underexplored, tenets of the riot grrrl ethos: there is strength to be gained when one makes oneself physically and emotionally vulnerable to the violence in the world. Risk and even violation are a part of living, and can enrich life. More than that, the social forces that would protect girls from any possibility of risk or violation—the heteronormative family, the politics of respectability, sexual prudishness, the law—are the same ones that enable and often perpetrate violence against girls.

In their focus on quotidian sites of violence such as school, home, and punk show, riot grrrl zines gave voice to experiences of violation that were often invisible in mainstream culture. Girls experienced recognition and attachment in response to Hanna's work, but they often expressed such feelings by, for example, crying at Bikini Kill concerts.[85] The wide-ranging forms of feminist shock that characterized Hanna's writing and music grew out of tensions she saw between punk aesthetics and feminist art. Like earlier avant-garde formations, riot grrrl explored taboo themes in order to enact a form of aggression against audiences, but such aggression also provoked experiences of recognition, joy, and mobilizing anger. By playfully reappropriating quotidian forms of violence, riot grrrl artists imagined alternative ways of engaging with the world. An anonymous zine writer, for example, wrote of her anger about rape on her campus, the school's mishandling of it, and "how shitty it is to live in fear." In response, her riot grrrl group "made up a secret plan and carried it out that night. we laughed and held hands and ran around in the dark and we were the ones you should be looking out for. in a girl gang i am the nite and and i feel i can't be raped and i feel so fuckin' free."[86] Here, the response to a culture of sexual violence is not in terms of a legal definition of consent but rather in terms of imaginative play, appropriation of "dangerous" space, and communal good feeling—feeling that might include imagining oneself as dangerous to others.[87] As an alternative to a legal discourse of consent, riot grrrl gave girls a model for articulating affect that imagined alternatives to the "good" victim and the traumatized survivor.

Undoing grammars of victimization can also help girls be self-understanding and critical about their own participation in the violence of white supremacy. We need only think back to Emmett Till to recall that white women have demonstrated plenty of capacity for violence in US culture. As in the example of Carolyn Bryant, who accused Till of whistling at her and sparked his lynching, this capacity for violence comports to, rather than challenges, the construction of white womanhood as innocent, passive, naive, and vulnerable.[88] In addition to claiming forms of bodily agency and a capacity for change that makes (white) girls' vulnerability less totalizing, imagining oneself as capable of violence can reorient one's relationship to the social. Not only could girls fight back, they could become more aware of their capacity to harm, their participation in upholding a violent culture. It is, I want to insist, precisely through the formal arrangements captured in the language of "grammar" that riot grrrl complicated notions of the passive white girl. Mimi Thi Nguyen's analysis of racism and classism in riot grrrl claims that critiques of riot grrrl from people of color are a central part of its cultural contribution, not evidence of its fragmentation or failure.[89] I want to add to her claims by pushing them beyond a notion of representational politics to highlight how the self-correcting, recursive dialectical gestures of the callout—often manifested in zine writing as well as meetings and other ephemeral conversations—echo Acker's approach to language, in which she manipulated grammar and punctuation to place recursion and revision in the body of her text. Recall how Acker used the colon to formalize expressing a thought, then revising it, and how she would lightly edit sections of her diary collaged into her novels to increase their polysemy. Like the broader collage aesthetic, this is a kind of collage ethic that brings recursion and revision into the work of the text. The collage ethic produces polyvocality by making its work that of checking, revising, and improvising.

One way we cognize shared cultural feeling is through contesting the particular meanings of shared language; the range of meanings embedded in our terms demonstrate how language is a ground of social change.[90] The language that builds around a structure of feeling is not just a reflection of the values that shape how we talk and think about that feeling, but the avenue for engaging those concepts. Changing the language helps change the structure of feeling. By invoking Raymond Williams I hope to connect Marcus's grammar of sexual violence to Hortense Spillers's grammar of gender, race, and the flesh. Spillers frames the logic of white supremacist violence and misogynoir through the concept of the "grammar book." The structuring grammar of American life also naturalizes ethnic categories that create whiteness and Blackness and, as part of that process, make racialized bodies vulnerable to both violence and metaphorical overdetermination.[91] Importantly, Spillers's grammar book accounts for the ways afterlives of slavery shape gender ideology, excluding Black women from an unproblematized category of "woman." Enslaved women were not only subject to rape but also to lynching and forms of violence coded masculine, highlighting the limitations of rape discourse as a discourse of female pain.[92] As Spillers demonstrates, the legacies of slavery complicate discourses of sexual violence, because "the customary lexis of sexuality . . . is thrown into unrelieved crisis."[93] Slavery ungenders Black people, complicating what Marcus would soon call the grammars of rape. As Marcus would in 1992, in 1987 Spillers proposed that undoing hegemonic "syntax" of American sexuality and developing "a new semantic field/fold" that was more attuned to historical conditions would be one important way to change a violent society.[94] Rather than making a way for Black women to fit in the hegemonic category of woman, Spillers sees the ungendered location of Black womanhood as a site for potential insurgency and remaking of gendered grammars.[95] This is a representational project that unfolds through language — language as medium for new modes of representation, but also language as material for remaking structures of feeling.

As Mimi Thi Nguyen has shown, the desire for a unified female experience has been one way white riot grrrls inflicted forms of pain on non-white grrrls. Universalizing concepts of girl love, which riot grrrls invoked, have held up a structure of symbolic violence that erases both the particular experience of non-white girls and the ways white girls were in fact participating, consciously or not, in the violent logics of white supremacy. What many non-white and poor girls recognized in riot grrrl was a familiar dynamic of exclusion, ignorance, or appropriation in the guise of empathy. Nguyen outlines the way a rhetorical gesture of calling out privilege became a prominent feature of zine culture and argues that such a gesture functions as a kind of absolution from that privilege for white grrrls. This rhetorical move also relied on declarations of intimacy that subsumed the embodied and emotional experiences of non-white "others" for a community that nevertheless remained fairly exclusive.[96] Hanna herself has often come under critique for her insufficient attempts to address racial inequality in riot grrrl communities.[97] White riot grrrls did not simply overlook the experiences of racial minorities, but in their attempts at an antiracist movement, also performed "confessional gestures and professed desires for intimacy with the other" that "produce[d] possessive investments in an antiracist whiteness."[98] The pain of engaging with what "hurts" in riot grrrl indicates some failures of riot grrrl, but it is also a generative discursive formation, one grounded in negative affect. One of Nguyen's key insights is to reframe antiracist critiques of riot grrrl as central to the formation, not antagonistic or ancillary. Nguyen situates the riot grrrl movement not only as a chapter in the history of the avantgarde but also as formed in the crucible of the 1991 Mount Pleasant riots in Washington, DC, which "erupted around immigration, race, and police brutality."[99] Rewriting the historiography of riot grrrl, Nguyen insists that its "woman of color feminist critique" is not a *course correction* of the movement but a central feature of the movement itself.[100] A movement formed as contestation and revision, its politics share the combinatory and recombinatory formal properties of the collage. Following on Nguyen's insights, I contrast the model of "course correction" to that of grammatical revision, the reworking practices of Acker and riot grrrl manifested through cutting and pasting, calling out, and other forms of rewriting.


## From Infantile Citizen to Collaged Subject

Interwoven with riot grrrl's political critique, its more unwieldy and senseless shock aesthetic invited more expansive, full ways of conceptualizing sexual violence by embracing the way girlhood is a category that complicates consent. As Lauren Berlant has demonstrated, anti-pornography legislation in the 1980s "helped to consolidate an image of the citizen [in general] as a minor, female, youthful victim who requires civil protection by the state whose adult citizens, especially adult men, seem mobilized by a sex- and capital-driven compulsion to foul their own national culture."[101] If anti-pornography legislation thus aligned the subject with the figure of the girl, whose ability to consent is highly contingent and proscribed, then it is no wonder that Acker's and Hanna's avant-garde approach to sexual violence centers on girlhood. In their work, girlhood is an identity formation that complicates clear-cut frameworks of consent by destabilizing the notion of a subject who is able to give consent. By reappropriating the figure of the girl—presumed by the law not to be able to give consent—this feminist avant-garde formation could raise questions about how much *any* subject can fully consent, given our vulnerability to unanticipated feelings and emotions that accompany sexual acts. As a liminal space in which sexuality, agency, and desire are fraught, girlhood challenges the notion that "consent" can fully resolve questions of sexual violation. A collage aesthetic exploring the radical possibilities of girlhood involved readers in embodied, affective dynamics of consent and shock, dynamics that cultivated an awareness of the affective power of texts over readers and of images over viewers without treating representations of sexual violence as interchangeable with real violence, as other strands of feminist thought tended to do.

In contrast to an anti-pornography ethos that shaped the socially legible responses women might have to sexual violation, collage offered an aesthetic strategy that embraced the affective power of texts over readers and of images over viewers. Berlant points to this textual aggression as a key to understanding the sex wars. Many critics believe that "texts are muscular active persons in some sense of the legal fiction that makes corporations into persons: texts can and do impose their will on consumers, innocent or consenting."[102] This belief fuels MacKinnon and Dworkin's assertion that, even if one leaves aside its conditions of production, pornography commits violence against women. Acker and Hanna, however, seem to welcome and encourage a text's ability to aggress against nonconsenting readers. Readers might, in fact, welcome the power of texts to act on them. The collage coupling of image and text, photograph and drawing, paired with an aesthetics informed by diary writing, figures girlhood as a "vulnerable," "public[,] and alive" identity.[103] Riot grrrl authors manipulated pornographic tropes and depictions of potential violence in order to explore the emotional complexity that MacKinnon and Dworkin's vision of female desire and oppression cannot accommodate, a vision that has been written into the legal framing of sexual violence.[104]

Riot grrrl zines countered the mainstream notion of the girl as an infantile citizen by articulating girlhood as a radical political subjectivity activated through a collage-based practice of *détournement,* "insisting on tentative, creative and contingent forms of political mobilisation."[105] Rather than a powerless victim or "empowered" postfeminist subject, this girl is a political subject who refuses the quotidian violence of a misogynistic society on the grounds of her own vulnerability.[106] An important chapter in the history of feminist collage, riot grrrl zines ground their political intervention not in a form of "coherence" but through "their jagged, fractured, discontinuities and . . . their startling juxtapositions, contrasts, and contradictions."[107] As Lisa Darms notes in her introduction to *The Riot Grrrl Collection,* "zines—although made to be shared, and often with strangers—could feel private and intimate, like an extension of a diary (but one with witnesses who had perhaps shared your experience and could attest to your sanity)."[108] Echoing Hanna's experience of shared "sanity" when reading *Blood and Guts,* this brief aside gestures toward a key strain of the politics of riot grrrl aesthetics: in a context where victims of gendered violence are often silenced by having their sanity and reliability questioned, the risks of confession are significant, but the counterpublic staged in zine exchanges offered an alternative space wherein these experiences were not dismissed by a patriarchal common sense. In fact, the conference proceedings of the infamous "Barnard Conference" at the heart of the sex wars were eventually published as the *Diary of a Conference on Sexuality,* taking shape as a collage text whose aesthetics anticipate riot grrrl zines, with proceedings from the academic presentations interspersed with found images, including sexually explicit ones, as well as handwriting and ephemera. Its cover is printed to look like a leather diary, with gold embossed writing and a lock. The title, however, uses collage aesthetics: "Diary of a Conference" appears to be embossed on the leatherlike cover, while "on SEXUALITY" appears as a cutout scrap of paper pasted, askew, on top.[109] The contingent aesthetics of collage give shape to a feminist politics grounded in the limits of self-knowledge.

Writing about feminist theory in the wake of the "affective turn," Clare Hemmings explains that affective conversion is central to feminism's political interventions. Hemmings describes her own experience of rejecting feminism as a young woman and, through the "affective dissonance" of seeing how her own sense of herself was discordant with the limitations of a sexist world,[110] coming into feminism through rage.[111] Engaging Elspeth Probyn's work on "feminist reflexivity," Hemmings makes the case that affect "gives feminism its life" because it can make sense of the disjunction between ontology and epistemology.[112] Grounded in the body, affect can mobilize feminist politics because it disorients, realigns, or conflicts with familiar, sexist worldviews. "Politics" she writes, "can be characterized as that which moves us, rather than that which affirms what we already know."[113] If affective conversion is central to feminist identification and epistemology, then a key question arises: how does feminist art move its audiences? What can the aesthetic do that other kinds of appeals to affect cannot? By deploying shock, feminist collage aesthetics can move audiences in ways that a more straightforward rehearsal of injustice might not. The conversions instantiated by Acker's and Hanna's avant-garde representations of sexual violence emphasize affect's central role in questions of sexual consent. By complicating readers' consent to an experience of represented violence, Acker and Hanna also expose the limitations of consent in accounting for the circulation of affect, power, and violation in sexual relationships.

The feminist collage aesthetics practiced by Acker and Hanna can point the way toward a renewed understanding of affect and feminist aesthetics in the current moment. By assaulting readers with representations of violence, shock prompted feminist readers to reflect on the complex nature of consent, and subsequently to think and feel the violation of shock alongside pleasure, absorption, and recognition. Formally intervening in ordering logics of composition, the collage intervenes in grammars of violence, race, and gender to break apart the seemingly natural order of sexual violence. Experienced by audiences as a shocking, aggressive, yet also recognizable and pleasurable reading experience, the feminist collage text challenges felt experiences of consent as part of the aesthetic work of rewriting grammars of violence.

Acker's and Hanna's aesthetic of shock, and the contradictory affects it provokes, reverberates in contemporary conversations around the aesthetics of sexual violence. Performance artist Emma Sulkowicz is an emblematic flashpoint: their undergraduate thesis at Columbia University, *Mattress Performance/Carry That Weight* (2014–15), in which they carried a mattress any time they were on campus for nine months, is often understood as a protest against the university's inept handling of their own sexual assault case. But as Sulkowicz repeatedly insists, *Mattress Performance* is primarily art, not protest. In the tradition of Chris Burden and Tehching Hsieh, Sulkowicz has created endurance art about rape, privacy, and consent.[114] Their choice of the endurance performance piece echoes the riot grrrl aesthetic of inhabiting pain to articulate it, and their use of the found object places Sulkowicz in the lineage of feminist collage.[115] Surprising and disorienting, if not shocking, *Mattress Performance* is an inheritor to the feminist avant-garde because it manifests vulnerability and explores bad feelings. Bearing a close relationship to Tracey Emin's *My Bed*, but modifying the shock effect of that piece by erasing the signs of female embodiment that are its hallmark,[116] *Mattress Performance* pairs the disorienting surprise of inserting the mattress into unexpected places (classrooms, libraries, graduation ceremonies) with an emphasis on pain—the immediate physical effort of schlepping the mattress echoes the absent-present pain of sexual violence. *Mattress Performance* also proclaims art as an alternative space to work through issues of sexual violence. Abandoning the legal system and the possibility of a criminal or civil case against their alleged rapist, Sulkowicz is implicitly claiming that their art project is a more productive or valuable way of processing their experiences than the legal system can offer.

Perhaps art is the place for an expansive, internally contradictory, and even incoherent affective field of responses to sexual violence. The kind of pain formalized through the collage complicates narratives of trauma around sexual violence and allows for the possibility of emotional responses that range in valence from numbed shock, to anger, to confusion, to interest, even to certain kinds of pleasure. This expanded emotional vocabulary may seem politically inconvenient in the fight to end sexual violence, but contemporary feminists might look to the model of affect articulated in this feminist avant-garde to imagine new discursive possibilities for refusal, failure, expression, and critique that come from a wider range of emotional standpoints. Acknowledging the presence of vulnerability and the impossibility of a safe and secure subject position might help feminists make better demands on the law, or even approach "the law" with skepticism, as Acker does. Feminist avant-garde shock enables a range of affective experiences and communal attachments precisely by making readers vulnerable to art and language. Like Barthes's language that "wounds or seduces,"[117] avant-garde shock can enable love through readerly pain.

# Coda

## *Aesthetics and the Senseless*

This book has traced aesthetic responses to discourses of violence in the United States in the second half of the twentieth century. Periodizing aesthetic treatments of suffering between World War II and September 11, 2001, and framing this time period as the long 1960s, the book has claimed that artistic responses of aesthetic violence formalized the complicated dynamic between structures of violence and the senseless feeling of suffering. In this coda, I would like to expand on why I end with 9/11 and how the impact of postwar aesthetics of violence linger in—and have the potential to further shape—contemporary US culture. Literary periods are often bracketed by wide-scale events of state violence: think of 1865 as a historically common dividing line for the American literature survey course, or the periodizing claim of the Space Between Society, which covers literary history between World War I and II.[1] And, of course, the demarcation of a *postwar* period itself illustrates my point. In periodizing this book, I have observed that aesthetic explorations of the meaning and structures of suffering both align with and transgress against this common sense of literary periodization: the aesthetic approach to suffering I have described developed partly in response to the legacies of World War II, and I argue in this conclusion that 9/11 effected a historical shift in the discourse of structural and senseless suffering. This moment traverses the development of neoliberalism; it anticipates contemporary discourses of so-called senseless violence that appear, like clockwork, in politicians' responses to terrorism, to mass shootings, and to gun violence. As Lucy Diavolo laments in an op-ed for the twentieth anniversary of the Columbine shooting, these events are frequently referred to as senseless violence; "if this violence is truly senseless, how are we supposed to make sense of it?"[2] A 2018 collection of psychology articles studying senseless violence calls the phenomenon "a twenty-first century epidemic" and explores topics as varied as school shootings, children's migration from Central America, the effects of violent video games, and the legacy of the Holocaust.[3] Discourses of senselessness continue to register overwhelming feelings in response to violence.

Let's revisit Joan Didion's nameless, naked woman standing on a ledge. Let's place her beside another figure, one who would index twenty-first-century discourses of violence. Captured in a now-iconic image taken by Associated Press photographer Richard Drew, the "falling man" either fell or jumped from a tower of the World Trade Center soon after the attacks of September 11, 2001.[4] The image has become a motif of this moment, as indicated by, for example, Don DeLillo's novel *Falling Man*. Similarly, Jonathan Safran Foer's *Extremely Loud and Incredibly Close,* another canonical work of 9/11 literature, invokes the falling man in its last pages, which feature a flipbook-style series of photographs that reverse the fall, imaginatively rewinding time to the moment before the attacks.[5] Invocations of the day's blue sky and language of falling are also frequent in criticism about 9/11 literature and culture.[6] If Didion's naked woman is a thought experiment reflecting ascendant cultural questions around the possibility of "authentically senseless" suffering, 9/11's iconography of falling marks a turn in this discourse, one marked by the deployment of discourses of suffering to justify state violence in the form of global war, legal constriction of civil rights through policies such as the PATRIOT Act, and policing and surveillance of racialized people.[7] Initially experienced by most US spectators as bewildering and random, the attacks were quickly swept up in "a profound instrumentalization of the event at the service of political and economic goals that were more ideologically continuous than disruptive."[8] The dominant framing of the attacks in the United States helped justify the war on terror, underwritten by notions that America is an innocent victim of violence that needs to defend itself. The imagined innocence of the United States has also been critiqued by those who would point to the long history of US neo-imperialism in the Middle East as a key context leading up to the attacks.[9] As Jay Shelat argues, literary critical discourse about 9/11 "centers whiteness" in a way that aligns with dominant political rhetoric around the attacks. Thus, the literary critical understanding of the event and its aftermath has largely bolstered a "flawed historical perspective that perpetuates narratives of white innocence and precariously deracializes the consequences of 9/11 altogether."[10] Discourses of senseless attacks—undergirded by deeply felt reactions to the event, to be sure—were mobilized toward a response like the call for "law and order" diagnosed by Stuart Hall in 1970s Britain. Indeed, as anthropologist Anton Blok has claimed, terrorism should not be thought of as "senseless," but it is often spoken of that way. For US residents largely ignorant of the broader geopolitical context that framed the rise of Al Qaeda, in this case, the "dominant perceptions and representations of violence" as senseless emerge from a point of view that cannot see a clear relationship between the "means" of terrorism and the "ends" of the group's broader goal.[11] To frame terrorist attacks as purely random or senseless betrays a racialized privilege, and like the mugging discourse it also justifies other kinds of violence through appeals to senselessness. The war on terror implicitly framed terrorism not in relationship to political goals but as a threat to the law,[12] and the figure of the terrorist echoes Hall's mugger, a senseless attacker who must be controlled through increasing law and order.

Similarly, Walter Benn Michaels sees the post-9/11 moment as a shift toward discourses of terrorism as senseless, and his 2004 monograph on the turn away from ideology critique concludes with a discussion of the terrorism moment: a fantasy of writing without meaning, as he puts it, and a turn away from the political to the biopolitical. He draws on Kathy Acker's 1988 novel *Empire of the Senseless* as his case study. For Michaels, the novel and other examples of "the literature of terror" seek to reenvision writing as a corporeal expression rather than a representation that carries meaning—this literature is senseless because "it is not the meaning of my words but the touch of my body that matters."[13] The novel's title registers structural violence by invoking both empire and the senseless, sensory experiences of embodiment—a collapse of the personal and the political. Its themes anticipate twenty-first-century concepts and discourses of violence, which may be one reason for the resurgence of critical interest in Acker's work in the twenty-first century.[14] *Empire of the Senseless* anticipates discourses of terror and suffering that would characterize the twenty-first century. In turn, it invites us to consider how aesthetic violence can illuminate contemporary questions around represented violence. Indeed, Alexandra Kleeman, in her introduction to Grove's 2018 reissue of the novel, calls it "a book that doesn't behave, that won't sit still and simply make sense." She also claims that "literary texts participate in real-world consequences," suggesting the continued relevance of aesthetic violence and its complicated attempt to blend text and life.[15] Acker's collage technique, along with her violent subject matter, makes it an aesthetically difficult, even violent text that reaches into the world via the complex reading experience it provokes. One of the book's protagonists, Thivai, illustrates this work when recalling a nightmare about his sister's death: "To my dead sister, dream somehow of paradise. It's the only thing that can now keep us alive. The sweetness of your mouth. Coming while not being bruised by the hatred of the one who's making you come. You no longer don't have to not exist."[16] This moment, which does not describe violence in particularly explicit terms, enacts aesthetic violence through the difficulty of parsing the language, especially the last sentence quoted. Its style evidences Acker's collage aesthetic that pushes toward nonsense with its ambiguous grammar, challenging interpretive protocols without fully collapsing into meaninglessness.

The discourse around terrorism that coalesced in the United States in the wake of 9/11 and the start of the Iraq War, as Michaels puts it, framed terrorism as senseless because the rationale or political goal of any terrorist act was considered to be immaterial—indeed, was nearly unspeakable, as indicated by the controversy around Reverend Jeremiah Wright's claims that US chickens were coming home to roost.[17] As Michaels has put it, "terrorism is our current name for political acts that seem to us to render whatever reasons might be given for them irrelevant."[18] Michaels, who claims that the "disarticulation of writing from representation is fundamental to the literature of terror,"[19] wants to turn away from the senseless and toward criticism's proper aim, which is interpretation of meaning rather than apprehension or experience of form. While I think Michaels effectively diagnoses a dynamic of the literature of terror and the post-9/11 turn toward a resolute, myopic invocation of the senseless, I believe attending to form and to affective experiences elicited by these aggressive texts remains a valuable goal, not a distraction from the work of literary criticism. Formalist critics have by now well established form's slipperiness. As Jonathan Kramnick and Anahid Nersessian put it, our definition of form is contingent on what we aim to do with the knowledge a formalist reading can reveal.[20] In the case of Acker's aesthetic violence, attention to form can illuminate how texts work in the world, and this knowledge is about affective, subjective experience, as well as meaning.

Aesthetic approaches can reveal the contours of our *sensus communis*, helping us limn the edges of what is speakable or imaginable in a particular cultural context. In the twenty years since the attacks, a line of thinking focused on the aesthetics of 9/11 has developed, though such aesthetic approaches to 9/11 were widely considered horrifying and offensive in the period immediately following the attacks. The avant-garde composer Karlheinz Stockhausen, for example, was almost universally condemned and disgraced for calling the attacks "the greatest work of art imaginable for the whole cosmos."[21] Though some scholars have more recently reappraised and complicated Stockhausen's ideas,[22] the responses they received at the time suggest that it was unthinkable to look at the form of the attacks for their aesthetic, rather than moral or political, elements. Claiming that the spectacle of 9/11 shares some commitments and effects with Artaudian cruelty, Richard Schechner suggests that "in our day, the walls between the real and the virtual have crumbled, the theatrical and the actual have merged. What

9/11 offered was a spectacle of cruelty in the Artaudian sense, 'terror . . . on a vast scale.'"[23] Schechner's cautious exploration of the relationship between avant-garde cruelty and the very real violence of the 9/11 attacks recalls Walter Benjamin's warning that aestheticizing violence encourages people to take pleasure in their own destruction.[24] Yet as I have tried to show in my reading of formalist approaches to suffering in postwar America, aesthetic interest is not necessarily the same thing as pleasure, and taking the aesthetic elements of violence into account might reveal ways to respond more ethically to violence, rather than to enjoy its spectacular presentation. In a moment when reality TV was becoming an increasingly significant form of entertainment and online platforms like YouTube helped make user-generated content a much larger part of the media landscape, "the boundaries between the real and the fictional" were increasingly becoming blurred. This dynamic exacerbated the repackaging of 9/11 as a Hollywood spectacle, and as Schechner puts it, "the television presentations of the 9/11 attacks soon took on the qualities of a made-for-television drama series."[25] The event became aestheticized even as an aesthetic response was disavowed as morally reprehensible. Given all this, can a resolutely aesthetic approach, one that brackets political interpretation, offer a useful response to the senseless moment of post-9/11 media?

I hope this book has shown that it can. The 9/11 moment also, as Rachel Greenwald Smith has shown, invites closer attention to the work of aesthetic abstraction and its relationship to affect in considerations of literary violence. In conversation with Brian Massumi and Alain Badiou, Smith highlights a politics of aesthetics that focuses on sensation in the body before it is put into language, while it is still an uneasy, muddy, ugly feeling. The politics of aesthetics Greenwald Smith describes do not manifest in art that expresses particular political positions or speaks from the standpoint of "the specificity of a particular subject position vis-à-vis globalization."[26] Instead, the political work of aesthetic experience happens through the ways forms of art also form audiences' sensory experiences. As she puts it, "in a situation where power is exercised by presenting sets of possible sensibilities that appear to be infinite, the political efficacy of art is embedded within its capacity to form countersensibilities."[27] Aesthetic violence, as it manifests in frames, happenings, grotesques, silhouettes, and collages of the long 1960s, offers a view of how art can help cultivate countersensibilities. Frames destabilize rhetorics of violence through proliferating perspectives, drawing audiences into a disorienting relationship to interpretation and shame. Through their use of chance procedures, happenings suspend audiences in the non-cathartic space of unresolved knowledge about violence. The grotesque uses structure or rule to modulate feeling and call into question sentimental assumptions about suffering and embodiment. The silhouette outlines scenes of subjection to cultivate aesthetic interest in violence, interest that disrupts fixed logics of racialized disgust. Finally, the collage intervenes in grammars of sexual violence to rework ideas about power and gender, modulating shock to capacitate new ways to envision gender and citizenship.

Art has the capacity to form countersensibilities, but no guarantee. One useful way to think about how aesthetic experience reaches beyond the dynamic between text and audience to participate in the world comes from Raymond Williams and his concept of structures of feeling. For Williams, art both reflects the society that produces it and "creates, by new perceptions and responses, elements which the society, as such, is not able to realise."[28] Art can reveal "evidence of the deadlocks and unsolved problems of the society: often admitted to consciousness for the first time in this way. Part of this evidence will show a false consciousness, designed to prevent any substantial recognition; part again a deep desire, as yet uncharted, to move beyond this."[29] Aesthetic violence, though not invented in the mid-twentieth century, marked an encounter with new kinds of problems. It confronted the demand to make sense of violence, to aim for its explanation, to assimilate violence into known narratives, grammars, and belief systems. Rather than protesting the violent dynamics of the postwar era and, by extension, participating in the dominant meaning-making strategies shaped by mainstream notions of gender, race, embodiment, and nation, aesthetic violence cultivates emotional and cognitive difficulty. Through such aesthetic experiences of violence, audiences might try out new ways to feel, might learn "a new feeling"[30] that confronts violence not through recourse to familiar explanatory mechanisms, but at the edge of understanding, where new, as-yet-unknown, insights might take shape.

The theory of structures of feeling speaks directly to the challenge of understanding one's present moment. For Lauren Berlant, writing a history of the present means tracing that movement through feeling. Berlant writes that "the present is perceived, first, affectively."[31] Williams had suggested this as well, claiming that this perception is captured in the arts, before there are theoretical framings of a present feeling. Berlant claims that "the sense of the present" can be apprehended in the "genre" of "the 'impasse.'"[32] The minor feeling, the formal structure managing or modulating feeling, the sense of impasse named by the instinct to call an act senseless: these are affective and aesthetic ways of apprehending changing material conditions. In this book, I have tried to show that one response to discourses of violence was through aesthetic violence, or mediations that effect "a perceptual wandering" that makes interpreting and orienting oneself in the work difficult through the collision of forms.[33] Aesthetic violence formalizes the pain experienced in the context of complex, overwhelming structures of inequality and violence. It also offers ways to think about suffering outside the framework of trauma. Commenting on trauma as an exhausted category in an era of continual crisis, Berlant argues that the framework of the traumatic exceptionalizes suffering that is produced through ongoing systems. Although it has roots in diagnostic contexts that describe severe transformations of physical health and life, "'trauma,'" according to Berlant, "has become the primary genre of the last eighty years for describing the historical present as the scene of an exception that has just shattered some ongoing, uneventful ordinary life that was supposed just to keep going on and with respect to which people felt solid and confident."[34] In a moment where trauma seems ascendent in literary culture, aesthetic violence turns attention to the ongoing formal structures that shape possibilities of embodiment and violation. The unresolved and difficult perceptive and emotional experience of aesthetic violence, in other words, should sensitize critics and audiences to the ways suffering can be known or approached through art. Aesthetic violence can cultivate attention to the particulars of suffering, against trauma's "fundamentally ahistoricizing logic."[35] Formalist readings of scenes that might be gathered under the rubric of trauma can question this logic and open a way into other things literature and the arts can do with suffering.

Contemporary US culture, characterized by these discourses of senseless suffering, also sees the rise of book bans and what Parul Sehgal calls "the trauma plot."[36] The trauma plot focuses on unearthing characters' traumatic pasts as a mechanism for making sense of plot points and character dynamics. It reflects "trauma's creep" into our conceptual landscape. The trauma plot also flattens an experience of fiction by resolving ambiguities and mysteries. It contains threats of incommensurability and difficult aesthetic encounters even as it thematically centers trauma. The trauma plot's logic—that difficult textual dynamics will become unlocked and fitted into a clear-cut worldview explained by the traumatic event—shares some underlying warrants with the anxieties fueling book banning. Certainly, these bans are generally bad-faith attempts to erase diverse viewpoints and lived experiences. But they implicitly make their case on the assumption that representations do predictable things to readers—that representations will imprint on a reader in a direct way to cause harm. Indeed, the most frequently cited reason for banning a book, according to PEN America's 2023 report, is its depiction of violence.[37] Resting on the notion that texts do things to readers and that difficult aesthetic experience is dangerous, the implicit logic fueling book bans is shared by the logic of the trauma plot: difficulty must be resolved or contained. The kind of aesthetic violence I have tracked in this project offers an alternative view. It invites us to stay with the difficulty of suffering rather than slip quickly into right feeling. Aesthetic violence seeks to show suffering without sensationalizing it—instead, it draws out more difficult and sustained emotional reckonings with violence, reckonings that may be unresolved, ambivalent, or non-cathartic, but that encourage attention to the relationship between form and feeling, to how our emotions about violence intersect with structures of violence. Such an aesthetic encounter offers space to experience new emotions, unlocking audiences from more familiar grammars of violence.

The generative struggle of aesthetic violence can be valuable in our contemporary moment of sensory media overload. Drawing on Williams's account of structures of feeling, Rebecca Coleman suggests that the present moment is characterized by the "pre-emergent" experience of structures of feeling, or the ways that the ideology of a historical moment is always coming into formation. This structure of feeling can be viewed by looking at art and culture, where new collisions of affect, new formal arrangements that give shape to feeling, open up space for ideologies to begin to develop or cohere. The structure of feeling is not fixed, but manifests in the "'active,' 'flexible' 'temporal present'" and is a phenomenon of "pre-emergence," a concept characterizing "that which is in the process of emerging, and hence is felt, but is 'not yet fully articulated.'"[38] "Structure[s] of feeling" can be "generated by textual forms."[39] The structure of feeling also attends to the interactions between an individual experience and a social phenomenon. As Coleman notes, "one of the primary ways in which digital media are experienced, embodied and engaged (with) is through feeling."[40] If the cell phone video is a nascent form of the digital era's relationship to violence, one that provokes and engages feeling, then a comparison with the silhouette of the long 1960s might reveal continuities and divergences that illuminate the politics and aesthetics of this nascent media form. Inspired by Sula's interested approach to violence, we might similarly look at representations of suffering for their aesthetic shape, setting aside, at least for the time being, questions of right and wrong. Distinguishing affective response to a violent image from an ethical judgment about that image, we might then take up an aesthetic interest in violence to more fully attend to how it works, to hesitate in an aesthetic experience that might affect us in unpredictable ways. If "forms are at work everywhere,"[41] then an aesthetic approach to represented violence not only centers the shaping, orienting, and rhetorical work of form, but also enables a new, richer view of the "work" done by violent images.

In her work on extreme performance art at the transgressive edge of the contemporary art world, Jennifer Doyle frames this work as difficult, rather than "either *controversial* or *extreme*."[42] She examines works that are far less mainstream than my assemblage here, yet her analysis of difficult work, such as the body art of Ron Athey, which often involves needles, bloodletting, and other extreme acts, is significant for my thinking about aesthetic violence. The performance art she discusses is often so controversial that it is difficult to critically assess—scholars talk about the controversy around the work, rather than the work itself. Glossing theories of difficult literature through the work of George Steiner and John Vincent, Doyle highlights the important variability of audiences and their receptiveness to difficult work. In Steiner's theorization of difficulty, a work may be difficult to interpret for four main reasons: the reader may lack knowledge about the topic of the text (contingent) or its context (modal); the author may want to challenge the interpretive skills of the reader (tactical) or push against the boundaries of what a text can be (ontological). Yet as Doyle points out, Steiner's theory assumes a reader who desires to make sense of the text, overlooking the other kinds of encounters audiences may desire.[43]

An aesthetics of violence can draw audiences into close, sensed relation with the violent scene, facilitating not only challenging affective experiences but also sharper attention to the shapes violence takes. While this form of attention does not translate directly into guidance for real-world political work, it does produce an experience that can inspire clear, deep thinking about how power and feeling work in the world. The aesthetic concerns sensation, judgment, community, and questions of order or form. As Anna Kornbluh puts it, "far from being an epiphenomenon dispelling politics, aesthetics amount to the core of politics: arrangement, patterning, and ordering of the socialities and indeed of the sensory bodily experience of everyday life."[44] Although many scholars in this aesthetic turn valorize the disruption or "collision" of forms as the site of possibility for radical politics,[45] Kornbluh focuses attention on the ability of forms to order or construct political life, arguing "that humans cannot exist without forms that scaffold sociability, even though the particular forms that human sociality takes are not fixed."[46]

Similarly, for Cara Lewis, forms are "dynamic" and *form* is a verb; literary and visual forms move and mutate our perception.[47] For this reason, however, "there can be no easy conclusions" about the social effects of forms.[48] If we foreclose or oversimplify the effects of form by looking for easy conclusions, I contend, we overlook important kinds of work the aesthetic does in the world. It cannot simply convey messages that are encoded in the minds of readers; it is a sensuous participant in the material experience of those readers. For Kandice Chuh, "aesthetics refers to the relationships among the senses and the processes and structures of value making by which certain sensibilities become common sense and others are disavowed, subjugated, or otherwise obscured."[49] Like Chuh, I am interested in the ways "aesthetic inquiry emphasizes sensibility as a crucial domain of knowledge and politics."[50] Susan Buck-Morss reminds us that "*Aisthitikos* is the ancient Greek word for that which is 'perceptive by feeling.'" The aesthetic senses, including the "nose, eyes, ears, mouth, [and] some of the most sensitive areas of skin[,] are located at the surface of the body, the mediating boundary between inner and outer." The parts of the body that sense thus "encounter[] the world prelinguistically . . . prior not only to logic but to meaning as well."[51] Aesthetic apperception itself has a moment of senselessness built into it, and thus representations of violence necessarily, at some level, echo the senseless experience of pain inflicted through violence. Affect theory reminds us that the circuitry of sensory and affective perception is intermeshed with linguistic and cultural forms, so much so that we cannot easily demarcate where "pure" sensation ends and cognition or meaning-making begins.[52] Though we may be unable to pinpoint and isolate textual moments that are prior to or outside of meaning-making, we might register that a senseless experience is imbricated in the aesthetic as such. This moment of senselessness might be said to live on the body, to be touched whenever we consume figurative violence.

The question of what aesthetic experience can do in the world forms a throughline in twentieth-century American literary culture. It also inflects contemporary debates in literary studies around the knowledge produced through interpretive methods such as reparative and surface reading. Indeed, one of the most important texts to inaugurate the postcritical turn, Eve Kosofsky Sedgwick's "Paranoid Reading, Reparative Reading, Or, You're So Paranoid, You Probably Think This Essay is About You," alights from a conversation that took place "back in the middle of the first decade of the AIDS epidemic,"[53] a context that gives shape to the critique of suspicion and turn to repair she famously articulates in the piece. The historical context of underrecognized, homophobic, and racist structural violence—a violence inflicted through failure or refusal to acknowledge or respond to the disease because it disproportionately affected marginalized people—highlights the enmeshed relationship between epistemology and violence. In her critique of the turn toward repair, Patricia Stuelke situates the "turn toward the reparative as a response to state violence,"[54] citing invocations of spectacular state-sanctioned violence in a number of the greatest hits of the postcritical turn. Indeed, Sedgwick and others situate the exhaustion of critique in the context of widely circulated images of spectacular state violence and a broader sense that what must be exposed is, in fact, already known. And, moreover, that exposing the violence hardly guarantees that it will then be undone.[55] The dynamic of senseless violence, interrogated in the aesthetic innovations of twentieth-century literary culture, might be understood as an important context for debates about critical method in the twenty-first century. Aesthetic violence, in affording audience experiences of a kind of violation and a sensuous engagement with suffering, offers literary critics a resource for postcritical readings of state violence that are open to knowledge, but also to the experience of not yet knowing.

Reflecting on formalist methods for studying postwar American literature, Timothy Aubry asks, "What happens after a work of art inspires a particular set of feelings or thoughts? How do these feelings and thoughts translate into material or institutional transformation? In many cases it may not be possible to offer a persuasive account of how the effects on a particular readership or audience lead to actual political change. The experience of the subject threatens, in other words, to exhaust all of the powers that the artwork can wield."[56] It is difficult to track how aesthetic experience participates in world-making, but we know from James Baldwin that simply feeling right is not enough. The aesthetic demands attention to suffering without resolving that attention into "right feeling." I am claiming that forms can do things to audiences, and these effects reach into a real world that is not fully cordoned off from aesthetic experience. At the same time, critics can explore what artworks do to audiences without claiming that they always and inevitably do specific, measurable, predictable things. To speak of the rhetorical or aesthetic work of senseless violence is to speak of audience, and audiences are unpredictable.

The perceptive and phenomenological engagement demanded by an aesthetics of senseless violence draws our attention to audience—to the people feeling senselessness. What is legible to some will be senseless to others, and as postcolonial scholars have suggested, claims of incomprehensibility can be wielded by the powerful to maintain unjust systems.[57] In turn, claims to not understand or see a dynamic unfolding can also be made by marginalized people in a kind of politics of refusal. This dynamic helps to account for why many of the writers and artists discussed in this book provoked controversy in their time: unresolvable scenes of violence that did not seem to align with the moral frameworks of audiences are experienced as senseless, without payoff or reason to exist. Without recourse to familiar narratives about violence, audiences for these works were stymied in how to make meaning from the violent scenes. This incomprehensibility could offend in its seeming refusal to make appropriate moral claims about violence. Yet this difficulty also challenged fixed narratives about violence in a strategy that enabled deeper attention to the relationship between reality and representation. And in opening up the possibility of other kinds of responses or approaches to violence, the aesthetic invites shared experiences across time. Coming together in the act of reading: whether in a classroom or alone in one's room, aesthetic experiences of suffering can offer something different than right feeling or consolation, can attune audiences to the forms pain finds, unfurling and mapping the senselessly overwhelming ways we are caught up in and complicit in suffering.

*Notes*

## Introduction

1. Didion, "The White Album," 11.

2. Didion, "The White Album," 11.

3. Didion, "The White Album," 45.

4. This dynamic finds a kind of synecdoche in the term "we," theorized variously by Susan Sontag in her exploration of war photography. Sontag historicizes new modes of "looking at other people's pain" to the revelation of Holocaust photographs in the wake of the war (Sontag, *Regarding the Pain of Others*, 7). Similarly, Judith Butler has critiqued notions of a "we" that includes grievable, recognizable lives framed through a Western perspective. Butler connects the public grief, shock, and rage in response to 9/11 to the "amorphous racism . . . rationalized by the claim of 'self defense'" both in daily US life and military policy after the attacks (Butler, *Precarious Life*, 39).Taking this idea up as it relates to 9/11 literature, Rachel Greenwald Smith argues that discourses of 9/11 as an exceptional trauma ignore geopolitical contexts that implicate US neo-imperialism and capitalist ideology in an ongoing, and much more complex, network of violences (Smith, "Organic Shrapnel," 158).

5. Xiang, *Tonal Intelligence*, 5–6.

6. As with other historical catastrophes, 9/11 was, in the United States, often inaccurately received as a radical break from history, in spite of some cultural critics responding to the attacks by contextualizing them in relation to US international policy and global hegemony (Smith, "Organic Shrapnel," 158). Indeed, as Jay Shelat has put it, "Dominant authorial concerns with 9/11 have been largely white and tend to represent the attacks without precedent or antecedent. Instead of historicizing and contextualizing responsibly, these initial responses by critics, authors, and artists alike exceptionalized the United States: how on earth could *America* be attacked?" (Jay Shelat, "Introduction: Legacies—9/11 and the War on Terror at Twenty," *Post45*, September 11, 2021, https://post45.org/2021/09/introduction-legacies-9-11-and-the-war-on-terror-at-twenty/) The discourse of catastrophe often, as it did in the case of the war on terror, "provided opportunities for the institution of new forms of authority," including the expansion of presidential executive power and the acceleration of neoliberal policies begun in the Reagan era (Smith, "Organic Shrapnel," 158–59).

7. Cole, *At the Violet Hour*, 12.

8. Bersani and Dutoit, "The Forms of Violence," 19.

9. Kuc, "Aesthetic Violence in the Anarchival Turn," 19.

10. Butler, *The Force of Nonviolence*, 2.

11. *OED Online*, "senseless, adj.," December 2021, https://www.oed.com/view/Entry/175960.

12. Yao, *Disaffected*, 6.

13. *OED Online*, "senseless, adj."

14. Of the 156 entries for "senseless violence" in the *Corpus of Contemporary American English*, for example, the vast majority are drawn from news reporting on mass shootings and gun violence, as well as from politicians' use of the phrase to describe these events as well as geopolitical issues like terrorist attacks (Mark Davies, *Corpus of Contemporary American English*, accessed November 14, 2024, https://www.english-corpora.org/coca/?c=coca&q=123104542). Research into the concept of senseless violence appears in psychology and anthropology, but the phrase is largely undertheorized in literary or language studies. Anthropologist Anton Blok, however, uses the example of terrorism to argue that no violence should be thought of as senseless, for even violence inflicted on innocent people is motivated and, moreover, communicates symbolically. Indeed, it is essential that the victims be imagined as innocent in order for terrorism to communicate as intended (Blok, "The Enigma of Senseless Violence").

15. Nixon, *Slow Violence and the Environmentalism of the Poor*, 14.

16. In Google's Ngram corpus, all three modifiers of violence—senseless, structural, and systemic—appear very rarely before 1940. "Senseless violence" increases in usage starting in 1960, and both "systemic" and "structural" begin to appear as modifiers for violence around 1970. After 2000, both "senseless" and "systemic" remain fairly steady in usage, but the usage rate of "structural violence" increases steadily and significantly (Google Books Ngram Viewer, accessed February 19, 2022, https://books.google.com/ngrams/graph?content=violence%3D%3Esenseless%2Cviolence%3D%3Estructural%2CvCviolen%3D%3Esystemic&year_start=1800&year_end=2019&corpus=28&smoothing=0).

17. Galtung, "Violence, Peace, and Peace Research," 171.

18. Hall et al., *Policing the Crisis*, 29.

19. Hall et al., *Policing the Crisis*, 55.

20. Hall et al., *Policing the Crisis*, vii.

21. Hinton, *America on Fire*, 4.

22. Hinton, *America on Fire*, 5–6.

23. "The Enemy is Without, Not Within," *The Lexington Advertiser*, Lexington, Mississippi, October 11, 1962, Chronicling America, Library of Congress, https://chroniclingamerica.loc.gov/lccn/sn84024271/1962-10-11/ed-1/seq-2/.

24. "The Enemy is Without, Not Within."

25. Hall et al., *Policing the Crisis*, vii

26. Baldwin, *Notes of a Native Son*, 19.

27. Baldwin, *Notes of a Native Son*, 19.

28. Melamed, *Represent and Destroy*, xii.

29. Melamed, *Represent and Destroy*, xii.

30. Martínez, *On Making Sense*, 14.

31. Martínez, *On Making Sense*, 3.

32. Martínez, *On Making Sense*, 65.

33. The "scopic regime of modernity" has been defined as a social formation that has privileged sight over other senses and has helped to construct Western categories of racial, gender, and sexual difference (Jay, "Scopic Regimes of Modernity," 4).

34. Amin, Musser, and Pérez, "Queer Form," 234.

35. Amin, Musser, and Pérez, "Queer Form," 227.

36. Streeby, *Radical Sensations*, 15.

37. Berlant, *The Female Complaint*, 64.

38. Hartman, *Scenes of Subjection*, 4.

39. Nelson, *Tough Enough*, 2.

40. Ngai, *Ugly Feelings*, 3.

41. Xiang, *Tonal Intelligence*, 251.

42. Yao, *Disaffected*, 3.

43. Friedman, "Unsentimental Historicizing," 115.

44. See in particular the work of Mark Seltzer, who argues that we live in a "wound culture" characterized by fascination with bodily violation and suffering. From media spectacles of emotional abjection to representations of physical trauma like the television show *ER*, "wound culture" brings emotional suffering and the torn body into the open public sphere, troubling the distinction between public and private (Seltzer, *Serial Killers*, 22).

45. Mitchell, "'Ut Pictura Theoria,'" 361.

46. Sontag, *Regarding the Pain of Others*, 20–21.

47. Doane, "Information, Crisis, Catastrophe," 225–27.

48. Sontag, *Regarding the Pain of Others*, 7.

49. Jannarone, *Artaud and His Doubles*, 11.

50. Harper, *Abstractionist Aesthetics*, 3.

51. Harper, *Abstractionist Aesthetics*, 2.

52. Harper, *Abstractionist Aesthetics*, 11.

53. Levine, *Forms*, 70.

54. Craig Dworkin develops this idea in *Reading the Illegible*.

55. Scholars including Martin Jay, Nicole Fleetwood, Nicholas Mirzoeff, and Kandice Chuh have articulated how Western modernity's privileging of sight above other senses participates in the epistemology of racial difference and racial hierarchy. As Chuh puts it, the "primacy of sight, of the privileged economy of the visual in the apparatuses of modernity . . . subtends the privileging and double meaning of representation as referring to both political standing and reflective image" (Chuh, *The Difference Aesthetics Makes*, 22).

56. Brinkema, *The Forms of the Affects*, 36.

57. Bersani and Dutoit, "The Forms of Violence," 19.

58. Bersani and Dutoit, "The Forms of Violence," 19.

59. Bersani and Dutoit, "The Forms of Violence," 27.

60. Bersani and Dutoit, "The Forms of Violence," 21.

61. Nancy, *The Ground of the Image*, 15, 24.

62. Nancy, *The Ground of the Image*, 24.

63. As Sally Bachner argues, the discourse of violence as unrepresentable is belied by the many significant depictions of violence in contemporary American literature. Starting in the 1960s, Bachner argues, violence became a central way for American writers to mark their works as serious literature, even as the notion that violence is unrepresentable became commonplace (Bachner, *The Prestige of Violence*, 2–3).

64. Debates about represented violence tend to understand it as enabling either cathartic or mimetic experiences. As long as it has been an object of philosophical inquiry, represented violence has been understood to relate to real-world violence, whether as a homeopathic prevention of violent affects that may spill into violent acts, or as an inducement to repeat violence for its own senseless sake (Lawtoo, "The Double Meaning of Violence: Catharsis and Mimesis," 158).

65. Castronovo, *Beautiful Democracy*, 6.

66. Susan Buck-Morss expands on this notion (Buck-Morss, "Aesthetics and Anaesthetics," 38), which is also found famously in the Futurist manifesto's celebration of war as a move toward aesthetic perfection.

67. Castronovo, *Beautiful Democracy*, 114–16.

68. In his "Critique of Violence," Walter Benjamin traces conceptual frameworks around violence to questions of morality, and thereby to the law. He notes that extralegal violence is always a threat to the law's command of sanctioned violence, as it challenges the common sense notion that the law must monopolize violence (Benjamin, "Critique of Violence," 281).

69. Rancière, *The Politics of Aesthetics*, 8.

70. Benjamin, "The Work of Art in the Age of Mechanical Reproduction," 241.

71. Buck-Morss, "Aesthetics and Anaesthetics," 4.

72. Buck-Morss, "Aesthetics and Anaesthetics," 5.

73. Buck-Morss, "Aesthetics and Anaesthetics," 5.

74. Chuh, *The Difference Aesthetics Makes*, 18.

75. Williams, *The Long Revolution*, 69.

76. Castronovo, *Beautiful Democracy*, 24.

77. Throughout the nineteenth century and up until World War II, aesthetic debates about taste and judgment also played a role in political debates about violence and democracy, with the Kantian notion of sensus communis, or "the common standard of aesthetic judgment in which individual perception tallies with general taste," bleeding into political theory and rhetoric (Castronovo, *Beautiful Democracy*, 21). Another way art might intervene in common sense, according to Caroline Levine, is through the collision of representational forms with material ones. When forms collide, even across these strata, surprising outcomes can emerge, even if they are unlikely or minor (Levine, *Forms*, 8).

78. Levine, *Forms*, 6.

79. Serpell, *Seven Modes of Uncertainty*, 9.

80. Serpell, *Seven Modes of Uncertainty*, 17–20.

81. Bradway, *Queer Experimental Literature*, vii.

82. Reed, *The Art of Protest*, 10, 395–96.

83. Such critiques of formalism have come most forcefully in pushback against the postcritical turn, as illustrated by Patricia Stuelke, *The Ruse of Repair*. See also Armstrong, *The Radical Aesthetic*; Amin, Musser, and Pérez, "Queer Form"; and Chuh, *The Difference Aesthetics Makes*.

84. Hartman, *Scenes of Subjection*, 3.

85. Marcus, "Fighting Bodies, Fighting Words," 385.

Chapter One

1. Chenoweth, "Rock, Paper, Scissors," 11.

2. Smith, "Narrating the Guillotine," 34.

3. Sontag, *Regarding the Pain of Others*, 20.

4. James Baldwin, "A Report from Occupied Territory," *The Nation*, July 11, 1966, https://www.thenation.com/article/culture/report-occupied-territory/.

5. Miller, "Separate and Unequal in Paris," 160–61.

6. Goldberg, "James Baldwin and the Anti-Black Force of Law," 528.

7. Goldberg, "James Baldwin and the Anti-Black Force of Law," 531.

8. Blok, "The Enigma of Senseless Violence," 23.

9. Blok, "The Enigma of Senseless Violence," 25.

10. Miller, "Separate and Unequal in Paris," 167.

11. Ross, "White Fantasies of Desire," 15.

12. For more on this line of thinking, see Ross, "White Fantasies of Desire"; Henderson, "James Baldwin"; Abdur-Rahman, "'Simply a Menaced Boy'"; and Stuart, "Finding the Jimmy in James."

13. Late in his life, Baldwin conducted an interview with David Adams Leeming that focused on his relationship to Henry James. Drawing on this interview and comparing *Giovanni's Room* to James's *The Ambassadors*, Christopher Stuart has argued that James and Baldwin shared a universalist belief that our common humanity, and the suffering it inevitably entails, draws us into relation with one another. In Stuart's reading, Baldwin reconceives the forms and themes he drew from *The Ambassadors* in his approach to *Giovanni's Room*, a novel that "argues that the most despicable crime is precisely the failure to recognize that our common humanity transcends social boundaries, such as race, class, and sexual orientation" (Stuart, "Finding the Jimmy in James," 56). Stuart recovers an important part of Baldwin's aesthetic project by emphasizing the limitations of reading Baldwin only through the lens of the African American literary tradition and its legacy of social protest.

14. Caws, *Reading Frames in Modern Fiction*, 3.

15. Baldwin, *Giovanni's Room*, 10.

16. Baldwin, *Giovanni's Room*, 163.

17. Henderson, "James Baldwin," 326.

18. Baldwin, *Giovanni's Room*, 155–57. While David may be rationalizing Giovanni's murder of Guillaume, biographical details suggest readers can trust that some version of this event happened. Baldwin was inspired, in part, by the murder of David Kammerer by the Columbia undergraduate Lucien Carr in Riverside Park in 1944, after Kammerer, a significantly older man, made repeated sexual advances to Carr. After attacking Kammerer with a Boy Scout knife, Carr dropped his body in the Hudson River and eventually confessed to the murder. The trial was a sensational event and closely followed by the media; it was an early instance of the "gay panic defense," and Carr served two years in prison for manslaughter (Lawlor, *Beat Culture*, 168). Baldwin has credited the incident as inspiration for Giovanni's murder of Guillaume (James Baldwin, "The Art of Fiction No. 78," interview by Jordan Elgrably, *Paris Review*, Spring 1984, https://www.theparisreview.org/interviews/2994/the-art-of-fiction-no-78-james-baldwin).

19. Hall et al., *Policing the Crisis*, 50–51.

20. Baldwin, *Giovanni's Room*, 148–49.

21. Baldwin, *Giovanni's Room*, 149.

22. Baldwin, *Giovanni's Room*, 5.

23. Baldwin, *Giovanni's Room*, 166.

24. Baldwin, *Giovanni's Room*, 167.

25. Baldwin, *Giovanni's Room*, 168.

26. Brooks, *Reading for the Plot*, 77.

27. Brooks Peters, "Through a Glass Noir: Thoughts on Giovanni's Room," *Creative Pinellas*, February 11, 2020, https://creativepinellas.org/magazine/through-a-glass-noir-thoughts-on-giovannis-room/.

28. Brooks, *Reading for the Plot*, 71–73.

29. Freeman, "Time Binds, or, Erotohistoriography," 61.

30. Brooks, *Reading for the Plot*, 65.

31. Brooks, *Reading for the Plot*, 65.

32. Baldwin, *Giovanni's Room*, 38.

33. Baldwin, *Giovanni's Room*, 169.

34. Baldwin, *Giovanni's Room*, 10.

35. Sedgwick and Frank, "Shame in the Cybernetic Fold," 114.

36. Bakhtin, *The Dialogic Imagination*, 250.

37. Munt, *Queer Attachments*, 3.

38. Flatley, *Affective Mapping*, 16.

39. Baldwin, *Giovanni's Room*, 42.

40. Stockton, *Beautiful Bottom, Beautiful Shame*, 153.

41. Stockton, *Beautiful Bottom, Beautiful Shame*, 153.

42. Stockton, *Beautiful Bottom, Beautiful Shame*, 153.

43. David Halperin and Valerie Traub's 2009 collection, *Gay Shame*, theorizes the role of shame in queer identity, offering a redemptive reading of shame as foundational to all identity and available as sustenance for a resistant, queer identity. Critiquing the consumerism and homonormativity of "gay pride," the collection, which was developed from a 2005 conference at the University of Michigan, reclaims the "abject materiality" of shame as constitutive of identity (Halberstam, "Shame and White Gay Masculinity," 223). In his critique of the conference, Jack Halberstam calls the embrace of shame a "white gay male" thing (Halberstam, "Shame and White Gay Masculinity," 220) that universalizes identity and elides the distinction of feminist and queer-of-color theories of shame (Halberstam, "Shame and White Gay Masculinity," 220, 225). See Halberstam, "Shame and White Gay Masculinity"; Stockton, *Beautiful Bottom, Beautiful Shame*; Halperin and Traub, *Gay Shame*; Reid-Pharr, "Tearing the Goat's Flesh"; and Love, *Feeling Backward*.

44. Love, *Feeling Backward*, 5.

45. Love, *Feeling Backward*, 18–19.

46. Freeman, "Time Binds, or, Erotohistoriography," 61.

47. Freeman, "Time Binds, or, Erotohistoriography," 66.

48. Bakhtin, *The Dialogic Imagination*, 250.

49. Bakhtin, *The Dialogic Imagination*, 254.

50. Ross, "White Fantasies of Desire," 25.

51. Ross, "White Fantasies of Desire," 25.

52. Flatley, *Affective Mapping*, 7.

53. Sontag, *Regarding the Pain of Others*, 24.

54. Sontag, *Regarding the Pain of Others*, 25.

55. Foster, "Death in America," 51.

56. Foster, "Death in America," 53.

57. Flatley, *Like Andy Warhol*, 198.

58. Capers, "On Andy Warhol's *Electric Chair*," 245.

59. Capers, "On Andy Warhol's *Electric Chair*," 249.

60. Capers, "On Andy Warhol's *Electric Chair*," 260.

61. Capers, "On Andy Warhol's *Electric Chair*," 247–49.

62. Collins, "Warhol's Modern Dance of Death," 50.

63. Flatley, *Like Andy Warhol*, 179.

64. Flatley, *Like Andy Warhol*, 201.

65. Quiñones, "Reading Color," 512.

66. See Flatley, *Like Andy Warhol*; Quiñones, "Reading Color"; and Wagner, "Warhol Paints History, or Race in America."

67. Quiñones, "Reading Color," 530–31.

68. Flatley, *Like Andy Warhol*, 201n55.

69. Sedgwick, "Queer Performativity," 135.

70. Sedgwick, "Queer Performativity," 139.

71. Chuh, *The Difference Aesthetics Makes*, 18.

72. Quiñones, "Reading Color," 512.

73. Andy Warhol, interview by Andrew Sarris, *Show on Shows*, Canadian Broadcasting Corporation, 1965.

74. Jonathan Flatley theorizes the notion of "feeling like" in Warhol's work, arguing that the ethic of "liking" enables audiences to feel "like" those that might be quite different from themselves (Flatley, *Like Andy Warhol*, 4).

75. Campany and Wolukau-Wanambwa, *Indeterminacy*, 37.

76. Campany and Wolukau-Wanambwa, *Indeterminacy*, 37.

77. Campany and Wolukau-Wanambwa, *Indeterminacy*, 39.

78. Michaels, *The Beauty of a Social Problem*, 39.

79. Michaels, *The Beauty of a Social Problem*, 41.

80. Best, *None like Us*, 45–47.


Chapter Two

1. In addition to my review of the show, work by Keegan Cook Finberg, Jane Malcolm, and Austin Allen has sought to reframe Ono as a poet. See Austin Allen, "'My Beautiful Never-Nevers': Yoko Ono's Poetry Revisited," *Los Angeles Review of Books*, April 4, 2022, https://lareviewofbooks.org/article/my-beautiful-never-nevers -yoko-onos-poetry-revisited/; Keegan Cook Finberg, "Assimilating the Arts: On Poetry and Difference in Yoko Ono's *Grapefruit*," *Amodern*, 11, October 2023, https://amodern .net/article/assimilating-the-arts/; Jane Malcolm, "Ono Optics: Toward a Theory of the

Perfectly Unreadable," *Amodern*, 11, October 2023, https://amodern.net/article/ono
-optics/; Anna Ioanes, "Observations on an Event: Yoko Ono: Poetry, Painting, Music,
Objects, Events, and Wish Trees," *ASAP/Review*, February 27, 2020, https://asapjournal
.com/observations-on-an-event-yoko-ono-poetry-painting-music-objects-events
-and-wish-trees-anna-ioanes/; and Claire Voon, "Is Yoko Ono Overlooked as a Poet?"
*Chicago Magazine*, May 6, 2019, https://www.chicagomag.com/Chicago-Magazine
/May-2019/Revisiting-Yoko-Onos-Poetry/.

2. Higgins, "Intermedia," 49.

3. Keegan Cook Finberg, "Assimilating the Arts: On Poetry and Difference in Yoko
Ono's *Grapefruit*," *Amodern*, 11, October 2023, https://amodern.net/article/assimilating
-the-arts/.

4. Seiler, *Midcentury Suspension*, 23.

5. Buck-Morss, "Aesthetics and Anaesthetics," 32–33.

6. Katz, "The Ethic of Expediency," 271.

7. Katz, "The Ethic of Expediency," 260.

8. Katz, "The Ethic of Expediency," 266.

9. This coinage is credited to performance artist Allan Kaprow, who staged such
performance art events and helped to define the term in his 1961 essay "Happenings
in the New York Scene."

10. Seiler, *Midcentury Suspension*, 17.

11. Saint-Amour, "Bombing and the Symptom," 60.

12. Saint-Amour, "Bombing and the Symptom," 59.

13. Saint-Amour, "Bombing and the Symptom," 60.

14. Saint-Amour, "Bombing and the Symptom," 60–61. The future-oriented, subjunctive experience of the nuclear era was, as Jessica Hurley argues, experienced differently based on social location. Though many people experienced "the arrival of
atomic weaponry . . . as an absolute novelty and historical rupture, subaltern writers, thinkers, and activists immediately connected the new technology to existing
forms of historical and structural violence" (Hurley, *Infrastructures of Apocalypse*, 3).
Coexisting with the suspended experience of "a damaging anticipation of disaster"
was ongoing nuclear violence, in the forms of ongoing nuclear testing (Hurley, *Infrastructures of Apocalypse*, 5–6). As Hurley's broader argument about the unrecognized,
ongoing, infrastructural violence of the nuclear era suggests, the suspensive feeling
of the Cold War era captures anticipation of a totalizing event but also reveals the
question whose answer seems continually suspended and unresolved: is this
violence?

15. On suspense, see Caroline Levine, "An Anatomy of Suspense" and *The Serious
Pleasures of Suspense* as well as Vera Tobin, who claims that "The experience of suspense isn't fundamentally about uncertainty, even if it seems like it is" (Tobin, *Elements of Surprise*, 40).

16. Seiler, *Midcentury Suspension*, 27–28.

17. Richards, *The Fury Archives*, 187.

18. Richards, *The Fury Archives*, 187.

19. Richards, *The Fury Archives*, 189.

20. Duberman, *Black Mountain*, 350–51.

21. Fetterman, *John Cage's Theatre Pieces*, 103–4.

22. Kaprow, "Happenings in the New York Scene," 19.

23. Ono, *Grapefruit*, n.p.

24. Cohen, "Ono in Opera," 51–52. The avant-garde composer La Monte Young collaborated with Ono to organize the series, but took credit for it and left her name off the program and other materials, excluding Ono from the very event she had enabled (Cohen, "Ono in Opera," 51).

25. Keegan Cook Finberg, "Assimilating the Arts: On Poetry and Difference in Yoko Ono's *Grapefruit*," *Amodern*, 11, October 2023, https://amodern.net/article/assimilating-the-arts/.

26. Dezeuze, "Origins of the Fluxus Score," 78.

27. Dezeuze, "Origins of the Fluxus Score," 79–80.

28. Kaprow, "Happenings in the New York Scene," 16.

29. Kaprow, "Happenings in the New York Scene," 15.

30. Kaprow, "Happenings in the New York Scene," 16.

31. Bohrer, *Suddenness*, 11.

32. Sontag, "Happenings," 268.

33. Sontag, "Happenings," 265.

34. Sontag, "Happenings," 266.

35. Kaprow, "Happenings in the New York Scene," 19.

36. Brill, *Shock and the Senseless in Dada and Fluxus*, 12.

37. Brill, *Shock and the Senseless in Dada and Fluxus*, 12.

38. Quayson, *Aesthetic Nervousness*, 18. In his reading of disability in contemporary Anglophone literature, Ato Quayson highlights the universal, if ignored, fact of bodily contingency. Writing about how representations of disability contain a trace reminder of universal bodily contingency, Quayson claims that "the causes of impairment can never be fully anticipated or indeed prepared for. Every/body is subject to chance and contingent events." This "sudden recognition of contingency is not solely a philosophical one—in fact, it hardly ever is at the moment of the social encounter itself—but is also and perhaps primarily an emotional and affective one" (Quayson, *Aesthetic Nervousness*, 17). This affective experience can be sustained, stretched across time, in the mode of suspension, where the sudden impact of the incomprehensible and violent act might then wrest a person into an experience of senselessness.

39. Bryan-Wilson, "Remembering Yoko Ono's *Cut Piece*," 101n2.

40. Cohen, "Ono in Opera," 42.

41. Cohen, "Ono in Opera," 43.

42. Cohen, "Ono in Opera," 46.

43. Cohen, "Ono in Opera," 49.

44. Carrigan, "Postcolonial Disaster, Pacific Nuclearization, and Disabling Environments," 256.

45. Xiang, *Tonal Intelligence*, 3–4.

46. Xiang, *Tonal Intelligence*, 4–5.

47. Xiang, *Tonal Intelligence*, 5.

48. Vivian Huang calls Ono's performance in *Cut Piece* "inscrutable," and she theorizes inscrutability in relationship to discourses of hospitality, parasitism, gender, and

racialization. Huang's "theory of inscrutability does not foreclose intimacy but rather gestures to the racialized and gendered systems of knowledge used to cognize sociality as such" (Huang, *Surface Relations*, 62). As we will see, inscrutability works in *Cut Piece* to foster some kinds of intimacy while foreclosing forms of knowledge, unsettling the racial and gender dynamics audience members would likely bring to their understanding of the performance event.

49. Xiang, *Tonal Intelligence*, 6.

50. Vimalassery, Pegues, and Goldstein, "Introduction," n.p.

51. Vimalassery, Pegues, and Goldstein, "Introduction," n.p.

52. Vimalassery, Pegues, and Goldstein, "Introduction," n.p.

53. Fisher, "Tangible Acts," 170.

54. Qtd. in Concannon, "Yoko Ono's *Cut Piece*," 82. In Simon and Schuster's 1970 republication of *Grapefruit*, the score reads simply: "Cut." It is followed by a description of Ono's performances, which also mentions that "the performer . . . does not have to be a woman" (Ono, *Grapefruit*, n.p.).

55. Bryan-Wilson, "Remembering Yoko Ono's *Cut Piece*," 106.

56. Kaprow, "Happenings in the New York Scene," 20.

57. Ono, Maysles, and Maysles. *Cut Piece*.

58. Ono, Maysles, and Maysles. *Cut Piece*.

59. Halberstam, *The Queer Art of Failure*, 137.

60. Ono, Maysles, and Maysles. *Cut Piece*.

61. Fisher, "Tangible Acts," 169.

62. Fisher, "Tangible Acts," 170.

63. Bryan-Wilson, "Remembering Yoko Ono's *Cut Piece*," 111.

64. Hendricks, qtd. in Concannon, "Yoko Ono's *Cut Piece*," 91.

65. Huang, *Surface Relations*, 55.

66. Huang, *Surface Relations*, 66.

67. Bryan-Wilson, "Remembering Yoko Ono's *Cut Piece*," 103.

68. Huang, *Surface Relations*, 53.

69. Huang, *Surface Relations*, 63.

70. Qtd. in Huang, *Surface Relations*, 65.

71. Huang, *Surface Relations*, 65.

72. Sontag, "Happenings," 266.

73. Levine, *The Serious Pleasures of Suspense*, 3.

74. Levine, *The Serious Pleasures of Suspense*, 4.

75. Levine, "An Anatomy of Suspense," 197.

76. Austin Allen, "'My Beautiful Never-Nevers': Yoko Ono's Poetry Revisited," *Los Angeles Review of Books*, April 4, 2022, https://lareviewofbooks.org/article/my-beautiful-never-nevers-yoko-onos-poetry-revisited/.

77. Matheson, "This Lousy Little Book," 237.

78. Vonnegut, *Slaughterhouse-Five*, 29.

79. Vonnegut, *Slaughterhouse-Five*, 2, 27, 93.

80. Vonnegut, *Slaughterhouse-Five*, 34.

81. Matheson, "This Lousy Little Book," 233.

82. These themes are explored in the extensive body of secondary literature on the novel. The novel's approach to meaningless suffering is addressed frequently in Harold Bloom's collection *Kurt Vonnegut's Slaughterhouse-Five*. See also Currie, *About Time*; Cole, *At the Violet Hour*; Gavins, *Reading the Absurd*; Gibbs, *Contemporary American Trauma Narratives*.

83. Concannon, "Not For Sale," 78.


Chapter Three

1. "Collage: Revolution from Refuse," *Time*, June 4, 1965; Flannery O'Connor Papers, Box 35, Folder 16, Stuart A. Rose Manuscript, Archives, and Rare Book Library, Emory University.

2. "The Medium: Taking Waste Out of the Wasteland," *Time*, May 30, 1969; Flannery O'Connor Papers, Box 35, Folder 16, Stuart A. Rose Manuscript, Archives, and Rare Book Library, Emory University.

3. Fodor, "Marketing Flannery O'Connor," 33.

4. Yaeger, "Flannery O'Connor and the Aesthetics of Torture," 200.

5. Fodor, "Marketing Flannery O'Connor," 33.

6. Fodor, "Marketing Flannery O'Connor," 34.

7. O'Donnell, *Radical Ambivalence*, 68–69. Other work exploring how O'Connor's letters, and the beliefs articulated therein, should shape reception of her fiction include Elie, *The Life You Save May Be Your Own*, Monica Carol Miller's introduction to the collected letters of O'Connor written while at the University of Iowa, *Dear Regina*, and Benjamin Mangrum's article "Flannery O'Connor, the Phenomenology of Race, and the Institutions of Irony."

8. James Goodwin names O'Connor one of the key figures of the twentieth-century American grotesque; Dieter Meindl discusses O'Connor under the rubric of the modernist grotesque, and both Anthony Di Renzo and Marshall Bruce Gentry devote monographs to O'Connor's relationship to the grotesque. See Goodwin, *Modern American Grotesque*; Meindl, *American Fiction and the Metaphysics of the Grotesque*; Gentry, *Flannery O'Connor's Religion of the Grotesque*; Di Renzo, *American Gargoyles*.

9. Rune Graulund, "Grotesque," in *Oxford Research Encyclopedia of Literature*, edited by John Frow, 2019, https://doi.org/10.1093/acrefore/9780190201098.013.1067.

10. Connelly, *Modern Art and the Grotesque*, 1.

11. Connelly, *Modern Art and the Grotesque*, 4.

12. Goodwin, *Modern American Grotesque*, 2.

13. Belletto, *No Accident, Comrade*, 26.

14. James, *Constraining Chance*, 10.

15. James, *Constraining Chance*, 192.

16. Wylot, *Reading Contingency*, 2.

17. On contingency and accidents, see Hamilton, *Accident*; Malabou, *The Ontology of the Accident*; Varsava, *Contingent Meanings*; and Virilio, *The Original Accident*.

18. Wylot, *Reading Contingency*, 3.

19. Connelly, *Modern Art and the Grotesque*, 4.

20. Theories of the grotesque appear in literary criticism as early as Ruskin, *The Stones of Venice*, vol. III. Classic studies on the grotesque include Harpham, *On the Grotesque*; Bakhtin, *Rabelais and His World*; Russo, *The Female Grotesque*; Thomson, *The Grotesque*; and Kayser, *The Grotesque in Art and Literature*.

21. Goodwin, *Modern American Grotesque*, 2.

22. Goodwin, *Modern American Grotesque*, 2.

23. Levine, *Forms*, 4.

24. Goodwin, *Modern American Grotesque*, 2.

25. O'Connor, "Some Aspects of the Grotesque in Southern Fiction," 40.

26. Harpham, *On the Grotesque*, 178.

27. O'Connor, "Some Aspects of the Grotesque in Southern Fiction," 43.

28. O'Connor, "Some Aspects of the Grotesque in Southern Fiction," 43.

29. Letter to Cecil Dawkins, in O'Connor, *Habit of Being*, 486.

30. McGurl, "Understanding Iowa," 531.

31. McGurl, "Understanding Iowa," 532.

32. Gerald, *Flannery O'Connor*, 101.

33. Gerald, *Flannery O'Connor*, 105.

34. Sketchbook, undated, Box 29, Folder 2, Flannery O'Connor Papers, Stuart A. Rose Manuscript, Archives, and Rare Book Library, Emory University.

35. Gerald, *Flannery O'Connor*, 116.

36. Wanzo, *The Content of Our Caricature*, 4.

37. Gerald, *Flannery O'Connor*, 48.

38. Clark, *American Graphic*, 49.

39. Clark, *American Graphic*, 54.

40. French, *Maryat Lee's EcoTheater*, 44.

41. French, *Maryat Lee's EcoTheater*, 44.

42. O'Donnell, *Radical Ambivalence*, 53–54.

43. O'Connor, *Habit of Being*, 329.

44. O'Donnell, *Radical Ambivalence*, 50.

45. Harris, "'The Pleasant Lady' in Flannery O'Connor's 'Revelation,'" 31.

46. O'Connor, *Habit of Being*, 200–201.

47. Brecht, "The Street Scene," 128.

48. French, *Maryat Lee's EcoTheater*, 26.

49. French, *Maryat Lee's EcoTheater*, 22–23.

50. Goodwin, *Modern American Grotesque*, 119.

51. Goodwin, *Modern American Grotesque*, 125.

52. Goodwin, *Modern American Grotesque*, 126–27.

53. Goodwin, *Modern American Grotesque*, 130.

54. Lee, *Four Men and a Monster*, 33.

55. Lee, *Four Men and a Monster*, 22.

56. Lee, *Four Men and a Monster*, 22.

57. Katz, "Flannery O'Connor's Rage of Vision," 54.

58. O'Connor, "On Her Own Work," 112.

59. Yaeger, "Flannery O'Connor and the Aesthetics of Torture," 184.

60. Yaeger, "Flannery O'Connor and the Aesthetics of Torture," 187.

61. Yaeger, "Flannery O'Connor and the Aesthetics of Torture," 189–90.

62. McGurl, "Understanding Iowa," 14.

63. O'Connor, "Some Aspects of the Grotesque in Southern Fiction," 42.

64. O'Connor, *The Complete Stories*, 119.

65. O'Connor, *The Complete Stories*, 125.

66. O'Connor, *The Complete Stories*, 125.

67. Hamilton, *Accident*, 16.

68. Hamilton, *Accident*, 21.

69. O'Connor, *The Complete Stories*, 132.

70. O'Connor, *The Complete Stories*, 133.

71. O'Connor, *The Complete Stories*, 133.

72. O'Connor, *The Complete Stories*, 132.

73. As Benjamin Mangrum has argued, "The Artificial Nigger," O'Connor's sixth story in *A Good Man Is Hard to Find* and one of her favorite stories, revolves around its similarly ambiguous climax. When the two protagonists, Nelson and Mr. Head, share a redemptive moment triggered by the presence of a racist lawn statue, the spiritual redemption invoked is also undercut by the racist symbolic violence of the scene. Mangrum calls the climactic encounter with the lawn figure "decisively metafictional, for it is the representational fiction of 'the plaster figure of a Negro' that reconciles Head and Nelson, in a moment framed as a scene of reading" (Mangrum, "Flannery O'Connor, the Phenomenology of Race, and the Institutions of Irony," 255–56). In this way, O'Connor's ironizing extends to the possibilities of fiction itself, raising the notion that literature's redemptive or progressive power is at best "ambivalent" (Mangrum, "Flannery O'Connor, the Phenomenology of Race, and the Institutions of Irony," 256). This ambiguity is heightened through O'Connor's use of irony—a structure of the story that can only render the moment of redemption at its end suspect and unresolvable. O'Connor's use of ironic narrative "*qualifies*—raises evaluative questions about—the narrative and existential contexts of the story's final episode" (Mangrum, "Flannery O'Connor, the Phenomenology of Race, and the Institutions of Irony," 251).

74. Quayson, *Aesthetic Nervousness*, 17.

75. Quayson, *Aesthetic Nervousness*, 17.

76. Quayson, *Aesthetic Nervousness*, 52.

77. Quayson, *Aesthetic Nervousness*, 49.

78. O'Connor, *The Complete Stories*, 267.

79. Libow, "Prosthesis Repurposed," 386.

80. Libow, "Prosthesis Repurposed," 389.

81. Libow, "Prosthesis Repurposed," 390.

82. Libow, "Prosthesis Repurposed," 390.

83. Bosco, "Consenting to Love," 287.

84. O'Connor, *The Complete Stories*, 291.

85. O'Connor, *The Complete Stories*, 289–90.

86. McGurl, "Understanding Iowa," 15.

87. Garland-Thomson, *Extraordinary Bodies*, xi.

88. Garland-Thomson, *Extraordinary Bodies*, 6–7.

89. Garland-Thomson, *Extraordinary Bodies*, 11.

90. Garland-Thomson, *Extraordinary Bodies*, 11.

91. Mitchell and Snyder, *Narrative Prosthesis*, 47.

92. Garland-Thomson, *Extraordinary Bodies*, 12.

93. O'Connor, *The Complete Stories*, 283.

94. O'Connor, *The Complete Stories*, 275.

95. O'Connor, *The Complete Stories*, 274.

96. Adams, *Sideshow U.S.A.*, 128.

97. Adams, *Sideshow U.S.A.*, 129.

98. Adams, *Sideshow U.S.A.*, 129.

99. Nelson, *Tough Enough*, 134.

100. Nelson, *Tough Enough*, 141.

101. Nelson, *Tough Enough*, 141.

102. Nelson, *Tough Enough*, 142.

103. Di Renzo, *American Gargoyles*, 9.

104. Mintz, *Hurt and Pain*, 4.

105. Siebers, *Disability Aesthetics*, 3.

106. Siebers, *Disability Aesthetics*, 34–36.

107. Nelson, *Tough Enough*, 126.


## Chapter Four

1. Françoise Mouly, "Kara Walker's Toni Morrison," *New Yorker*, August 8, 2019, https://www.newyorker.com/culture/cover-story/cover-story-2019-08-19.

2. Françoise Mouly, "Kara Walker's Toni Morrison," *New Yorker*, August 8, 2019, https://www.newyorker.com/culture/cover-story/cover-story-2019-08-19.

3. Brinkema, *The Forms of the Affects*, 115.

4. Menninghaus, *Disgust*, 103.

5. Vigarello, *The Silhouette*, 16.

6. Vigarello, *The Silhouette*, 21.

7. Vigarello, *The Silhouette*, 18.

8. Vigarello, *The Silhouette*, 30.

9. English, *How to See a Work of Art in Total Darkness*, 92.

10. For a further examination of Sarah Baartman, violence, and visual culture, see Gilman, "Black Bodies, White Bodies"; Hobson, *Venus in the Dark*; and Brown, *The Black Female Body in American Literature and Art*. For a discussion of lynching photography, see Apel and Smith, *Lynching Photographs*; Apel, *Imagery of Lynching*; Wood, *Lynching and Spectacle*; Carbonell, "The Afterlife of Lynching"; and Park, "Lynching and Antilynching."

11. Wiegman, "The Anatomy of Lynching," 446. Also see Castronovo, "Beauty along the Color Line"; Carby, "'On the Threshold of Woman's Era'"; and Rushdy, "Exquisite Corpse."

12. Eatman, *Ecologies of Harm*, 18.

13. Eatman, *Ecologies of Harm*, 19.

14. Eatman, *Ecologies of Harm*, 28.

15. Alexander, "Can You Be Black and Look at This?," 78.

16. Goldsby, "The High and Low Tech of It," 254–55.

17. Goldsby, "The High and Low Tech of It," 259.

18. Rushdy, "Exquisite Corpse," 72–73.

19. Douglas, qtd. in Miller, *The Anatomy of Disgust*, 44. Along these lines, Sandy Alexandre invokes Mary Douglas to theorize the ways Till himself was a form of "matter out of place" as an urbane Chicagoan in Money, Mississippi. His lynching was, among other things, a form of patrolling imaginary boundaries between the urban North and the rural South (Alexandre, *The Properties of Violence*, 171).

20. Claudia Rankine, "'The Condition of Black Life Is One of Mourning,'" *New York Times*, June 22, 2015, https://www.nytimes.com/2015/06/22/magazine/the-condition -of-black-life-is-one-of-mourning.html.

21. Claudia Rankine, "'The Condition of Black Life Is One of Mourning,'" *New York Times*, June 22, 2015, https://www.nytimes.com/2015/06/22/magazine/the-condition -of-black-life-is-one-of-mourning.html.

22. See, in particular, Mirzoeff, *The Right to Look*; Sharpe, *Monstrous Intimacies*; Mitchell, *Seeing Through Race*; and Smith, "Guest Editor's Introduction."

23. Fleetwood, *Troubling Vision*.

24. Kristeva, *Powers of Horror*, 1–2.

25. Hartman, *Scenes of Subjection*, 20.

26. Hilton Als, "The Shadow Act," *New Yorker*, October 8, 2007, https://www .newyorker.com/magazine/2007/10/08/the-shadow-act.

27. Shaw, *Seeing the Unspeakable*, 20–21.

28. Shaw, *Seeing the Unspeakable*, 24.

29. Shaw, *Seeing the Unspeakable*, 25.

30. I am grateful to Laura Goldblatt for this insight.

31. English, *How to See a Work of Art in Total Darkness*, 75.

32. Bersani and Dutoit, "The Forms of Violence," 19.

33. Harper, *Abstractionist Aesthetics*, 24.

34. Harper, *Abstractionist Aesthetics*, 24–27.

35. This dynamic reemerged forcefully in Walker's 2014 installation at the Domino Sugar Factory, when patrons were encouraged to post images of the exhibit to social media sites using the hashtag #karawalkerdomino. A Google image search of this hashtag will reveal offensive poses and captions that symbolically perform the very racial and sexual violence that the work highlights and critiques.

36. English, *How to See a Work of Art in Total Darkness*, 112.

37. Hartman, *Scenes of Subjection*, 3.

38. Like Hartman, Christina Sharpe insists that repeating the horror of Black violation "does not make the violence of everyday black subjection undeniable" and "does not confirm or confer humanity on the suffering black body" (Sharpe, *Monstrous Intimacies*, 2).

39. As a form of anti-aesthetic for figures ranging from Kant to Bataille, disgust marks the limit of aesthetic engagement, "the rejected other," what is "definitionally, structurally, necessarily excluded" from aesthetic engagement (Brinkema, *The Forms of the Affects*, 123–24). Following Winfried Menninghaus, Eugenie Brinkema frames

disgust as central to the formation of aesthetics as a discipline, which was "concerned primarily with the conditions of possibility for aesthetic judgment and the radical exclusion or omission at the center of that system" (Brinkema, *The Forms of the Affects*, 124).

40. The relationship between violence, the silhouette, and disgust is further emphasized by the proliferation of feces and aspects of anality in Walker's silhouettes and *Sula*. Yasmil Raymond identifies "feces and semen" as a key motif in Walker's installations (Raymond, "Maladies of Power," 361), echoing Kathryn Bond Stockton's argument that *Sula* reworks Freudian associations between excrement and money by embracing forms of abjection in "the Bottom" (Stockton, "Heaven's Bottom," 89–90).

41. Brinkema, *The Forms of the Affects*, 139–41.

42. Brinkema, *The Forms of the Affects*, 141.

43. Keizer, "Gone Astray in the Flesh," 1671.

44. Along these lines, Caroline Levine defines form broadly to characterize "all shapes and configurations, all ordering principles, all patterns of repetition and difference" (Levine, *Forms*, 3). When I contend that any depiction of violence is in some way an aesthetic construct, I echo Levine's argument by claiming that a depiction must have a form and, additionally, that its affective force—its effect on an audience—is mediated through an aesthetic encounter. In a complementary argument, drawing on Deleuze's aesthetic theory, renée c. hoogland reminds us that affect and sensation have long been central to aesthetic theory, that "aesthetics [is], first, a question of feeling" (hoogland, *A Violent Embrace*, 2).

45. Kara Walker, "In Conversation: Kara Walker and Hamza Walker," interview by Hamza Walker, September 27, 2021, https://towardcommoncause.org/calendar/in -conversation-kara-walker-and-hamza-walker/.

46. Walker, qtd. in Brown, *The Black Female Body in American Literature and Art*, 63.

47. See Menninghaus, *Disgust*; Ngai, *Ugly Feelings*; and Korsmeyer, *Savoring Disgust*.

48. Carolyn Korsmeyer distinguishes between "core" disgust, a visceral reaction "to foul and contaminated objects in close proximity" and "moral" disgust, or a reaction to "persons or behaviors that transgress social norms" (Korsmeyer, *Savoring Disgust*, 5). For Korsmeyer, no inherent connection exists between core and moral disgust, though moral outrage may be felt as a visceral sense of revulsion.

49. Pindell, qtd. in Hilton Als, "The Shadow Act," *New Yorker*, October 8, 2007, https://www.newyorker.com/magazine/2007/10/08/the-shadow-act.

50. As Martin Berger has demonstrated, after 1945 in the United States, such forms of violent desire were captured in photographs that circulated widely in the civil rights era, prompting a wide range of emotional and political responses (Berger, *Seeing through Race*, 52). Along these lines, see Abel, "Skin, Flesh, and the Affective Wrinkles of Civil Rights Photography"; and Torres, *Black, White, and in Color*.

51. Tang, "Postmodern Repetitions," 152.

52. Keizer, "Gone Astray in the Flesh," 1670.

53. Keizer, "Gone Astray in the Flesh," 1666.

54. This is Stephen Best's term for a methodological approach to the archives of transatlantic slavery that imagines scholarship as "a kind of crime scene investigation in which the forensic imagination is directed toward the recovery of a 'we' at the

point of 'our' violent origin. It participates in a broader intellectual matrix within black studies that assumes slavery as the point of origin of this we" (Best, *None like Us*, 21). Best advocates for a turn away from the impossible recovery project of melancholy historicism toward an embrace of that very impossibility, and looks toward contemporary visual art as a model for "an *aesthetics of the intransmissible*" that envisions modes of freedom through detachment from demands for an "authentic" Black experience rooted in historical continuity (Best, *None like Us*, 22).

55. McDowell, "'The Self and the Other,'" 77–99.

56. Namwali Serpell uses the term "uncertainty" to define the ways literary form can produce an "agonistic, unsettling experience" that unfolds as a reader engages with fiction "over time" (Serpell, *Seven Modes of Uncertainty*, 9). One of Serpell's seven "modes" of uncertainty is "adjacency," in which a novel's characters provide multiple, competing, and unresolved viewpoints on "key images, characters, and events" as a way of "troubl[ing] the ontological status of persons and events" (Serpell, *Seven Modes of Uncertainty*, 127). Serpell defines adjacency through an analysis of Morrison's *Beloved*, claiming that the novel's "structure of multiplicity affords *adjacency*, a tenuous, momentary contiguity that offers a countermodel to the dysfunctional communities its characters experience in its storyline" (Serpell, *Seven Modes of Uncertainty*, 132). In *Sula*, I argue, Morrison's form of uncertainty is characterized by the silhouette.

57. Hartman, *Scenes of Subjection*, 22.

58. Morrison, *Playing in the Dark*, xi.

59. Abel, "Black Writing, White Reading," 477.

60. Morrison, "Recitatif," 175.

61. Morrison, "Recitatif," 162.

62. Morrison, "Recitatif," 169.

63. Morrison, "Recitatif," 172.

64. Morrison, "Recitatif," 162.

65. Morrison, "Recitatif," 161.

66. Morrison, *Sula*, 119.

67. Morrison, *Sula*, 60–61.

68. Morrison, *Sula*, 64.

69. Morrison, *Sula*, 64.

70. Jackson, "A 'Headless Display,'" 374–75. This is hardly the only place Morrison addresses lynching iconography in her work. Her little-known play, *Dreaming Emmett*, has Emmett Till return to the scene of his lynching and confront the murderers. The murder is mentioned in *Song of Solomon*, and *Beloved* takes up lynching through tree imagery (Alexandre, *The Properties of Violence*, 123).

71. Morrison, *Sula*, 63.

72. Morrison, *Sula*, 63–64.

73. Korsmeyer, *Savoring Disgust*, 4–5.

74. Moten, *In the Break*, 198.

75. Moten, *In the Break*, 201.

76. This awareness of a disgust response held in abeyance echoes the Kantian sublime, characterized as the ability to transcend being overcome by unsettling forms of

magnitude through reason (Kant, *Critique of Judgment*, 97). Like the Kantian sublime, the silhouette enables an aesthetic interest in something horrific. However, it also provokes a hermeneutic impasse that undermines reason.

77. Tang, "Postmodern Repetitions," 152.

78. Serpell, *Seven Modes of Uncertainty*, 9.

79. Wu, "Doing Things with Ethics," 782.

80. Wu, "Doing Things with Ethics," 782. Also see Nissen, "Form Matters."

81. Wu, "Doing Things with Ethics," 787.

82. Novak, "'Circles and Circles of Sorrow,'" 187.

83. Menninghaus, *Disgust*, 11.

84. Menninghaus, *Disgust*, 15.

85. Ngai, *Ugly Feelings*, 335.

86. Morrison, *Sula*, 112.

87. Morrison, *Sula*, 113.

88. Morrison, *Sula*, 113.

89. Tomkins, "What Are Affects?," 34.

90. Hemmings, "Invoking Affect," 561.

91. Lorde, *Sister Outsider*, 147.

92. Hemmings, "Invoking Affect," 561.

93. Miller, *The Anatomy of Disgust*, 137.

94. Johnson, "'Aesthetic' and 'Rapport' in Toni Morrison's *Sula*," 8.

95. Johnson, "'Aesthetic' and 'Rapport' in Toni Morrison's *Sula*," 9.

96. Morrison, *Sula*, 75.

97. Morrison, *Sula*, 76.

98. Morrison, *Sula*, 77.

99. Morrison, *Sula*, 78, my emphasis.

100. Morrison, *Sula*, 76.

101. Brinkema, *The Forms of the Affects*, 129.

102. Baker, "When Lindbergh Sleeps with Bessie Smith," 85.

103. Johnson, "'Aesthetic' and 'Rapport' in Toni Morrison's *Sula*," 10.

104. Wood, *Lynching and Spectacle*, 75. See also Goldsby, *A Spectacular Secret*; and Eatman, *Ecologies of Harm*.

105. Toni Morrison, interview by Charlie Rose, *Charlie Rose*, January 19, 1998. https://charlierose.com/videos/17664.

106. Alexandre, *The Properties of Violence*, 28.

107. Alexandre, *The Properties of Violence*, 28.

108. Alexandre, *The Properties of Violence*, 27.

109. Alexandre, *The Properties of Violence*, 27.

110. Alexandre, *The Properties of Violence*, 34.

111. As Jacqueline Goldsby argues, lynching has been both spectacular and "a cultural secret" throughout its history in the US (Goldsby, *A Spectacular Secret*, 27).

112. I echo Stephen Best and Sharon Marcus's description of "surface reading" as a way to "let ghosts be ghosts, instead of saying what they are ghosts *of*" (Best and Marcus, "Surface Reading," 13).

Chapter Five

1. Nelson, *Jane*, 223.

2. Nelson, *Jane*, 125.

3. Seltzer, *Serial Killers*, 2.

4. Seltzer, *Serial Killers*, 7.

5. Seltzer, *Serial Killers*, 5.

6. Seltzer, *Serial Killers*, 22.

7. Susan Brownmiller's *Against Our Will* is the foundational text of this intervention. As Angela Davis and Estelle Friedman have argued, beliefs about rape are bound up in ideologies of race, with the dominant narrative about rape imagining a pure and virtuous white woman attacked by a Black man; this ideological formation was also an operative justification for the widespread lynching that took place in America in the postbellum era and through the 1930s. In her overview of the rhetoric of rape in American literary history, Sabine Sielke argues that "American rape narratives are over determined by a distinct history of racial conflict" (Sielke, *Reading Rape*, 2) shaped by the foundation of plantation slavery, which maintained itself in part through systemic rape committed by white plantation owners against enslaved women, whose children would also be born into slavery (Sielke, *Reading Rape*, 184). In her reading of nineteenth-century American "seduction narratives," Sielke argues that contemporary feminist discourses of rape and consent often reproduce assumptions about gender and power that infantilize women and frame authentic consent as always already impossible because they define sexuality as "the violation of women by men" (Sielke, *Reading Rape*, 29).

8. Edgar Allan Poe, "The Philosophy of Composition," *Poetry Foundation*, October 11, 2009, https://www.poetryfoundation.org/articles/69390/the-philosophy-of -composition.

9. Nelson, *Jane*, 215.

10. Alcoff, "Sexual Violations and the Question of Experience," 445.

11. Ulmer, "The Object of Post-Criticism," 94.

12. Perloff, *The Futurist Moment*, 51.

13. Cran, *Collage in Twentieth-Century Art, Literature, and Culture*, 9.

14. Burroughs and Gysin, *The Third Mind*, 34.

15. Qtd. in Kraus, *After Kathy Acker*, 65.

16. Higgins, *Collage and Literature*, 24.

17. Cran, *Collage in Twentieth-Century Art, Literature, and Culture*, 7–15.

18. Cran, *Collage in Twentieth-Century Art, Literature, and Culture*, 28–29.

19. Cran, *Collage in Twentieth-Century Art, Literature, and Culture*, 30.

20. McLeod and Kuenzli, "I Collage, Therefore I Am," 2–3.

21. McLeod and Kuenzli, "I Collage, Therefore I Am," 10–11.

22. Sweet, "Where's the Booty?," 31.

23. I borrow this term from Sondra Bacharach, who uses it to describe the dynamics of consent in street art. Like street art, collage is a form that relies on an aconsensual dynamic for its political and aesthetic force (Bacharach, "Street Art and Consent," 486). Street artists do not ask for consent to paint on others' property, and the

assumption that consent would not be granted plays a key role in the artwork's subversive, ephemeral, and critical style. The aconsensual relationship between artist and property owner extends to the relationship between artwork and viewer as well. Because street art appears in public spaces, its audiences are rarely seeking out an art experience when they encounter a work. In contrast to the experience of going to an art gallery or deciding to open a book, the audience for street art is often simply confronted with the work.

24. Indeed, Harding claims that greater critical attention to feminist collage practices would rewrite the history of the avant-garde *tout court* (Harding, *Cutting Performances*, 7). Even as its most visible practitioners demonstrated thoroughgoing misogyny, the classical avant-garde was always preoccupied with gender, or rather, with a guiding language that takes "man" and "woman" as structuring metaphors. Modernism was marked by its exploration of the category "woman" (Jardine, qtd. Suleiman, *Subversive Intent*, 13). Whether that exploration took the shape of the Futurist celebration of masculine aggression and "contempt for woman," or of the Surrealists' abiding interest in the female body, the "putting into discourse of 'woman'" was a structuring interest of modernist aesthetic practice (Jardine, qtd. in Suleiman, *Subversive Intent*, 13). While the classical European avant-garde had a distinctly masculine cast, it would be incorrect to suggest that women were simply excised from avant-garde formations. Female avant-garde artists such as Mina Loy and Valentine de Saint-Point drafted their own manifestoes in part to respond to the misogyny of many avant-garde artists (Lyon, *Manifestoes*, 90). Thus, the later feminist avant-garde formation that took shape in the United States does not merely provide an antidote to the sexism of earlier avant-garde formations. Indeed, the feminist avant-garde's preoccupation with the structural violence that maintains gender inequality can be seen as a point of continuity, rather than rupture, between earlier and later avant-garde formations.

25. Harding, *Cutting Performances*, 23.

26. Richards, *The Fury Archives*, 42.

27. Harding, *Cutting Performances*, 29.

28. Kathy Acker, "Dummy for Blood and Guts," n.d., Kathy Acker Papers, Box 4, Folder 2, David M. Rubenstein Rare Book and Manuscript Library, Duke University.

29. Colby, *Kathy Acker*, 70, 77–78.

30. Colby, *Kathy Acker*, 80.

31. Kraus, *After Kathy Acker*, 147.

32. Acker, *Blood and Guts in High School*, 129.

33. As MacKinnon has put it, "the appearance of choice or consent [in pornography], with their attribution to inherent nature, are crucial in concealing the reality of force. Love of violation, variously termed female masochism and consent, comes to define female sexuality, legitimizing this political system [of patriarchal oppression of women and the naturalization of rape] by concealing the force on which it is based" (MacKinnon, *Toward a Feminist Theory of the State*, 141).

34. Clune, "Blood Money," 500.

35. Rubin, "Blood Under the Bridge," 29.

36. Felski, "Redescriptions of Female Masochism," 127.

37. Freeman, *Time Binds*, 142.

38. Foucault, "Sex, Power, and the Politics of Identity," 165.

39. Felski, "Redescriptions of Female Masochism," 134.

40. MacKinnon, *Toward a Feminist Theory of the State*, 175.

41. Russell and Griffin, "On Pornography," 12.

42. Russell and Griffin, "On Pornography," 13.

43. Kipnis, *Bound and Gagged*, 140.

44. Wark, *Philosophy for Spiders*, 156.

45. Berry, *Women's Experimental Writing*, 5.

46. Colby, *Kathy Acker*, 14.

47. Colby, *Kathy Acker*, 101.

48. This is Sianne Ngai's term for a "concatenation of boredom and astonishment—a bringing together of what 'dulls' and what 'irritates' or agitates; of sharp, sudden excitation and prolonged desensitization, exhaustion, or fatigue" (Ngai, *Ugly Feelings*, 271). Acker's collage practice often removes grammatical or syntactical elements that help readers make meaning from her text, but she also repeats acts of violence in such a way as to test readers' ability to continue to be shocked by such images, simultaneously "forc[ing] the reader to go on in spite of its equal enticement to readers [to] give up" (Ngai, *Ugly Feelings*, 272).

49. Colby also highlights critical tendency to overlook the specific formal features of Acker's work that provoke a violent experience (Colby, *Kathy Acker*, 3).

50. Milletti, "Violent Acts, Volatile Words," 353.

51. Acker, *Blood and Guts in High School*, 19.

52. Kathy Acker, "Dummy for Blood and Guts," n.d., Kathy Acker Papers, Box 4, Folder 2. David M. Rubenstein Rare Book and Manuscript Library, Duke University.

53. Acker, *Blood and Guts in High School*, 137.

54. Wark, *Philosophy for Spiders*, 141, 150.

55. Milks, "Janey and Genet in Tangier," 99.

56. Barthes and Duisit, "An Introduction to the Structural Analysis of Narrative," 244–45.

57. Culler, qtd. in Milletti, "Violent Acts, Volatile Words," 359.

58. Felski, *Uses of Literature*, 113.

59. Felski, *Uses of Literature*, 110.

60. Felski, *Uses of Literature*, 113.

61. Cvetkovich, *An Archive of Feelings*, 4.

62. Littau, *Theories of Reading*, 2.

63. Cvetkovich, *An Archive of Feelings*, 51.

64. For a further elaboration of these ideas, see Greenblatt and Valens, *Querying Consent*.

65. Alcoff, "Sexual Violations and the Question of Experience," 447.

66. Alcoff, "Sexual Violations and the Question of Experience," 448.

67. Alcoff, "Sexual Violations and the Question of Experience," 448.

68. Marcus, *Girls to the Front*, 32.

69. Stosuy, *Up Is Up, but So Is Down*, 26.

70. Piepmeier, *Girl Zines*, 18.

71. Piepmeier, *Girl Zines*, 79.

72. Kathleen Hanna, *The Most Beautiful Girl Is a Dead Girl*, 1992, Box 11, Folder 1, ms. 271, Kathleen Hanna Papers, Fales Library and Special Collections, New York University Libraries. I thank Lisa Darms for drawing my attention to this zine.

73. Marcus, "Fighting Bodies, Fighting Words," 396.

74. Marcus, "Fighting Bodies, Fighting Words," 386.

75. Marcus, "Fighting Bodies, Fighting Words," 387.

76. Marcus, "Fighting Bodies, Fighting Words," 400.

77. Marcus, "Fighting Bodies, Fighting Words," 395.

78. Marcus, "Fighting Bodies, Fighting Words," 392.

79. Marcus, "Fighting Bodies, Fighting Words," 395.

80. Kathleen Hanna, *My Life with Evan Dando, Popstar*, Box 2, Folder 7, mss. 271, Kathleen Hanna Papers, Fales Library and Special Collections, New York University. In Darms, *The Riot Grrrl Collection*, 201.

81. Kathleen Hanna, *My Life with Evan Dando, Popstar*, Box 2, Folder 7, mss. 271, Kathleen Hanna Papers, Fales Library and Special Collections, New York University. In Darms, *The Riot Grrrl Collection*, 208.

82. Kathleen Hanna, *My Life with Evan Dando, Popstar*, Box 2, Folder 7, mss. 271, Kathleen Hanna Papers, Fales Library and Special Collections, New York University. In Darms, *The Riot Grrrl Collection*, 201, 214.

83. Marcus, "Fighting Bodies, Fighting Words," 392.

84. Qtd. in Darms, *The Riot Grrrl Collection*, 170.

85. Kathleen Hanna, "Q&A: Kathleen Hanna on Love, Illness, and the Life-Affirming Joy of Punk Rock," interview by Matt Diehl, *T: The New York Times Style Magazine*, November 20, 2013, http://tmagazine.blogs.nytimes.com/2013/11/20/q-a-kathleen-hanna-on-love-illness-and-the-life-affirming-joy-of-punk-rock/?_r=0.

86. Qtd. in Darms, *The Riot Grrrl Collection*, 186.

87. Hanna herself has emphasized the pleasure in danger that riot grrrl culture enabled. Of performing at punk shows, she says: "I felt that in Bikini Kill—we walked into these spaces that were *so* male, and where the promoters treated us like garbage and a lot of the audience treated us like garbage, but the girls *took over*, and all of a sudden this really horrible male space became a place where women were welcome. To watch a room change like that, and to still have the fear that those front two rows of girls were going to get the shit kicked out of them, or that we were going to get the shit kicked out of us, but then seeing the solidarity of the girls in the front row singing the lyrics—I do miss that excitement and fear, that feeling that *anything* could happen" (Kathleen Hanna, "This Is My Thing: An Interview with Kathleen Hanna," interview by Lena Singer, *Rookie*, September 16, 2013, http://www.rookiemag.com/2013/09/kathleen-hanna-interview/).

88. For an excellent exploration of white women's capacity for direct, physical violence as depicted in narratives of the circum-Atlantic plantation, see King, *Grotesque Touch*.

89. Nguyen, "Riot Grrrl, Race, and Revival," 187.

90. Williams, *Keywords*, xxv. As Williams puts it in his introduction to *Keywords*, much of his inquiry into culture was sparked by exploring the meaning of that word

with his adult education students, then seeing it as structurally linked to other terms. When looking up "culture" in the *Oxford English Dictionary*, Williams saw traces of this "structure" of relation between words in how the dictionary tracked changes in the definition of "culture" over time. In this example, we see how the structure of feeling in the arts manifests, at least in part, through language itself. Vocabulary captures the ways a society works out values and meanings, and grammar, I add in the spirit of Marcus and Spillers, captures the organizing principles of this structure. Like vocabulary, grammar contains forms of contestation and can intervene in the social. To put it in Williams's terms, our ability to view the "historical shape" of ideas through language can also aid us in "understanding [our] immediate world" (Williams, *Keywords*, xxv).

91. Spillers, "Mama's Baby, Papa's Maybe," 66.

92. Spillers, "Mama's Baby, Papa's Maybe," 68.

93. Spillers, "Mama's Baby, Papa's Maybe," 76.

94. Spillers, "Mama's Baby, Papa's Maybe," 79.

95. Spillers, "Mama's Baby, Papa's Maybe," 80.

96. Nguyen, "Riot Grrrl, Race, and Revival," 179–82.

97. Laina Dawes, "Why I Was Never a Riot Grrrl," *Bitch*, May 15, 2013, https://bitchmedia.org/post/why-i-was-never-a-riot-grrl (site discontinued).

98. Nguyen, "Riot Grrrl, Race, and Revival," 183.

99. Nguyen, "Riot Grrrl, Race, and Revival," 174.

100. Nguyen, "Riot Grrrl, Race, and Revival," 190.

101. Berlant, *The Queen of America Goes to Washington City*, 67.

102. Berlant, *The Queen of America Goes to Washington City*, 67.

103. Berlant, *The Queen of America Goes to Washington City*, 71.

104. As Kathryn Abrams details, a number of sexual harassment cases were influenced by MacKinnon's groundbreaking account of sexual harassment as a form of gender discrimination, and her legal work helped to define legal definitions of sexual harassment (Abrams, "Sex Wars Redux," 304n2). Later, MacKinnon and Dworkin would help draft antipornography ordinances that passed in some US cities but were later ruled unconstitutional. MacKinnon and Dworkin's work is documented in their 1988 book *Pornography and Civil Rights*.

105. Lusty, "Riot Grrrl Manifestos and Radical Vernacular Feminism," 228–29.

106. Here I echo McKenzie Wark's theorization of girlhood in Acker's writing. She claims that, in Acker's work, "a girl is a node of attraction but also of vulnerability, whose actions are constrained by others' desires and violence—by men's desires and violence. Their vulnerability is their agency. . . . Girls enter masculine identities, penetrate them, through the senses, through the projection of their own penetrability" (Wark, *Philosophy for Spiders*, 149).

107. Radway, "Girl Zine Networks, Underground Itineraries, and Riot Grrrl History," 28.

108. Darms, *The Riot Grrrl Collection*, 10.

109. Love, "Diary of a Conference on Sexuality, 1982," 51.

110. Hemmings, "Affective Solidarity," 148.

111. Hemmings, "Affective Solidarity," 150.

112. Hemmings, "Affective Solidarity," 150.

113. Hemmings, "Affective Solidarity," 151.

114. Katie Van Syckle, "The Columbia Student Carrying a Mattress Everywhere Says Reporters Are Triggering Rape Memories," *The Cut*, September 4, 2014, https://www.thecut.com/2014/09/columbia-emma-sulkowicz-mattress-rape-performance-interview.html.

115. James Harding has highlighted connections between collage and feminist performance art. Similarly, Vivian Huang situates Sulkowicz in line with Ono's performance work. See Harding, *Cutting Performances*; and Huang, *Surface Relations*.

116. Rebecca Mead, "Two Beds and the Burdens of Feminism," *New Yorker*, April 6, 2015, https://www.newyorker.com/culture/cultural-comment/two-beds-and-the-burdens-of-feminism.

117. Barthes, *The Pleasure of the Text*, 38.

## Coda

1. The Space Between Society, "About," *The Space Between: Literature and Culture, 1914–1945*. Accessed February 2, 2024, https://spacebetweensociety.com/home/about.

2. Lucy Diavolo, "20 Years after Columbine, What Do We Make of 'Senseless' Violence?" *Teen Vogue*, April 20, 2019, https://www.teenvogue.com/story/columbine-shooting-20th-anniversary-make-sense-of-senseless-violence.

3. Rokach, *Senseless Violence and Its Ramifications*, 1.

4. Pozorski, *Falling after 9/11*, 63.

5. Namwali Serpell's *Seven Modes of Uncertainty*, which taxonomizes formal strategies for producing multiple, ambiguous interpretive experiences in postwar Anglophone literature, concludes with a critique of *Extremely Loud and Incredibly Close*, treating it as a failed attempt at uncertainty "that manipulates techniques for uncertainty with which readers are deeply familiar. Rather than unsettling our values," Serpell argues, "this novel's flashy moves conduce to a set of clichéd ideas about uncertainty while stirring a generic, sentimental affective response" (Serpell, *Seven Modes of Uncertainty*, 269).

6. A number of monographs and edited collections have theorized 9/11 literature, among them Richard Gray's *After the Fall*; Susana Araújo's *Transatlantic Fictions of 9/11 and the War on Terror*; *Literature after 9/11*, edited by Ann Keniston and Jeanne Follansbee Quinn; Aimee Pozorski's *Falling after 9/11*; and Kristiaan Versluys's *Out of the Blue*.

7. Jay N. Shelat, "Pattern Recognition: The Enduring Whiteness of 9/11 Literary Studies," *Post45*, September 11, 2021, https://post45.org/2021/09/pattern-recognition-the-enduring-whiteness-of-9–11-literary-studies/.

8. Smith, "Organic Shrapnel," 155.

9. Published on the twentieth anniversary of 9/11, a *Contemporaries* cluster at *Post45* considers the continuities of neo-imperialism that traversed the 9/11 moment. In particular, Jay Shelat's introduction highlights how presumptions of US innocence and victimhood also helped justify anti-Muslim sentiment and racist treatment of Black and Brown people in the wake of the attacks. Liliana Naydan's contribution to the cluster highlights the role of media in how mainstream American culture has nar-

 rativized 9/11 in an oversimplified, flattened way (Liliana M. Naydan, "Texturizing 9/11 in the Flat World: Screen Culture, Endless War, and the Literature of Terror," *Post45*, September 11, 2021, https://post45.org/2021/09/texturizing-9-11-in-the-flat -world-screen-culture-endless-war-and-the-literature-of-terror/).

10. Jay N. Shelat, "Pattern Recognition : The Enduring Whiteness of 9/11 Literary Studies," *Post45*, September 11, 2021, https://post45.org/2021/09/pattern-recognition -the-enduring-whiteness-of-9-11-literary-studies/.

11. Blok, "The Enigma of Senseless Violence," 24.

12. Michaels, *The Shape of the Signifier*, 171.

13. Michaels, *The Shape of the Signifier*, 175.

14. Khakpour, "Ackerphilia."

15. Kleeman, Alexandra, "Introduction," in *Empire of the Senseless*, xii.

16. Acker, *Empire of the Senseless*, 38.

17. For a strong analysis of Jeremiah Wright's rhetorical style and a useful contextualization of the "chickens coming home to roost" speech, which was cherry-picked and reported on to stoke controversy around Barack Obama, a one-time parishioner of Wright's, see Gunn and McPhail, "Coming Home to Roost."

18. Michaels, *The Shape of the Signifier*, 175.

19. Michaels, *The Shape of the Signifier*, 175.

20. Kramnick and Nersessian, "Form and Explanation," 661.

21. Qtd. in Schechner, "9/11 as Avant-Garde Art?," 1820.

22. Stockhausen quickly walked back and contextualized his comments, stating clearly that he joined others in "mourning this atrocity" (qtd. in Terry Castle, "Stockhausen, Karlheinz," *New York Magazine*, August 27, 2011, https://nymag.com/news /9-11/10th-anniversary/karlheinz-stockhausen/). Like performance studies scholar Richard Schechner and literary critic Terry Castle, the literary scholars Frank Lentricchia and Jody McAuliff have reassessed Stockhausen's comments in their book *Crimes of Art and Terror*, exploring the connections between avant-garde invocations of violence and the spectacle of the attacks.

23. Schechner, "9/11 as Avant-Garde Art?," 1821.

24. Benjamin, "The Work of Art in the Age of Mechanical Reproduction," 242.

25. Schechner, "9/11 as Avant-Garde Art?," 1822.

26. Smith, "Organic Shrapnel," 160.

27. Smith, "Organic Shrapnel," 161.

28. Williams, *The Long Revolution*, 91.

29. Williams, *The Long Revolution*, 91.

30. Williams, *The Long Revolution*, 91.

31. Berlant, *Cruel Optimism*, 4.

32. Berlant, *Cruel Optimism*, 4.

33. Bersani and Dutoit, "The Forms of Violence," 19.

34. Berlant, *Cruel Optimism*, 9–10.

35. Berlant, *Cruel Optimism*, 10.

36. Parul Sehgal, "The Case Against the Trauma Plot," *New Yorker*, December 27, 2021, https://www.newyorker.com/magazine/2022/01/03/the-case-against-the-trauma -plot.

37. Kasey Meehan, Tasslyn Magnusson, Sabrina Baêta, and Jonathan Freedman. "Banned in the USA: The Mounting Pressure to Censor." *PEN America*, September 1, 2023. https://pen.org/report/book-bans-pressure-to-censor/.

38. Coleman, "Theorizing the Present," 601.

39. Coleman, "Theorizing the Present," 606.

40. Coleman, "Theorizing the Present," 608.

41. Levine, *Forms*, 2.

42. Doyle, *Hold It against Me*, 15.

43. Doyle, *Hold It against Me*, xii.

44. Kornbluh, *The Order of Forms*, 3.

45. Levine, *Forms*, 16.

46. Kornbluh, *The Order of Forms*, 5.

47. Lewis, *Dynamic Form*, 227.

48. Lewis, *Dynamic Form*, 227.

49. Chuh, *The Difference Aesthetics Makes*, xii.

50. Chuh, *The Difference Aesthetics Makes*, 3.

51. Buck-Morss, "Aesthetics and Anaesthetics," 6.

52. Leys, "The Turn to Affect," 458.

53. Sedgwick, *Touching Feeling*, 123.

54. Stuelke, *The Ruse of Repair*, 7.

55. Sedgwick, *Touching Feeling*, 124.

56. Timothy Aubry, "Form Contra Aesthetics," *Post45: Peer Reviewed*, January 15, 2021, https://post45.org/2021/01/aubry-form-contra-aesthetics/.

57. Vimalassery, Pegues, and Goldstein, "Introduction," n.p.

# *Bibliography*

Archival Sources

Atlanta, GA
  Emory University
    Stuart A. Rose Manuscript, Archives, and Rare Book Library
      Flannery O'Connor Papers
Durham, NC
  Duke University
    David M. Rubenstein Rare Book and Manuscript Library
      Kathy Acker Papers
New York, NY
  New York University
    Fales Library and Special Collections
      Kathleen Hanna Papers

Newspapers and Periodicals

*Bitch Magazine*
*Chicago Magazine*
*Creative Pinellas*
*Cut*
*Lexington Advertiser*
*Los Angeles Review of Books*
*Nation*
*New Yorker*
*New York Magazine*
*New York Times*
*Paris Review*
*Rookie*
*Teen Vogue*

Other Sources

Abdur-Rahman, Aliyyah I. "'Simply a Menaced Boy': Analogizing Color, Undoing Dominance in James Baldwin's *Giovanni's Room*." *African American Review* 41, no. 3 (2007): 477–86.

Abel, Elizabeth. "Black Writing, White Reading: Race and the Politics of Feminist Interpretation." *Critical Inquiry* 19, no. 3 (Spring 1993): 470–98.

———. "Skin, Flesh, and the Affective Wrinkles of Civil Rights Photography." *Qui Parle* 20, no. 2 (2012): 35–69. https://doi.org/10.5250/quiparle.20.2.0035.

Abrams, Kathryn. "Sex Wars Redux: Agency and Coercion in Feminist Legal Theory." *Columbia Law Review* 95, no. 2 (March 1995): 304–76. https://doi.org/10.2307/1123232.

Acker, Kathy. *Blood and Guts in High School*. New York: Grove Press, 1984.

———. *Empire of the Senseless*. New York: Grove Press, 1988.

Adams, Rachel. *Sideshow U.S.A.: Freaks and the American Cultural Imagination*. Chicago: University of Chicago Press, 2001.

Alcoff, Linda Martín. "Sexual Violations and the Question of Experience." *New Literary History* 45, no. 3 (2014): 445–62. https://doi.org/10.1353/nlh.2014.0030.

Alexander, Elizabeth. "'Can You Be Black and Look at This?': Reading the Rodney King Video(s)." *Public Culture* 7, no. 1 (October 1, 1994): 77–94. https://doi.org/10.1215/08992363-7-1-77.

Alexandre, Sandy. *The Properties of Violence: Claims to Ownership in Representations of Lynching*. Jackson: University Press of Mississippi, 2012.

Amin, Kadji, Amber Jamilla Musser, and Roy Pérez. "Queer Form: Aesthetics, Race, and the Violences of the Social." *ASAP/Journal* 2, no. 2 (2017): 227–39. https://doi.org/10.1353/asa.2017.0031.

Apel, Dora. *Imagery of Lynching: Black Men, White Women, and the Mob*. New Brunswick, NJ: Rutgers University Press, 2004.

Apel, Dora, and Shawn Michelle Smith. *Lynching Photographs: Defining Moments in American Photography*. Berkeley: University of California Press, 2007.

Araújo, Susana. *Transatlantic Fictions of 9/11 and the War on Terror: Images of Insecurity, Narratives of Captivity*. London: Bloomsbury, 2015.

Armstrong, Isobel. *The Radical Aesthetic*. Oxford, UK: Blackwell, 2000.

Bacharach, Sondra. "Street Art and Consent." *British Journal of Aesthetics* 55, no. 4 (2015): 481–95.

Bachner, Sally. *The Prestige of Violence: American Fiction, 1962–2007*. Athens: University of Georgia Press, 2011.

Baker, Houston. "When Lindbergh Sleeps with Bessie Smith: The Writing of Place in *Sula*." In *The Difference Within: Feminism and Critical Theory*, edited by Elizabeth A. Meese and Alice A. Parker, 85–114. Amsterdam: John Benjamins, 1989.

Bakhtin, M. M. *The Dialogic Imagination: Four Essays*. Translated by Caryl Emerson and Michael Holquist. Austin: University of Texas Press, 1981, 2008.

———. *Rabelais and His World*. Translated by Hélène Iswolsky. Bloomington: Indiana University Press, 1984.

Baldwin, James. *Giovanni's Room*. New York: Delta, 1956.

———. *Notes of a Native Son*. New York: Beacon Press, 1955.

Barthes, Roland. *The Pleasure of the Text*. Translated by Richard Miller. New York: Hill and Wang, 1975.

Barthes, Roland, and Lionel Duisit. "An Introduction to the Structural Analysis of Narrative." *New Literary History* 6, no. 2 (1975): 237. https://doi.org/10.2307/468419.

Belletto, Steven. *No Accident, Comrade: Chance and Design in Cold War American Narratives*. New York: Oxford University Press, 2012.

Benjamin, Walter. "Critique of Violence." In *Reflections: Essays, Aphorisms, Autobiographical Writing*, 277–300. Translated by Edmund Jephcott. New York: Schocken Books, 1986.

———. "The Work of Art in the Age of Mechanical Reproduction." In *Illuminations: Essays and Reflections*, 217–251. Translated by Harry Zohn. New York: Schocken Books, 1968.

Berger, Martin A. *Seeing through Race: A Reinterpretation of Civil Rights Photography*. Berkeley: University of California Press, 2011.

Berlant, Lauren. *Cruel Optimism*. Durham, NC: Duke University Press, 2011.

———. *The Female Complaint: The Unfinished Business of Sentimentality in American Culture*. Durham, NC: Duke University Press, 2008.

———. *The Queen of America Goes to Washington City: Essays on Sex and Citizenship*. Durham, NC: Duke University Press, 1997.

Berry, Ellen E. *Women's Experimental Writing: Negative Aesthetics and Feminist Critique*. London: Bloomsbury Publishing, 2017.

Bersani, Leo, and Ulysse Dutoit. "The Forms of Violence." *October* 8 (1979): 17–29. http://www.jstor.org/stable/778223.

Best, Stephen Michael. *None like Us: Blackness, Belonging, Aesthetic Life*. Durham, NC: Duke University Press, 2018.

Best, Stephen, and Sharon Marcus. "Surface Reading: An Introduction." *Representations* 108, no. 1 (November 1, 2009): 1–21.

Blok, Anton. "The Enigma of Senseless Violence." In *Meanings of Violence: A Cross Cultural Perspective*, edited by Goran Aijmer and Jon Abbink, 23–38. Oxford, UK: Berg, 2000.

Bloom, Harold. *Kurt Vonnegut's Slaughterhouse-Five*. New York: Infobase Publishing, 2007.

Bohrer, Karl Heinz. *Suddenness: On the Moment of Aesthetic Appearance*. New York: Columbia University Press, 1981.

Bosco, Mark. "Consenting to Love: Autobiographical Roots of 'Good Country People.'" *The Southern Review* 41, no. 2 (2005): 283–95.

Bradway, Teagan. *Queer Experimental Literature: The Affective Politics of Bad Reading*. New York: Palgrave Macmillan, 2017.

Brecht, Bertolt. "The Street Scene: A Basic Model for an Epic Theatre." In *Brecht on Theatre: The Development of an Aesthetic*, 121–29. Translated by John Willett. New Delhi: Radha Krishna, 1978.

Brill, Dorothée. *Shock and the Senseless in Dada and Fluxus*. Hanover, NH: Dartmouth College Press, 2010.

Brinkema, Eugenie. *The Forms of the Affects*. Durham, NC: Duke University Press, 2014.

Brooks, Peter. *Reading for the Plot: Design and Intention in Narrative*. Cambridge, MA: Harvard University Press, 1992.

Brown, Caroline A. *The Black Female Body in American Literature and Art: Performing Identity*. New York: Routledge, 2012.

Brownmiller, Susan. *Against Our Will: Men, Women and Rape*. New York: Simon and Schuster, 1975.

Bryan-Wilson, Julia. "Remembering Yoko Ono's *Cut Piece*." *Oxford Art Journal* 26, no. 1 (2003): 99–123.

Buck-Morss, Susan. "Aesthetics and Anaesthetics: Walter Benjamin's Artwork Essay Reconsidered." *October* 62 (1992): 3–41. https://doi.org/10.2307/778700.

Burroughs, William S., and Brion Gysin. *The Third Mind*. New York: Viking Press, 1978.

Butler, Judith. *The Force of Nonviolence: An Ethico-Political Bind*. London: Verso, 2020.

———. *Precarious Life: The Powers of Mourning and Violence*. London: Verso, 2004.

Campany, David, and Stanley Wolukau-Wanambwa. *Indeterminacy: Thoughts on Time, the Image, and Race(Ism)*. New York: MACK, 2022.

Capers, Bennett. "On Andy Warhol's *Electric Chair*." *California Law Review* 94, no. 1 (2006): 243–60.

Carbonell, Bettina. "The Afterlife of Lynching: Exhibitions and the Re-compostion of Human Suffering." *The Mississippi Quarterly* 61, no. 1–2 (2008): 197–215.

Carby, Hazel. "'On the Threshold of Woman's Era': Lynching, Empire, and Sexuality in Black Feminist Theory." *Critical Inquiry* 12, no. 1 (1985): 262–77.

Carrigan, Anthony. "Postcolonial Disaster, Pacific Nuclearization, and Disabling Environments." *Journal of Literary & Cultural Disability Studies* 4, no. 3 (January 2010): 255–72. https://doi.org/10.3828/jlcds.2010.22.

Castronovo, Russ. *Beautiful Democracy: Aesthetics and Anarchy in a Global Era*. Chicago: University of Chicago Press, 2009.

———. "Beauty along the Color Line: Lynching, Aesthetics, and the Crisis." *PMLA* 121, no. 5 (October 2006): 1443–59. https://doi.org/10.1632/pmla.2006.121.5.1443.

Caws, Mary Anne. *Reading Frames in Modern Fiction*. Princeton, NJ: Princeton University Press, 1985.

Chenoweth, Katie. "Rock, Paper, Scissors: On Media Revolution and the Death Penalty." *Discourse* 39, no. 1 (2017): 3–30.

Chuh, Kandice. *The Difference Aesthetics Makes: On the Humanities "after Man."* Durham, NC: Duke University Press, 2019.

Clark, Rebecca B. *American Graphic: Disgust and Data in Contemporary Literature*. Stanford, CA: Stanford University Press, 2022.

Clune, Michael. "Blood Money: Sovereignty and Exchange in Kathy Acker." *Contemporary Literature* 45, no. 3 (2004): 486–515. https://doi.org/10.1353/cli.2004.0020.

Cohen, Brigid. "Ono in Opera: A Politics of Art and Action, 1960–1962." *ASAP/Journal* 3, no. 1 (2018): 41–66. https://doi.org/10.1353/asa.2018.0002.

Colby, Georgina. *Kathy Acker: Writing the Impossible*. Edinburgh: Edinburgh University Press, 2018.

Cole, Sarah. *At the Violet Hour: Modernism and Violence in England and Ireland*. New York: Oxford University Press, 2012.

Coleman, Rebecca. "Theorizing the Present: Digital Media, Pre-Emergence and Infra-Structures of Feeling." *Cultural Studies* 32, no. 4 (2018): 600–622. https://doi.org/10.1080/09502386.2017.1413121.

Collins, Bradford R. "Warhol's Modern Dance of Death: Work and Text." *American Art* 30, no. 2 (June 2016): 32–57. https://doi.org/10.1086/688590.

Concannon, Kevin. "Not For Sale: Yoko Ono's Discounted Advertising Art." *Athanor* 17 (1999): 77–85.

———. "Yoko Ono's *Cut Piece*: From Text to Performance and Back Again." *PAJ: A Journal of Performance and Art* 30, no. 3 (September 2008): 81–93. https://doi.org/10.1162/pajj.2008.30.3.81.

Connelly, Frances S., ed. *Modern Art and the Grotesque*. New York: Cambridge University Press, 2003.

Cran, Rona. *Collage in Twentieth-Century Art, Literature, and Culture: Joseph Cornell, William Burroughs, Frank O'Hara, and Bob Dylan*. London: Routledge, 2014.

Currie, Mark. *About Time*. Edinburgh: Edinburgh University Press, 2010.

Cvetkovich, Ann. *An Archive of Feelings: Trauma, Sexuality, and Lesbian Public Cultures*. Durham, NC: Duke University Press, 2003.

Darms, Lisa. *The Riot Grrrl Collection*. New York: The Feminist Press at CUNY, 2013.

Dezeuze, Anna. "Origins of the Fluxus Score: From Indeterminacy to the 'Do-It-Yourself' Artwork." *Performance Research* 7, no. 3 (January 2002): 78–94. https://doi.org/10.1080/13528165.2002.10871876.

Didion, Joan. "The White Album." In *The White Album: Essays*, 11–47. New York: Farrar, Straus and Giroux, 2009.

Di Renzo, Anthony. *American Gargoyles: Flannery O'Connor and the Medieval Grotesque*. Carbondale: Southern Illinois University Press, 1995.

Doane, Mary Ann. "Information, Crisis, Catastrophe." In *Logics of Television: Essays in Cultural Criticism*, edited by Patricia Mellencamp, 222–39. Bloomington: Indiana University Press, 1990.

Doyle, Jennifer. *Hold It against Me: Difficulty and Emotion in Contemporary Art*. Durham, NC: Duke University Press, 2013.

Duberman, Martin. *Black Mountain: An Exploration in Community*. Evanston, IL: Northwestern University Press, 2009.

Dworkin, Craig. *Reading the Illegible*. Evanston, IL: Northwestern University Press, 2003.

Eatman, Megan. *Ecologies of Harm: Rhetorics of Violence in the United States*. Columbus: Ohio State University Press, 2020.

Elie, Paul. *The Life You Save May Be Your Own: An American Pilgrimage*. New York: Farrar, Straus and Giroux, 2004.

English, Darby. *How to See a Work of Art in Total Darkness*. Cambridge, MA: MIT Press, 2010.

Felski, Rita. "Redescriptions of Female Masochism." *Minnesota Review* 2005, no. 63–64 (2005): 127–39. https://doi.org/10.1215/00265667-2005-63-64-127.

———. *Uses of Literature*. Malden, MA: Wiley-Blackwell, 2008.

Fetterman, William. *John Cage's Theatre Pieces: Notations and Performances*. London: Taylor and Francis, 1996.

Fisher, Jennifer. "Tangible Acts: Touch Performances." In *The Senses in Performance*, edited by Sally Barnes and André Lepecki, 166–78. New York: Routledge, 2007.

Flatley, Jonathan. *Affective Mapping: Melancholia and the Politics of Modernism*. Cambridge, MA: Harvard University Press, 2009.

———. *Like Andy Warhol*. Chicago: University of Chicago Press, 2017.

Fleetwood, Nicole R. *Troubling Vision: Performance, Visuality, and Blackness*. Chicago: University of Chicago Press, 2011.

Fodor, Sarah J. "Marketing Flannery O'Connor: Institutional Politics and Literary Evaluation." In *Flannery O'Connor: New Perspectives*, edited by Sura P. Rath and Mary Neff Shaw, 12–37. Athens: University of Georgia Press, 1996.

Foster, Hal. "Death in America." *October* 75 (1996): 37–59.

Foucault, Michel. "Sex, Power, and the Politics of Identity." In *Ethics: Subjectivity and Truth*, edited by Paul Rabinow. New York: The New Press, 1997.

Freeman, Elizabeth. "Time Binds, or, Erotohistoriography." *Social Text* 23, no. 3–4 (84–85) (2005): 57–68. https://doi.org/10.1215/01642472-23-3-4_84-85-57.

———. *Time Binds: Queer Temporalities, Queer Histories*. Durham, NC: Duke University Press, 2010.

French, William W. *Maryat Lee's EcoTheater: A Theater for the Twenty-First Century*. Morgantown: West Virginia University Press, 1998.

Friedman, Gabriella. "Unsentimental Historicizing: The Neo-Slave Narrative Tradition and the Refusal of Feeling." *American Literature* 93, no. 1 (March 1, 2021): 115–43. https://doi.org/10.1215/00029831-8878542.

Galtung, Johan. "Violence, Peace, and Peace Research." *Journal of Peace Research* 6, no. 3 (1969): 167–91.

Garland-Thomson, Rosemarie. *Extraordinary Bodies: Figuring Physical Disability in American Culture and Literature*. New York: Columbia University Press, 1997.

Gavins, Joanna. *Reading the Absurd*. Edinburgh: Edinburgh University Press, 2013.

Gentry, Marshall Bruce. *Flannery O'Connor's Religion of the Grotesque*. Jackson: University Press of Mississippi, 1986.

Gerald, Kelly, ed. *Flannery O'Connor: The Cartoons*. Seattle: Fantagraphics, 2012.

Gibbs, Alan. *Contemporary American Trauma Narratives*. Edinburgh: Edinburgh University Press, 2014.

Gilman, Sander L. "Black Bodies, White Bodies: Toward an Iconography of Female Sexuality in Late Nineteenth-Century Art, Medicine, and Literature." *Critical Inquiry* 12 (1985): 204–42.

Goldberg, Jess A. "James Baldwin and the Anti-Black Force of Law: On Excessive Violence and Exceeding Violence." *Public Culture* 31, no. 3 (2019): 521–38.

Goldsby, Jacqueline. "The High and Low Tech of It: The Meaning of Lynching and the Death of Emmett Till." *Yale Journal of Criticism* 9, no. 2 (1996): 245–82. https://doi.org/10.1353/yale.1996.0016.

———. *A Spectacular Secret: Lynching in American Life and Literature*. Chicago: University of Chicago Press, 2006.

Goodwin, James. *Modern American Grotesque: Literature and Photography*. Columbus: Ohio State University Press, 2009.

Gray, Richard. *After the Fall: American Literature Since 9/11*. Malden, MA: Wiley, 2011.

Greenblatt, Jordana, and Keja L. Valens, eds. *Querying Consent: Beyond Permission and Refusal*. New Brunswick, NJ: Rutgers University Press, 2018.

Gunn, Joshua, and Mark Lawrence McPhail. "Coming Home to Roost: Jeremiah Wright, Barack Obama, and the (Re) Signing of (Post) Racial Rhetoric." *Rhetoric Society Quarterly* 45, no. 1 (2015): 1–24.

Halberstam, Jack. *The Queer Art of Failure*. Durham, NC: Duke University Press, 2011.

———. "Shame and White Gay Masculinity." *Social Text* 23, no. 3–4 (2005): 219–33. https://doi.org/10.1215/01642472-23-3-4_84-85-219.

Hall, Stuart, Chas Critcher, Tony Jefferson, John Clarke, and Brian Roberts. *Policing the Crisis: Mugging, the State and Law and Order*. London: Macmillan, 1987.

Halperin, David M., and Valerie Traub, eds. *Gay Shame*. Chicago: University of Chicago Press, 2009.

Hamilton, Ross. *Accident: A Philosophical and Literary History*. Chicago: University of Chicago Press, 2007.

Harding, James M. *Cutting Performances: Collage Events, Feminist Artists, and the American Avant-Garde*. Ann Arbor: University of Michigan Press, 2012.

Harper, Phillip Brian. *Abstractionist Aesthetics: Artistic Form and Social Critique in African American Culture*. New York: New York University Press, 2015.

Harpham, Geoffrey Galt. *On the Grotesque: Strategies of Contradiction in Art and Literature*. Princeton, NJ: Princeton University Press, 1982.

Harris, Carole K. "'The Pleasant Lady' in Flannery O'Connor's 'Revelation': Maryat Lee Talks Back." *Flannery O'Connor Review* 16 (2018): 30–55.

Hartman, Saidiya V. *Scenes of Subjection: Terror, Slavery, and Self-Making in Nineteenth-Century America*. New York: Oxford University Press, 1997.

Hemmings, Clare. "Affective Solidarity: Feminist Reflexivity and Political Transformation." *Feminist Theory* 13, no. 2 (2012): 147–61.

———. "Invoking Affect: Cultural Theory and the Ontological Turn." *Cultural Studies* 19, no. 5 (September 2005): 548–67. https://doi.org/10.1080/09502380500365473.

Henderson, Mae G. "James Baldwin: Expatriation, Homosexual Panic, and Man's Estate." *Callaloo* 23, no. 1 (2000): 313–27. https://doi.org/10.1353/cal.2000.0032.

Higgins, Dick. "Intermedia." *Leonardo* 34, no. 1 (2001): 49–54.

Higgins, Scarlett. *Collage and Literature: The Persistence of Vision*. New York: Routledge, 2018.

Hinton, Elizabeth. *America on Fire: The Untold History of Police Violence and Black Rebellion Since the 1960s*. New York: Liveright Publishing, 2021.

Hobson, Janell. *Venus in the Dark: Blackness and Beauty in Popular Culture*. 2nd ed. New York: Routledge, 2018.

hoogland, renée c. *A Violent Embrace: Art and Aesthetics after Representation*. Hanover, NH: Dartmouth College Press, 2014.

Huang, Vivian L. *Surface Relations: Queer Forms of Asian American Inscrutability*. Durham, NC: Duke University Press, 2022.

Hurley, Jessica. *Infrastructures of Apocalypse: American Literature and the Nuclear Complex*. Minneapolis: University of Minnesota Press, 2020.

Jackson, Chuck. "A 'Headless Display': *Sula*, Soldiers, and Lynching." *MFS: Modern Fiction Studies* 52, no. 2 (2006): 374–92. https://doi.org/10.1353/mfs.2006.0048.

James, Alison. *Constraining Chance: Georges Perec and the Oulipo*. Evanston, IL: Northwestern University Press, 2009.

Jannarone, Kimberly. *Artaud and His Doubles*. Ann Arbor: University of Michigan Press, 2012.

Jay, Martin. "Scopic Regimes of Modernity." In *Vision and Visuality: Discussions in Contemporary Culture*, edited by Hal Foster, 3–23. Seattle: Bay Press, 1988.

Johnson, Barbara. "'Aesthetic' and 'Rapport' in Toni Morrison's *Sula*." In *The Aesthetics of Toni Morrison: Speaking the Unspeakable*, edited by Mark C. Connor, 3–11. Jackson: University Press of Mississippi, 2000.

Kant, Immanuel. *Critique of Judgment*. Translated by Werner S. Pluhar. Indianapolis: Hackett, 1987.

Kaprow, Allan. "Happenings in the New York Scene." In *Essays on the Blurring of Art and Life*, edited by Jeff Kelley, 15–26. Berkeley: University of California Press, 1993.

Katz, Claire. "Flannery O'Connor's Rage of Vision." *American Literature* 46, no. 1 (1974): 54–67.

Katz, Steven B. "The Ethic of Expediency: Classical Rhetoric, Technology, and the Holocaust." *College English* 54, no. 3 (March 1992): 255–75. https://doi.org/10.2307/378062.

Kayser, Wolfgang Johannes. *The Grotesque in Art and Literature*. New York: Columbia University Press, 1981.

Keizer, Arlene R. "Gone Astray in the Flesh: Kara Walker, Black Women Writers, and African American Postmemory." *PMLA* 123, no. 5 (October 2008): 1649–72. https://doi.org/10.1632/pmla.2008.123.5.1649.

Keniston, Ann, and Jeanne Follansbee Quinn, eds. *Literature after 9/11*. New York: Routledge, 2013.

Khakpour, Porochista. "Ackerphilia: On the Recent Kathy Acker Craze." *Virginia Quarterly Review* 94, no. 4 (Fall 2017): 213–15. https://www.jstor.org/stable/26434902.

King, Amy K. *Grotesque Touch: Women, Violence, and Contemporary Circum-Caribbean Narratives*. Chapel Hill: University of North Carolina Press, 2021.

Kipnis, Laura. *Bound and Gagged: Pornography and the Politics of Fantasy in America*. Durham, NC: Duke University Press, 1996.

Kleeman, Alexandra. Introduction to *Empire of the Senseless*, by Kathy Acker. New York: Grove, 2018.

Kornbluh, Anna. *The Order of Forms: Realism, Formalism, and Social Space*. Chicago: University of Chicago Press, 2019.

Korsmeyer, Carolyn. *Savoring Disgust: The Foul and the Fair in Aesthetics*. New York: Oxford University Press, 2011.

Kramnick, Jonathan, and Anahid Nersessian. "Form and Explanation." *Critical Inquiry* 43, no. 3 (2017): 650–69.

Kraus, Chris. *After Kathy Acker*. New York: Semiotext(e), 2017.

Kristeva, Julia. *Powers of Horror: An Essay on Abjection*. Translated by Leon S. Roudiez. New York: Columbia University Press, 1982.

Kuc, Kamila. "Aesthetic Violence in the Anarchival Turn: On the Infinite Visions of History." *Found Footage* 5 (March 2019): 78–93.

Lawlor, William T. *Beat Culture: Lifestyles, Icons, and Impact*. New York: Bloomsbury, 2005.

Lawtoo, Nidesh. "The Double Meaning of Violence: Catharsis and Mimesis." In *Violence and Meaning*, edited by Lode Lauwaert, Laura Katherine Smith, and Christian Sternad, 137–65. Palgrave Macmillan, 2019.

Lee, Maryat. *Four Men and a Monster: A Drama in One Act*. London: Samuel French, 1969.

Lentricchia, Frank, and Jody McAuliffe. *Crimes of Art and Terror*. Chicago: University of Chicago Press, 2003.

Levine, Caroline. "An Anatomy of Suspense: The Pleasurable, Critical, Ethical, Erotic Middle of *The Woman in White*." In *Narrative Middles: Navigating the Nineteenth-Century British Novel*, edited by Caroline Levine and Mario Ortiz-Robles, 195–214. Columbus: Ohio State University Press, 2011.

———. *Forms: Whole, Rhythm, Hierarchy, Network*. Princeton, NJ: Princeton University Press, 2015.

———. *The Serious Pleasures of Suspense: Victorian Realism and Narrative Doubt*. Charlottesville: University of Virginia Press, 2003.

Lewis, Cara L. *Dynamic Form: How Intermediality Made Modernism*. Ithaca, NY: Cornell University Press, 2020.

Leys, Ruth. "The Turn to Affect: A Critique." *Critical Inquiry* 37, no. 3 (2011): 434–72. https://doi.org/10.1086/659353.

Libow, Jess. "Prosthesis Repurposed: Gender and Rehabilitation in Flannery O'Connor's Fiction." *Journal of Literary & Cultural Disability Studies* 11, no. 4 (November 2017): 385–401. https://doi.org/10.3828/jlcds.2017.31.

Littau, Karin. *Theories of Reading: Books, Bodies, and Bibliomania*. Cambridge, UK: Polity Press, 2006.

Lorde, Audre. *Sister Outsider: Essays and Speeches*. Freedom, CA: Crossing Press, 1998.

Love, Heather. "Diary of a Conference on Sexuality, 1982." *GLQ: A Journal of Lesbian and Gay Studies* 17, no. 1 (January 1, 2011): 49–78. https://doi.org/10.1215/10642684-2010-016.

———. *Feeling Backward: Loss and the Politics of Queer History*. Cambridge, MA: Harvard University Press, 2007.

Lusty, Natalya. "Riot Grrrl Manifestos and Radical Vernacular Feminism." *Australian Feminist Studies* 32, no. 93 (2017): 219–39. https://doi.org/10.1080/08164649.2017.1407638.

Lyon, Janet. *Manifestoes: Provocations of the Modern*. Ithaca, NY: Cornell University Press, 1999.

MacKinnon, Catharine A. *Toward a Feminist Theory of the State*. Cambridge, MA: Harvard University Press, 1989.

MacKinnon, Catharine, and Andrea Dworkin. *Pornography and Civil Rights: A New Day for Women's Equality*. Minneapolis: Organizing Against Pornography, 1988.

Malabou, Catherine. *Ontology of the Accident: An Essay on Destructive Plasticity*. Cambridge, UK: Polity Press, 2012.

Mangrum, Benjamin. "Flannery O'Connor, the Phenomenology of Race, and the Institutions of Irony." *Twentieth-Century Literature* 65, no. 3 (September 1, 2019): 237–60. https://doi.org/10.1215/0041462X-7852075.

Marcus, Sara. *Girls to the Front: The True Story of the Riot Grrrl Revolution*. New York: HarperPerennial, 2010.

Marcus, Sharon. "Fighting Bodies, Fighting Words: A Theory and Politics of Rape Prevention." In *Feminists Theorize the Political*, edited by Judith Butler and Joan W. Scott, 385–403. New York: Routledge, 1992.

Martínez, Ernesto Javier. *On Making Sense: Queer Race Narratives of Intelligibility*. Stanford, CA: Stanford University Press, 2012.

Matheson, T. J. "'This Lousy Little Book': The Genesis and Development of 'Slaughterhouse-Five' as Revealed in Chapter One." *Studies in the Novel* 16, no. 2 (1984): 228–40.

McDowell, Deborah. "'The Self and the Other': Reading Toni Morrison's *Sula* and the Black Female Text." In *Critical Essays on Toni Morrison*, edited by Nellie Y. McKay, 77–89. Boston: G. K. Hall, 1988.

McGurl, Mark. "Understanding Iowa: Flannery O'Connor, B.A., M.F.A." *American Literary History* 19, no. 2 (Summer 2007): 527–45.

McLeod, Kembrew, and Rudolf Kuenzli. "I Collage, Therefore I Am: An Introduction to Cutting Across Media." In *Cutting Across Media: Appropriation Art, Interventionist Collage, and Copyright Law*, edited by Kembrew McLeod and Rudolf Kuenzli, 1–23. Durham, NC: Duke University Press, 2011.

Meindl, Dieter. *American Fiction and the Metaphysics of the Grotesque*. Columbia: University of Missouri Press, 1996.

Melamed, Jodi. *Represent and Destroy: Rationalizing Violence in the New Racial Capitalism*. Minneapolis: University of Minnesota Press, 2011.

Menninghaus, Winfried. *Disgust: Theory and History of a Strong Sensation*. Albany, NY: SUNY Press, 2003.

Michaels, Walter Benn. *The Beauty of a Social Problem*. Chicago: University of Chicago Press, 2015.

———. *The Shape of the Signifier: 1967 to the End of History*. Princeton, NJ: Princeton University Press, 2004.

Milks, Megan. "Janey and Genet in Tangier: Power Plagiarism in Kathy Acker's *Blood and Guts in High School*." In *Kathy Acker and Transnationalism*, edited by Polina Mackay and Kathryn Nicol, 91–114. Newcastle Upon Tyne, UK: Cambridge Scholars Publishing, 2009.

Miller, D. Quentin. "Separate and Unequal in Paris: *Notes of a Native Son* and the Law." In *James Baldwin: America and Beyond*, edited by Cora Kaplan and Bill Schwarz, 159–72. Ann Arbor: University of Michigan Press, 2011.

Miller, Monica Carol. "Introduction." In *Dear Regina: Flannery O'Connor's Letters from Iowa*, edited by Monica Carol Miller, vii–xvii. Athens: University of Georgia Press, 2022.

Miller, William Ian. *The Anatomy of Disgust*. Cambridge, MA: Harvard University Press, 1998.

Milletti, Christina. "Violent Acts, Volatile Words: Kathy Acker's Terrorist Aesthetic." *Studies in the Novel* 36, no. 3 (2004): 352–73.

Mintz, Susannah B. *Hurt and Pain: Literature and the Suffering Body*. London: Bloomsbury, 2013.

Mirzoeff, Nicholas. *The Right to Look: A Counterhistory of Visuality*. Durham, NC: Duke University Press, 2011.

Mitchell, David T., and Sharon L. Snyder. *Narrative Prosthesis: Disability and the Dependencies of Discourse.* Ann Arbor: University of Michigan Press, 2000.

Mitchell, W. J. T. *Seeing Through Race.* Cambridge, MA: Harvard University Press, 2012.

———. "'Ut Pictura Theoria': Abstract Painting and the Repression of Language." *Critical Inquiry* 15, no. 2 (January 1989): 348–71. https://doi.org/10.1086/448488.

Morrison, Toni. *Playing in the Dark: Whiteness and the Literary Imagination.* Cambridge, MA: Harvard University Press, 1992.

———. "Recitatif." In *The Oxford Book of Women's Writing in the United States*, edited by Linda Wagner-Martin and Cathy N. Davidson, 159–75. Oxford, UK: Oxford University Press, 1995.

———. *Sula.* New York: Alfred A. Knopf, 1973.

Moten, Fred. *In the Break: The Aesthetics of the Black Radical Tradition.* Minneapolis: University of Minnesota Press, 2003.

Munt, Sally. *Queer Attachments: The Cultural Politics of Shame.* Aldershot, UK: Ashgate, 2007.

Nancy, Jean-Luc. *The Ground of the Image.* Translated by Jeff Fort. New York: Fordham University Press, 2005.

Nelson, Deborah. *Tough Enough: Arbus, Arendt, Didion, McCarthy, Sontag, Weil.* Chicago: University of Chicago Press, 2017.

Nelson, Maggie. *Jane: A Murder.* New York: Soft Skull Press, 2005.

Ngai, Sianne. *Our Aesthetic Categories: Zany, Cute, Interesting.* Cambridge, MA: Harvard University Press, 2012.

———. *Ugly Feelings.* Cambridge, MA: Harvard University Press, 2005.

Nguyen, Mimi T. "Riot Grrrl, Race, and Revival." *Feminist Theory* 22, no. 2–3 (2012): 173–96.

Nissen, Axel. "Form Matters: Toni Morrison's *Sula* and the Ethics of Narrative." *Contemporary Literature* 40, no. 2 (1999): 263–85. https://doi.org/10.2307/1208913.

Nixon, Rob. *Slow Violence and the Environmentalism of the Poor.* Cambridge, MA: Harvard University Press, 2011.

Novak, Phillip. "'Circles and Circles of Sorrow': In the Wake of Morrison's *Sula.*" *PMLA* 114, no. 2 (March 1999): 184–93. https://doi.org/10.2307/463390.

O'Connor, Flannery. *The Complete Stories.* New York: Farrar, Straus and Giroux, 1971.

———. *The Habit of Being.* New York: Farrar, Straus and Giroux, 1999.

———. "On Her Own Work." In *Mystery and Manners: Occasional Prose*, 107–119. New York: Farrar, Straus and Giroux, 1969.

———. "Some Aspects of the Grotesque in Southern Fiction." In *Mystery and Manners: Occasional Prose*, 36–49. New York: Farrar, Straus and Giroux, 1969.

O'Donnell, Angela Alaimo. *Radical Ambivalence: Race in Flannery O'Connor.* New York: Fordham University Press, 2020.

Ono, Yoko. *Grapefruit: A Book of Instructions and Drawings by Yoko Ono.* New York: Simon and Schuster, 1970.

Ono, Yoko, Albert Maysles, and David Maysles. *Cut Piece.* New York: Maysles Films, Inc., 1966.

Park, Marlene. "Lynching and Antilynching: Art and Politics in the 1930s." *Prospects* 18 (October 1993): 311–65. https://doi.org/10.1017/S0361233300004944.

Perloff, Marjorie. *The Futurist Moment: Avant-Garde, Avant Guerre, and the Language of Rupture*. Chicago: University of Chicago Press, 2003.

Piepmeier, Alison. *Girl Zines: Making Media, Doing Feminism*. New York: New York University Press, 2009.

Pozorski, Aimee. *Falling after 9/11: Crisis in American Art and Literature*. New York: Bloomsbury, 2014.

Quayson, Ato. *Aesthetic Nervousness: Disability and the Crisis of Representation*. New York: Columbia University Press, 2007.

Quiñones, Carmen Merport. "Reading Color: Looking Through Language in Warhol." *Criticism* 59, no. 4 (2017): 511–38. https://doi.org/10.13110/criticism.59.4.0511.

Radway, Janice. "Girl Zine Networks, Underground Itineraries, and Riot Grrrl History: Making Sense of the Struggle for New Social Forms in the 1990s and Beyond." *Journal of American Studies* 50, no. 1 (February 2016): 1–31. https://doi.org/10.1017/S0021875815002625.

Rancière, Jacques. *The Politics of Aesthetics*. New York: Bloomsbury, 2013.

Raymond, Yasmil. "Maladies of Power: A Kara Walker Lexicon." In *My Complement, My Enemy, My Oppressor, My Love*, 347–70. Minneapolis: Walker Art Center, 2007.

Reed, Thomas Vernon. *The Art of Protest: Culture and Activism from the Civil Rights Movement to the Streets of Seattle*. Minneapolis: University of Minnesota Press, 2005.

Reid-Pharr, Robert F. "Tearing the Goat's Flesh: Crisis, Homosexuality, Abjection, and the Production of a Late-Twentieth-Century Black Masculinity." *Studies in the Novel* 28, no. 3 (1996): 372–94.

Richards, Juno Jill. *The Fury Archives: Female Citizenship, Human Rights, and the International Avant-Gardes*. New York: Columbia University Press, 2020.

Rokach, Ami, ed. *Senseless Violence and Its Ramifications*. London: Routledge, 2018.

Ross, Marlon B. "White Fantasies of Desire: Baldwin and the Racial Identities of Sexuality." In *James Baldwin Now*, edited by Dwight A. McBride, 13–55. New York: New York University Press, 1999.

Rubin, Gayle. "Blood Under the Bridge: Reflections on 'Thinking Sex.'" *GLQ: A Journal of Lesbian and Gay Studies* 17, no. 1 (January 1, 2011): 15–48. https://doi.org/10.1215/10642684-2010-015.

Rushdy, Ashraf. "Exquisite Corpse." *Transition*, no. 83 (2000): 70–77.

Ruskin, John. *The Stones of Venice*. Vol. III. San Francisco: Chronicle, 2017.

Russell, Diana, and Susan Griffin. "On Pornography: Two Feminists' Perspectives." *Chrysalis* 4 (1977): 11–19.

Russo, Mary J. *The Female Grotesque: Risk, Excess, and Modernity*. New York: Routledge, 1995.

Saint-Amour, Paul K. "Bombing and the Symptom: Traumatic Earliness and the Nuclear Uncanny." *Diacritics* 30, no. 4 (2000): 59–82. https://doi.org/10.1353/dia.2000.0034.

Schechner, Richard. "9/11 as Avant-Garde Art?" *PMLA* 124, no. 5 (2009): 1820–29.

Sedgwick, Eve Kosofsky. "Queer Performativity: Warhol's Shyness/Warhol's Whiteness." In *Pop Out: Queer Warhol*, edited by Jennifer Doyle, Jonathan Flatley, and José Esteban Muñoz, 134–43. Durham, NC: Duke University Press, 1996.

———. *Touching Feeling: Affect, Pedagogy, Performativity*. Durham, NC: Duke University Press, 2003.

Sedgwick, Eve Kosofsky, and Adam Frank. "Shame in the Cybernetic Fold: Reading Silvan Tomkins." In *Touching Feeling: Affect, Pedagogy, Performativity*, by Eve Kosofsky Sedgwick, 93–121. Durham, NC: Duke University Press, 2003.

Seiler, Claire. *Midcentury Suspension: Literature and Feeling in the Wake of World War II*. New York: Columbia University Press, 2020.

Seltzer, Mark. *Serial Killers: Death and Life in America's Wound Culture*. New York: Routledge, 1998.

Serpell, C. Namwali. *Seven Modes of Uncertainty*. Cambridge, MA: Harvard University Press, 2014.

Sharpe, Christina Elizabeth. *Monstrous Intimacies: Making Post-Slavery Subjects*. Durham, NC: Duke University Press, 2010.

Shaw, Gwendolyn DuBois. *Seeing the Unspeakable: The Art of Kara Walker*. Durham, NC: Duke University Press, 2004.

Siebers, Tobin. *Disability Aesthetics*. Ann Arbor: University of Michigan Press, 2010.

Sielke, Sabine. *Reading Rape: The Rhetoric of Sexual Violence in American Literature and Culture, 1790–1990*. Princeton, NJ: Princeton University Press, 2009.

Smith, Philip. "Narrating the Guillotine: Punishment Technology as Myth and Symbol." *Theory, Culture & Society* 20, no. 5 (2003): 27–51. https://doi.org/10.1177/02632764030205002.

Smith, Rachel Greenwald. "Organic Shrapnel: Affect and Aesthetics in September 11 Fiction." *American Literature* 83, no. 1 (January 1, 2011): 153–74.

Smith, Shawn Michelle. "Guest Editor's Introduction: Visual Culture and Race." *MELUS: Multi-Ethnic Literature of the United States* 39, no. 2 (June 1, 2014): 1–11. https://doi.org/10.1093/melus/mlu016.

Sontag, Susan. "Happenings: An Art of Radical Juxtaposition." In *Against Interpretation and Other Essays*, 263–74. New York: Delta, 1966.

———. *Regarding the Pain of Others*. New York: Farrar, Straus and Giroux, 2003.

Spillers, Hortense J. "Mama's Baby, Papa's Maybe: An American Grammar Book." *Diacritics* 17, no. 2 (1987): 64–81. https://doi.org/10.2307/464747.

Stockton, Kathryn Bond. *Beautiful Bottom, Beautiful Shame: Where "Black" Meets "Queer."* Durham, NC: Duke University Press, 2006.

———. "Heaven's Bottom: Anal Economics and the Critical Debasement of Freud in Toni Morrison's 'Sula.'" *Cultural Critique*, no. 24 (1993): 81–118. https://doi.org/10.2307/1354130.

Stosuy, Brandon. *Up Is Up, but So Is Down: New York's Downtown Literary Scene*. New York: New York University Press, 2006.

Streeby, Shelley. *Radical Sensations: World Movements, Violence, and Visual Culture*. Durham, NC: Duke University Press, 2013.

Stuart, Christopher. "Finding the Jimmy in James: How James Baldwin Discovered Giovanni's Room in Lambert Strether's Paris." *MELUS: Multi-Ethnic Literature of*

*the United States* 40, no. 2 (June 1, 2015): 53–73. https://doi.org/10.1093/melus
/mlv006.

Stuelke, Patricia. *The Ruse of Repair: US Neoliberal Empire and the Turn from Critique.*
Durham, NC: Duke University Press, 2021.

Suleiman, Susan. *Subversive Intent: Gender, Politics, and the Avant-Garde.* Cambridge,
MA: Harvard University Press, 1990.

Sweet, Paige. "Where's the Booty?: The Stakes of Textual and Economic Piracy as
Seen Through the Work of Kathy Acker." *Darkmatter* 5 (2009): 23–33.

Tang, Amy. "Postmodern Repetitions: Parody, Trauma, and the Case of Kara
Walker." *Differences* 21, no. 2 (September 1, 2010): 142–72. https://doi.org/10.1215
/10407391-2010-006.

Thomson, Philip. *The Grotesque.* London: Taylor and Francis, 1972.

Tobin, Vera. *Elements of Surprise: Our Mental Limits and the Satisfactions of Plot.*
Cambridge, MA: Harvard University Press, 2018.

Tomkins, Silvan. "What Are Affects?" In *Shame and Its Sisters: A Silvan Tomkins
Reader,* edited by Eve Kosofsky Sedgwick and Adam Frank, 33–74. Durham, NC:
Duke University Press, 1995.

Torres, Sasha. *Black, White, and in Color: Television and Black Civil Rights.* Princeton,
NJ: Princeton University Press, 2003.

Ulmer, Gregory. "The Object of Post-Criticism." In *The Anti-Aesthetic: Essays on
Postmodern Culture,* edited by Hal Foster. New York: The New Press, 1988.

Varsava, Jerry A. *Contingent Meanings: Postmodern Fiction, Mimesis, and the Reader.*
Tallahassee: Florida State University Press, 1990.

Versluys, Kristiaan. *Out of the Blue: September 11 and the Novel.* New York: Columbia
University Press, 2009.

Vigarello, Georges. *The Silhouette: From the 18th Century to the Present Day.* London:
Bloomsbury, 2016.

Vimalassery, Manu, Juliana Hu Pegues, and Alyosha Goldstein. "Introduction: On
Colonial Unknowing." *Theory & Event* 19, no. 4 (2016). https://muse.jhu.edu
/article/633283.

Virilio, Paul. *The Original Accident.* Cambridge, UK: Polity Press, 2007.

Vonnegut, Kurt. *Slaughterhouse-Five.* New York: Dial Press, 1999.

Wagner, Anne M. "Warhol Paints History, or Race in America." *Representations,*
no. 55 (1996): 98–119. https://doi.org/10.2307/3043740.

Wanzo, Rebecca. *The Content of Our Caricature: African American Comic Art and
Political Belonging.* New York: New York University Press, 2020.

Wark, McKenzie. *Philosophy for Spiders: On the Low Theory of Kathy Acker.* Durham,
NC: Duke University Press, 2021.

Wiegman, Robyn. "The Anatomy of Lynching." *Journal of the History of Sexuality* 3,
no. 3 (1993): 445–67.

Williams, Raymond. *Keywords: A Vocabulary of Culture and Society.* New York: Oxford
University Press, 1985.

———. *The Long Revolution.* Cardigan, Wales: Parthian Books, 2013.

Wood, Amy Louise. *Lynching and Spectacle: Witnessing Racial Violence in America,
1890-1940.* Chapel Hill: University of North Carolina Press, 2011.

Wu, Yung-Hsing. "Doing Things with Ethics: *Beloved, Sula,* and the Reading of Judgment." *MFS: Modern Fiction Studies* 49, no. 4 (2003): 780–805. https://doi.org/10.1353/mfs.2003.0067.

Wylot, David. *Reading Contingency: The Accident in Contemporary Fiction.* New York: Routledge, 2019.

Xiang, Sunny. *Tonal Intelligence: The Aesthetics of Asian Inscrutability During the Long Cold War.* New York: Columbia University Press, 2020.

Yaeger, Patricia. "Flannery O'Connor and the Aesthetics of Torture." In *Flannery O'Connor: New Perspectives,* edited by Sura P. Rath and Mary Neff Shaw, 183–206. Athens: University of Georgia Press, 1996.

Yao, Xine. *Disaffected: The Cultural Politics of Unfeeling in Nineteenth-Century America.* Durham, NC: Duke University Press, 2021.

Black people (cont.)
freedom movements, 7; Black men,
173n7; Black women, 112, 137;
lynching of, 97–98, 109, 115–17,
171n70; structural violence and, 6–7,
23–24, 82. *See also* race; racism
Black suffering, 95, 97–98, 105, 108–16
"Black Tarantula." *See* Acker, Kathy
blank spaces, 41–43, 99–100, 102
Blok, Anton, 24, 144, 156n14
*Blood and Guts in High School* (Acker),
120, 123–30, 132–33
bodily contingency, 87, 88–93, 94, 163n38
bodily precarity, 51, 56
book bans, 149–50
Brecht, Bertolt, 46, 79–80
Brinkema, Eugenie, 13, 102
Brooks, Peter, 30–31
Brownmiller, Susan, 134, 173n7
Buck-Morss, Susan, 15–16, 152
*bukimi*, 50–51, 56, 66–67
Burroughs, William S., 121

Cage, John, 52–53, 54, 57
cameras, 60. *See also* photography
capital punishment, 38–40, 44–45
caricature, 77, 100–101
cause and effect, 26, 73, 84. *See also*
accidents
Caws, Mary Ann, 26, 118
Chambers Street Loft series (Ono), 54
chance operations, 49, 52–53, 55–57, 64,
74. *See also* narrative chance
chance procedures, 49, 52–53, 56–58,
60, 67, 69
Chuh, Kandice, 152, 157n55
classism, 46, 52, 99–100, 136
close-ups, 60–63, 102
Cold War era, 49, 50–51, 58, 59
Coleman, Rebecca, 150
collage: aesthetic violence of, 145–46; *Blood
and Guts in High School* (Acker), 120,
123–30, 132–33; consent and, 121–23,
129, 139, 173n23, 175n48; copyright
and, 122; feminism and, 123, 134; as

form, 119; *Jane: A Murder* (Nelson),
118–20; language and, 126, 128,
136–37; masochism and, 129; sense-
making narratives in, 127–28. *See also*
Acker, Kathy; Hanna, Kathleen; zines
collateral damage, 48–50, 65, 67
colonialism, 58, 59, 67, 128, 178n9
common sense, 15–16, 158n77
consent, 119–26, 129–31, 138–41,
173n23, 174n33, 175n48
constraints, 73–75, 77. *See also* rules and
instructions; scores and scripts
contingency, 48, 52, 73–74, 87–93, 94
contrastive structure, 75
copyright, 122
cruelty, 12, 14, 16, 55, 124, 129, 146–47
*Cut* (Walker), 102–3, 104
*Cut Piece* (film), 60–66, 63, 64
*Cut Piece* (Ono), 56, 57, 58, 59–68, 63,
64, 163n48
"cut up" texts, 121. *See also* collage

Dando, Evan, 134–35
*Death and Disaster* series (Warhol), 37–46
decomposition, 33–34, 46–47
decontextualization, 11, 41–42, 45–46
defamiliarization, 12, 44–45, 46, 80
desire, 25, 34, 36, 105, 110–12, 117, 124
*Diary of a Conference on Sexuality*, 140
Didion, Joan, 1, 144
disabilities, 72, 76, 87–93, 94, 163n38
disasters, 38, 41, 44–45
disgust, 102, 105, 109–15, 117, 169n39,
170n40, 170n48, 171n76
"The Displaced Person" (O'Connor), 83
*Dope!* (Lee), 73, 79
Doyle, Jennifer, 151
*Dreaming Emmett* (Morrison), 171n70
Drew, Richard, 144
Dutoit, Ulysse, 4, 13–14, 42, 100
Dworkin, Andrea, 125, 139, 177n104

electric chairs, 38–39, 45, 46
*Electric Chair* series (Warhol), 38–41
emotion, 76, 93